UNDERSTANDING EDGE COMPUTING

UNDERSTANDING EDGE COMPUTING

Jose Benjamim Silva
Brian Heslo

Kruger Brentt
Publishers

2025

Kruger Brentt Publishers UK. LTD.
Company Number 9728962

Regd. Office: 68 St Margarets Road, Edgware, Middlesex HA8 9UU

ISBN: 978-1-78715-360-8

For information on all our publications visit our website at http://krugerbrentt.com/

PREFACE

Edge computing represents a transformative approach in the realm of computing architectures, aiming to decentralize data processing and computation closer to the point of data generation. This departure from traditional centralized cloud computing models is driven by the increasing demand for real-time data processing, low-latency applications, and efficient use of network resources across diverse industries.

At its core, edge computing shifts computational tasks and data storage from centralized data centers to distributed nodes closer to where data is generated, known as the "edge." This proximity minimizes the distance data travels, thereby reducing latency and enhancing the performance of applications that require instantaneous response times. Edge computing leverages a hierarchical architecture that includes devices (such as IoT sensors and gateways), edge nodes (local servers or gateways), and centralized cloud servers. This architecture enables data to be processed, analyzed, and acted upon locally, while also allowing for aggregation and further analysis in the cloud when necessary.

Key components of edge computing include edge devices equipped with sensors, actuators, and embedded systems that collect and transmit data. Edge nodes act as intermediaries between devices and centralized cloud servers, performing data preprocessing, filtering, and initial analysis. These nodes are crucial for optimizing bandwidth usage and improving the efficiency of data transmission by prioritizing critical data and reducing unnecessary data traffic.

Technologies that support edge computing encompass a wide range of tools and frameworks, including edge analytics, edge AI (Artificial Intelligence), and edge security solutions. Edge analytics processes data locally to derive immediate insights, making it ideal for applications such as predictive maintenance and real-time monitoring. Edge AI integrates machine learning models directly onto edge devices, enabling autonomous decision-making and intelligent data processing without continuous reliance on cloud services.

Edge computing finds applications across various domains, including: Facilitating real-time monitoring and control of connected devices, optimizing energy usage, and enhancing operational efficiency. Managing traffic flows, monitoring environmental conditions, and improving public safety through distributed edge infrastructure. Enabling remote patient monitoring, real-time diagnostics, and personalized treatment plans using edge computing's low-latency capabilities. Supporting predictive maintenance, quality control, and process optimization in smart factories through local data processing and analytics. Processing sensor data in real-time to enable autonomous decision-making and enhance vehicle-to-vehicle communication.

Despite its benefits, edge computing poses several challenges, including security vulnerabilities, interoperability issues across heterogeneous devices and platforms, and the complexity of managing distributed edge infrastructure. Addressing these challenges requires robust security protocols, standardized communication frameworks, and scalable management solutions to ensure seamless integration and deployment of edge computing technologies.

Looking ahead, the future of edge computing is poised for significant advancements, driven by the integration of 5G networks, advancements in edge AI, and the proliferation of IoT devices. These trends will further enhance edge computing's capabilities in delivering real-time insights, supporting mission-critical applications, and enabling innovative solutions across industries.

Jose Benjamim Silva
Brian Heslo

CONTENTS

CHAPTER 1
INTRODUCTION TO EDGE COMPUTING

1.1 DEFINITION AND CONCEPT OF EDGE COMPUTING

1.1.1 Definition of Edge Computing

Edge computing is a distributed computing paradigm that brings computation and data storage closer to the location where it is needed, to improve response times and save bandwidth. Instead of relying solely on a central data center, edge computing processes data on devices or local servers at the "edge" of the network—near the source of the data.

1.1.2 Concept of Edge Computing

The concept of edge computing revolves around decentralizing computing resources to enhance efficiency and reduce latency. Here are key components and ideas underpinning edge computing:

- **Proximity to Data Sources:** Edge computing places processing power near the data generation points, such as sensors, cameras, or other IoT devices. This proximity allows for real-time data processing and analysis, which is crucial for applications requiring immediate feedback.
- **Latency Reduction:** By processing data locally, edge computing significantly reduces the latency associated with sending data to centralized cloud servers. This is particularly important for time-sensitive applications like autonomous vehicles, industrial automation, and augmented reality.
- **Bandwidth Efficiency:** Edge computing minimizes the amount of data transmitted to and from central data centers by performing initial processing locally. This reduces the bandwidth required, which is beneficial in environments with limited connectivity or high data volumes.
- **Data Privacy and Security:** Processing data closer to its source can enhance privacy and security by keeping sensitive information on local

devices rather than transmitting it over the internet. This is critical in sectors like healthcare and finance, where data security is paramount.

- **Scalability and Flexibility:** Edge computing allows for more scalable and flexible architectures. Devices at the edge can operate independently and continue functioning even if the connection to the central server is interrupted. This decentralization supports the growth of IoT ecosystems by enabling more devices to be connected and managed efficiently.

1.2 EVOLUTION FROM CLOUD COMPUTING

Cloud computing has revolutionized how businesses and individuals manage data and applications, providing scalable resources over the internet. However, as technology continues to advance, new challenges and demands have emerged, leading to the evolution of edge computing. This progression from centralized cloud computing to a more decentralized model has profound implications for efficiency, speed, and security. The evolution from cloud computing to edge computing represents a significant shift in how data and applications are managed. By bringing computation closer to the source of data generation, edge computing addresses the limitations of traditional cloud models, providing reduced latency, optimized bandwidth, and enhanced security. As technology continues to advance, the integration of edge and cloud computing will drive innovation across various industries, enabling new applications and improving efficiency and performance.

1.2.1 Origins of Cloud Computing

Cloud computing emerged in the early 2000s, fundamentally changing the IT landscape by allowing users to access computing resources on-demand over the internet. Major players like Amazon Web Services (AWS), Microsoft Azure, and Google Cloud provided infrastructure, platforms, and software as services, eliminating the need for businesses to maintain costly and complex on-premises data centers. This model offered several benefits, including:

- **Scalability:** Businesses could scale their computing needs up or down quickly in response to demand.
- **Cost Efficiency:** The pay-as-you-go model reduced capital expenditures and allowed for more predictable operational costs.
- **Accessibility:** Applications and data could be accessed from anywhere, facilitating remote work and global collaboration.

Despite these advantages, cloud computing has some inherent limitations, particularly concerning latency, bandwidth, and data privacy.

1.2.2 The Limitations of Centralized Cloud Computing

While cloud computing has been a game-changer, certain applications and industries began to encounter limitations that centralized cloud models could not adequately address:

- **Latency:** Sending data back and forth between the central cloud and end-user devices can introduce significant delays. This latency is unacceptable for time-sensitive applications like autonomous driving, augmented reality, and real-time analytics.
- **Bandwidth:** With the explosion of Internet of Things (IoT) devices generating vast amounts of data, transmitting all this data to a central cloud for processing can strain network bandwidth and lead to higher costs.
- **Data Privacy and Security:** Sensitive data transmitted to and from the cloud can be vulnerable to interception and breaches. For industries like healthcare and finance, where data privacy is paramount, these risks are particularly concerning.

1.2.3 The Emergence of Edge Computing

Edge computing arose as a solution to these challenges. By decentralizing computing power and bringing it closer to the source of data generation, edge computing reduces latency, optimizes bandwidth usage, and enhances data security.

- **Proximity:** Edge computing involves processing data at or near the point where it is generated. This proximity reduces the distance data must travel, thereby decreasing latency and enabling real-time processing.
- **Bandwidth Optimization:** By processing data locally, only relevant or aggregated information is sent to the central cloud, significantly reducing bandwidth requirements and associated costs.
- **Enhanced Security:** Keeping data local reduces the exposure risk associated with transmitting sensitive information over networks. This localized processing is particularly beneficial in regulatory environments where data privacy is critical.

1.2.4 How Edge Computing Works

Edge computing leverages a variety of technologies and architectures to bring processing closer to the data source:

- **Edge Devices:** These include sensors, actuators, and other IoT devices that generate and sometimes process data locally. Examples include smart cameras, industrial robots, and connected vehicles.

- **Edge Servers and Gateways:** These are intermediate devices that aggregate data from edge devices, perform initial processing, and may interact with the central cloud. They serve as a bridge between edge devices and the broader network, handling tasks that require more computing power than edge devices can provide.
- **Localized Data Centers:** Smaller data centers located closer to end-users than traditional central clouds, providing additional processing power and storage.

1.2.5 Key Benefits of Edge Computing

Edge computing brings several distinct advantages over traditional cloud computing:

- **Reduced Latency:** Real-time applications benefit significantly from the reduced latency provided by edge computing. This is crucial for autonomous vehicles, industrial automation, and augmented reality.
- **Improved Reliability:** By processing data locally, edge computing can continue to operate even if connectivity to the central cloud is lost, enhancing the reliability of critical applications.
- **Cost Savings:** Reducing the volume of data sent to central clouds lowers bandwidth costs and reduces the need for extensive data center infrastructure.
- **Scalability:** Edge computing can be scaled more easily to accommodate growing numbers of IoT devices and data volumes, as processing is distributed rather than centralized.

1.2.6 Challenges and Considerations

While edge computing offers numerous benefits, it also presents challenges that need to be addressed:

- **Infrastructure Complexity:** Deploying and managing a distributed network of edge devices and servers can be complex and requires robust infrastructure and management tools.
- **Security Risks:** While edge computing can enhance data privacy, it also introduces new security challenges, as each edge device becomes a potential attack vector.
- **Interoperability:** Ensuring seamless communication and compatibility between diverse edge devices and central systems is critical for the success of edge computing implementations.
- **Scalability and Maintenance:** Managing a large number of edge devices can be challenging in terms of updates, maintenance, and scalability.

1.2.7 The Future of Computing: Edge and Cloud Synergy

Rather than replacing cloud computing, edge computing complements it. The future of computing likely lies in a hybrid approach that leverages the strengths of both paradigms:

- **Hybrid Architectures:** Combining edge and cloud computing enables optimized data processing, where time-sensitive tasks are handled at the edge, and more complex, resource-intensive processing is offloaded to the cloud.
- **AI and Machine Learning:** Edge computing facilitates real-time AI and machine learning applications by processing data locally, allowing for rapid decision-making and adaptation.
- **IoT and 5G Integration:** The rollout of 5G networks will further enhance the capabilities of edge computing by providing faster, more reliable connectivity for edge devices, enabling new applications and services.

1.3 KEY CHARACTERISTICS AND ADVANTAGES

Cloud computing has transformed the way businesses and individuals access and manage data and applications, providing a flexible, scalable, and cost-effective alternative to traditional on-premises IT infrastructure. Cloud computing's key characteristics and advantages have made it a cornerstone of modern IT infrastructure. By offering on-demand, scalable, and flexible resources, cloud computing supports cost efficiency, accessibility, and innovation. Its various models, including public, private, hybrid, and multi-cloud, provide tailored solutions to meet diverse business needs, ensuring optimal performance, security, and control. As technology continues to evolve, cloud computing will remain integral to driving business transformation and growth.

1.3.1 Key Characteristics of Cloud Computing

- **On-Demand Self-Service:** Users can access computing resources such as server time and network storage as needed, automatically, without requiring human intervention from the service provider.
- **Broad Network Access:** Cloud services are accessible over the network through standard mechanisms, promoting use by heterogeneous thin or thick client platforms (e.g., mobile phones, tablets, laptops, and workstations).
- **Resource Pooling:** The provider's computing resources are pooled to serve multiple consumers using a multi-tenant model, with different physical and virtual resources dynamically assigned and reassigned

according to demand. This pooling provides economies of scale and resource efficiency.

- **Rapid Elasticity:** Capabilities can be elastically provisioned and released, in some cases automatically, to scale rapidly outward and inward commensurate with demand. For consumers, the capabilities available for provisioning often appear to be unlimited and can be purchased in any quantity at any time.
- **Measured Service:** Cloud systems automatically control and optimize resource use by leveraging a metering capability at some level of abstraction appropriate to the type of service (e.g., storage, processing, bandwidth, and active user accounts). Resource usage can be monitored, controlled, and reported, providing transparency for both the provider and consumer.

1.3.2 Advantages of Cloud Computing

- **Cost Efficiency:** Cloud computing reduces the capital expense of buying hardware and software and setting up and running on-site data centers. Instead, it provides a pay-as-you-go or subscription-based model, converting capital expenditures to operational expenditures.
- **Scalability and Flexibility:** Businesses can easily scale up or down their IT resources as needed, ensuring that they only pay for what they use. This flexibility supports growth and adapts to varying workloads.
- **Accessibility and Collaboration:** Cloud computing allows users to access applications and data from anywhere with an internet connection. This facilitates remote work and collaboration among teams distributed across different locations.
- **Disaster Recovery and Backup:** Cloud services provide robust disaster recovery solutions, ensuring that data is backed up and easily recoverable in case of hardware failures, natural disasters, or cyberattacks.
- **Automatic Updates and Maintenance:** Cloud providers manage the underlying infrastructure, including hardware maintenance and software updates, ensuring that users always have access to the latest technology and security features.
- **Performance:** Cloud computing services run on a worldwide network of secure data centers, which are upgraded to the latest generation of fast and efficient computing hardware. This offers several benefits over a single corporate data center, including reduced network latency for applications and greater economies of scale.

- **Security:** Cloud providers offer a set of policies, technologies, and controls that strengthen security posture overall, helping to protect data, applications, and infrastructure from potential threats. This includes physical security of data centers and compliance with regulatory standards.
- **Innovation and Speed:** The cloud provides access to a wide range of tools and technologies, such as artificial intelligence, machine learning, and big data analytics, which can drive innovation. Businesses can quickly develop, test, and deploy applications, speeding up time to market.

1.3.3 Specific Advantages of Different Cloud Models

Public Cloud:

- **Accessibility:** Services are delivered over the public internet, making them accessible to anyone.
- **Cost-Effective:** Ideal for workloads that require significant scalability without significant up-front investment.

Private Cloud:

- **Control and Security:** Provides enhanced security and control over data and infrastructure, suitable for industries with stringent regulatory requirements.
- **Customization:** Can be tailored to specific business needs and performance requirements.

Hybrid Cloud:

- **Flexibility:** Combines the best of both public and private clouds, allowing businesses to run sensitive workloads in a private cloud while taking advantage of public cloud resources for non-sensitive workloads.
- **Optimized Resource Utilization:** Enables workload portability and resource optimization based on specific needs.

Multi-Cloud:

- **Risk Mitigation:** Reduces dependency on a single cloud provider, enhancing resilience and flexibility.
- **Best-of-Breed Services:** Allows businesses to leverage the strengths of different cloud providers for various workloads.

1.4 USE CASES AND APPLICATIONS

Cloud computing has become a fundamental technology across numerous industries due to its flexibility, scalability, and cost-efficiency. Cloud computing's diverse applications across various industries showcase its transformative impact on how businesses operate and innovate.

From data storage and disaster recovery to AI, IoT, and virtual desktops, the cloud provides the necessary tools and infrastructure to support modern digital demands.

As technology evolves, the integration of cloud computing will continue to drive efficiency, scalability, and innovation in numerous sectors.

1.4.1 Data Storage and Backup

- **Use Case:** Storing and backing up data.
- **Applications:** Companies use cloud storage services like Amazon S3, Google Cloud Storage, and Microsoft Azure Blob Storage to securely store and back up their data. This ensures data is easily accessible from anywhere, and redundancy features help in data recovery in case of hardware failures or disasters.

1.4.2 Disaster Recovery

- **Use Case:** Implementing disaster recovery solutions.
- **Applications:** Cloud-based disaster recovery services such as AWS Disaster Recovery, Azure Site Recovery, and Google Cloud Disaster Recovery provide affordable and efficient recovery options. Businesses can replicate critical IT systems and data in the cloud, ensuring business continuity with minimal downtime.

1.4.3 Big Data Analytics

- **Use Case:** Analyzing large datasets to derive insights.
- **Applications:** Platforms like Google BigQuery, Amazon Redshift, and Azure Synapse Analytics allow companies to process and analyze vast amounts of data in real-time. This enables better decision-making, predictive analytics, and business intelligence.

1.4.4 Software Development and Testing

- **Use Case:** Developing, testing, and deploying applications.
- **Applications:** Cloud services like AWS CodePipeline, Azure DevOps, and Google Cloud Build provide environments for continuous integration and continuous deployment (CI/CD). These services allow developers to quickly build, test, and release software, speeding up the development lifecycle.

1.4.5 Content Delivery and Streaming

- **Use Case:** Delivering content globally with low latency.
- **Applications:** Content delivery networks (CDNs) like Amazon CloudFront, Azure CDN, and Google Cloud CDN distribute content such as videos, images, and software updates efficiently across the globe. Streaming services like Netflix and YouTube rely on these platforms to deliver high-quality content to millions of users.

1.4.6 IoT (Internet of Things)

- **Use Case:** Managing and analyzing IoT devices and data.
- **Applications:** Cloud platforms such as AWS IoT, Azure IoT Hub, and Google Cloud IoT Core provide tools to connect, monitor, and manage IoT devices. These platforms also enable the processing and analysis of data generated by these devices, facilitating smart applications in industries like agriculture, manufacturing, and healthcare.

1.4.7 Artificial Intelligence and Machine Learning

- **Use Case:** Building and deploying AI and ML models.
- **Applications:** Cloud-based AI and ML services like AWS SageMaker, Google AI Platform, and Azure Machine Learning offer powerful tools to develop, train, and deploy machine learning models. These services help businesses integrate AI capabilities into their applications, improving processes and customer experiences.

1.4.8 Virtual Desktops and Remote Work

- **Use Case:** Providing remote access to desktops and applications.
- **Applications:** Solutions like Amazon WorkSpaces, Azure Virtual Desktop, and Google Cloud's VDI provide secure and scalable virtual desktop environments. These services support remote work by allowing employees to access their work desktops from anywhere, ensuring productivity and security.

1.4.9 E-commerce

- **Use Case:** Powering online retail platforms.
- **Applications:** E-commerce giants like Amazon and Alibaba use cloud computing to handle large-scale transactions, manage inventory, and process payments securely. Cloud services support features such as scalable infrastructure, customer analytics, and personalized shopping experiences.

1.4.10 Healthcare

- **Use Case:** Enhancing patient care and managing health records.
- **Applications:** Cloud platforms like AWS HealthLake, Azure Health Data Services, and Google Cloud Healthcare API enable healthcare providers to store, analyze, and share medical records securely. Telemedicine applications also leverage cloud computing to provide remote consultations and monitoring.

1.4.11 Education

- **Use Case:** Delivering online education and managing educational resources.
- **Applications:** Educational institutions use cloud services like Google Classroom, Microsoft Teams, and AWS Educate to provide virtual classrooms, online courses, and collaborative tools. These platforms support remote learning and streamline educational management.

1.4.12 Gaming

- **Use Case:** Hosting and streaming online games.
- **Applications:** Cloud gaming services like Google Stadia, NVIDIA GeForce Now, and Microsoft's Xbox Cloud Gaming enable gamers to stream high-quality games without needing powerful local hardware. Game developers also use cloud infrastructure to manage multiplayer game servers and game development pipelines.

1.4.13 Financial Services

- **Use Case:** Managing financial transactions and data analysis.
- **Applications:** Banks and financial institutions use cloud services to process transactions, analyze financial data, and detect fraud. Platforms like AWS Financial Services Cloud, Azure for Financial Services, and Google Cloud Financial Services provide tools for secure and compliant operations.

1.4.14 Media and Entertainment

- **Use Case:** Producing and distributing digital content.
- **Applications:** Media companies use cloud services for video editing, rendering, and distribution. Platforms like AWS Media Services, Azure Media Services, and Google Cloud Media Solutions provide the infrastructure for content creation, streaming, and analytics.

1.4.15 Enterprise Resource Planning (ERP)

- **Use Case:** Managing business processes and operations.
- **Applications:** Cloud-based ERP solutions like SAP S/4HANA Cloud, Oracle ERP Cloud, and Microsoft Dynamics 365 enable businesses to integrate and manage their core processes in finance, human resources, supply chain, and more. These solutions offer scalability, flexibility, and real-time insights.

CHAPTER 2
FUNDAMENTALS OF EDGE COMPUTING

2.1 EDGE DEVICE AND ENDPOINTS

Edge computing involves processing data closer to where it is generated, at the "edge" of the network, rather than relying solely on a centralized cloud infrastructure. Edge devices and endpoints are crucial components in this paradigm, enabling localized data processing and reducing latency. Edge devices and endpoints are integral to the edge computing paradigm, providing the necessary infrastructure for localized data processing and real-time decision-making. They encompass a wide range of technologies and applications, from simple sensors to complex industrial machines, all contributing to enhanced efficiency, reduced latency, and improved security in modern computing environments. As the demand for real-time processing and intelligent systems continues to grow, the role of edge devices and endpoints will become increasingly vital in various industries and applications.

2.1.1 Edge Devices

Edge devices are hardware components that perform data processing at the edge of the network. They collect, analyze, and act on data locally, often in real-time, before sending relevant information to centralized cloud servers or other systems for further processing or storage. These devices include a wide range of technologies and can be categorized based on their function and capabilities.

Types of Edge Devices

Sensors

A sensor is a device that produces an output signal for the purpose of detecting a physical phenomenon.

In the broadest definition, a sensor is a device, module, machine, or subsystem that detects events or changes in its environment and sends the information to other electronics, frequently a computer processor.

Sensors are used in everyday objects such as touch-sensitive elevator buttons (tactile sensor) and lamps which dim or brighten by touching the base, and in innumerable applications of which most people are never aware. With advances in micromachinery and easy-to-use microcontroller platforms, the uses of sensors have expanded beyond the traditional fields of temperature, pressure and flow measurement, for example into MARG sensors.

Analog sensors such as potentiometers and force-sensing resistors are still widely used. Their applications include manufacturing and machinery, airplanes and aerospace, cars, medicine, robotics and many other aspects of our day-to-day life. There is a wide range of other sensors that measure chemical and physical properties of materials, including optical sensors for refractive index measurement, vibrational sensors for fluid viscosity measurement, and electro-chemical sensors for monitoring pH of fluids.

A sensor's sensitivity indicates how much its output changes when the input quantity it measures changes. For instance, if the mercury in a thermometer moves 1 cm when the temperature changes by 1 °C, its sensitivity is 1 cm/°C (it is basically the slope dy/dx assuming a linear characteristic). Some sensors can also affect what they measure; for instance, a room temperature thermometer inserted into a hot cup of liquid cools the liquid while the liquid heats the thermometer. Sensors are usually designed to have a small effect on what is measured; making the sensor smaller often improves this and may introduce other advantages.

Technological progress allows more and more sensors to be manufactured on a microscopic scale as microsensors using MEMS technology. In most cases, a microsensor reaches a significantly faster measurement time and higher sensitivity compared with macroscopic approaches. Due to the increasing demand for rapid, affordable and reliable information in today's world, disposable sensors—low-cost and easy-to-use devices for short-term monitoring or single-shot measurements—have recently gained growing importance. Using this class of sensors, critical analytical information can be obtained by anyone, anywhere and at any time, without the need for recalibration and worrying about contamination.

Classification of Measurement Errors

A good sensor obeys the following rules:

- it is sensitive to the measured property,
- it is insensitive to any other property likely to be encountered in its application, and
- it does not influence the measured property.

Most sensors have a linear transfer function. The sensitivity is then defined as the ratio between the output signal and measured property. For example, if a sensor measures temperature and has a voltage output, the sensitivity is constant with the units [V/K]. The sensitivity is the slope of the transfer function. Converting the sensor's electrical output (for example V) to the measured units (for example K) requires dividing the electrical output by the slope (or multiplying by its reciprocal). In addition, an offset is frequently added or subtracted. For example, -40 must be added to the output if 0 V output corresponds to -40 C input.

For an analog sensor signal to be processed or used in digital equipment, it needs to be converted to a digital signal, using an analog-to-digital converter.

Since sensors cannot replicate an ideal transfer function, several types of deviations can occur which limit sensor accuracy:

- Since the range of the output signal is always limited, the output signal will eventually reach a minimum or maximum when the measured property exceeds the limits. The full scale range defines the maximum and minimum values of the measured property.
- The sensitivity may in practice differ from the value specified. This is called a sensitivity error. This is an error in the slope of a linear transfer function.
- If the output signal differs from the correct value by a constant, the sensor has an offset error or bias. This is an error in the y-intercept of a linear transfer function.
- Nonlinearity is deviation of a sensor's transfer function from a straight line transfer function. Usually, this is defined by the amount the output differs from ideal behavior over the full range of the sensor, often noted as a percentage of the full range.
- Deviation caused by rapid changes of the measured property over time is a dynamic error. Often, this behavior is described with a bode plot showing sensitivity error and phase shift as a function of the frequency of a periodic input signal.
- If the output signal slowly changes independent of the measured property, this is defined as drift. Long term drift over months or years is caused by physical changes in the sensor.
- Noise is a random deviation of the signal that varies in time.
- A hysteresis error causes the output value to vary depending on the previous input values. If a sensor's output is different depending on whether a specific input value was reached by increasing vs. decreasing the input, then the sensor has a hysteresis error.
- If the sensor has a digital output, the output is essentially an approximation of the measured property. This error is also called quantization error.

- If the signal is monitored digitally, the sampling frequency can cause a dynamic error, or if the input variable or added noise changes periodically at a frequency near a multiple of the sampling rate, aliasing errors may occur.

All these deviations can be classified as systematic errors or random errors. Systematic errors can sometimes be compensated for by means of some kind of calibration strategy. Noise is a random error that can be reduced by signal processing, such as filtering, usually at the expense of the dynamic behavior of the sensor.

The *sensor resolution* or *measurement resolution* is the smallest change that can be detected in the quantity that is being measured. The resolution of a sensor with a digital output is usually the numerical resolution of the digital output. The resolution is related to the precision with which the measurement is made, but they are not the same thing. A sensor's accuracy may be considerably worse than its resolution.

- For example, the distance resolution is the minimum distance that can be accurately measured by any distance measuring devices. In a time-of-flight camera, the distance resolution is usually equal to the standard deviation (total noise) of the signal expressed in unit of length.
- The sensor may to some extent be sensitive to properties other than the property being measured. For example, most sensors are influenced by the temperature of their environment.

Chemical Sensor

A chemical sensor is a self-contained analytical device that can provide information about the chemical composition of its environment, that is, a liquid or a gas phase. The information is provided in the form of a measurable physical signal that is correlated with the concentration of a certain chemical species (termed as analyte).

Two main steps are involved in the functioning of a chemical sensor, namely, recognition and transduction. In the recognition step, analyte molecules interact selectively with receptor molecules or sites included in the structure of the recognition element of the sensor. Consequently, a characteristic physical parameter varies and this variation is reported by means of an integrated transducer that generates the output signal. A chemical sensor based on recognition material of biological nature is a biosensor. However, as synthetic biomimetic materials are going to substitute to some extent recognition biomaterials, a sharp distinction between a biosensor and a standard chemical sensor is superfluous. Typical biomimetic materials used in sensor development are molecularly imprinted polymers and aptamers.

A chemical sensor array is a sensor architecture with multiple sensor components that create a pattern for analyte detection from the additive responses of individual sensor components. There exist several types of chemical sensor arrays including electronic, optical, acoustic wave, and potentiometric devices. These chemical sensor arrays can employ multiple sensor types that are cross-reactive or tuned to sense specific analytes.

Biosensor

In biomedicine and biotechnology, sensors which detect analytes thanks to a biological component, such as cells, protein, nucleic acid or biomimetic polymers, are called biosensors. Whereas a non-biological sensor, even organic (carbon chemistry), for biological analytes is referred to as sensor or nanosensor. This terminology applies for both in-vitro and in vivo applications. The encapsulation of the biological component in biosensors, presents a slightly different problem that ordinary sensors; this can either be done by means of a semipermeable barrier, such as a dialysis membrane or a hydrogel, or a 3D polymer matrix, which either physically constrains the sensing macromolecule or chemically constrains the macromolecule by bounding it to the scaffold.

Neuromorphic Sensors

Neuromorphic sensors are sensors that physically mimic structures and functions of biological neural entities. One example of this is the event camera.

MOS Sensors

Metal–oxide–semiconductor (MOS) technology originates from the MOSFET (MOS field-effect transistor, or MOS transistor) invented by Mohamed M. Atalla and Dawon Kahng in 1959, and demonstrated in 1960. MOSFET sensors (MOS sensors) were later developed, and they have since been widely used to measure physical, chemical, biological and environmental parameters.

Biochemical Sensors:

- A number of MOSFET sensors have been developed, for measuring physical, chemical, biological, and environmental parameters. The earliest MOSFET sensors include the open-gate field-effect transistor (OGFET) introduced by Johannessen in 1970, the ion-sensitive field-effect transistor (ISFET) invented by Piet Bergveld in 1970, the adsorption FET (ADFET) patented by P.F. Cox in 1974, and a hydrogen-sensitive MOSFET demonstrated by I. Lundstrom, M.S. Shivaraman, C.S. Svenson and L. Lundkvist in 1975. The ISFET is a special type of MOSFET with a gate at a certain distance, and where the metal gate is replaced by an ion-sensitive membrane, electrolyte solution and reference electrode. The

ISFET is widely used in biomedical applications, such as the detection of DNA hybridization, biomarker detection from blood, antibody detection, glucose measurement, pH sensing, and genetic technology.

- By the mid-1980s, numerous other MOSFET sensors had been developed, including the gas sensor FET (GASFET), surface accessible FET (SAFET), charge flow transistor (CFT), pressure sensor FET (PRESSFET), chemical field-effect transistor (ChemFET), reference ISFET (REFET), biosensor FET (BioFET), enzyme-modified FET (ENFET) and immunologically modified FET (IMFET). By the early 2000s, BioFET types such as the DNA field-effect transistor (DNAFET), gene-modified FET (GenFET) and cell-potential BioFET (CPFET) had been developed.

Image Sensors:

- MOS technology is the basis for modern image sensors, including the charge-coupled device (CCD) and the CMOS active-pixel sensor (CMOS sensor), used in digital imaging and digital cameras. Willard Boyle and George E. Smith developed the CCD in 1969. While researching the MOS process, they realized that an electric charge was the analogy of the magnetic bubble and that it could be stored on a tiny MOS capacitor. As it was fairly straightforward to fabricate a series of MOS capacitors in a row, they connected a suitable voltage to them so that the charge could be stepped along from one to the next. The CCD is a semiconductor circuit that was later used in the first digital video cameras for television broadcasting.
- The MOS active-pixel sensor (APS) was developed by Tsutomu Nakamura at Olympus in 1985. The CMOS active-pixel sensor was later developed by Eric Fossum and his team in the early 1990s.
- MOS image sensors are widely used in optical mouse technology. The first optical mouse, invented by Richard F. Lyon at Xerox in 1980, used a 5 μm NMOS sensor chip. Since the first commercial optical mouse, the IntelliMouse introduced in 1999, most optical mouse devices use CMOS sensors.

Monitoring Sensors:

- MOS monitoring sensors are used for house monitoring, office and agriculture monitoring, traffic monitoring (including car speed, traffic jams, and traffic accidents), weather monitoring (such as for rain, wind, lightning and storms), defense monitoring, and monitoring temperature, humidity, air pollution, fire, health, security and lighting. MOS gas detector sensors are used to detect carbon monoxide, sulfur dioxide, hydrogen sulfide, ammonia, and other gas substances. Other MOS sensors include intelligent sensors and wireless sensor network (WSN) technology.

Actuators

An actuator is a component of a machine that produces force, torque, or displacement, usually in a controlled way, when an electrical, pneumatic or hydraulic input is supplied to it in a system (called an actuating system). An actuator converts such an input signal into the required form of mechanical energy. It is a type of transducer. In simple terms, it is a "mover".

An actuator requires a control device (controlled by control signal) and a source of energy. The control signal is relatively low energy and may be electric voltage or current, pneumatic, or hydraulic fluid pressure, or even human power. In the *electric, hydraulic*, and *pneumatic* sense, it is a form of automation or automatic control.

The displacement achieved is commonly linear or rotational, as exemplified by linear motors and rotary motors, respectively. Rotary motion is more natural for small machines making large displacements. By means of a leadscrew, rotary motion can be adapted to function as a linear actuator (a linear motion, but not a linear motor).

Another broad classification of actuators separates them into two types: incremental-drive actuators and continuous-drive actuators. Stepper motors are one type of incremental-drive actuators. Examples of continuous-drive actuators include DC torque motors, induction motors, hydraulic and pneumatic motors, and piston-cylinder drives (rams).

Soft Actuator

A soft actuator is one that changes its shape in response to stimuli including mechanical, thermal, magnetic, and electrical. Soft actuators mainly deal with the robotics of humans rather than industry which is what most of the actuators are used for. For most actuators they are mechanically durable yet do not have an ability to adapt compared to soft actuators. The soft actuators apply to mainly safety and healthcare for humans which is why they are able to adapt to environments by disassembling their parts. This is why the driven energy behind soft actuators deal with flexible materials like certain polymers and liquids that are harmless to humans.

Hydraulic

The hydraulic actuator consists of cylinder or fluid motor that uses hydraulic power to facilitate mechanical operation. The mechanical motion gives an output in terms of linear, rotatory or oscillatory motion. As liquids are nearly impossible to compress, a hydraulic actuator can exert a large force. The drawback of this approach is its limited acceleration. The hydraulic cylinder consists of a hollow cylindrical tube along which a piston can slide. The term *single acting* is used when the fluid pressure is applied to just one side of the piston. The piston can move in only one direction, a spring being frequently used to give the piston a return stroke. The term *double acting* is used when pressure is applied on each side of the piston; any difference in force between the two sides of the piston moves the piston to one side or the other.

Pneumatic

Pneumatic actuators enable considerable forces to be produced from relatively small pressure changes. Pneumatic energy is desirable for main engine controls because it can quickly respond in starting and stopping as the power source does not need to be stored in reserve for operation.

Moreover, pneumatic actuators are cheaper, and often more powerful than other actuators. These forces are often used with valves to move diaphragms to affect the flow of air through the valve. The advantage of pneumatic actuators consists exactly in the high level of force available in a relatively small volume. While the main drawback of the technology consists in the need for a compressed air network composed of several components such as compressors, reservoirs, filters, dryers, air treatment subsystems, valves, tubes, etc. which makes the technology energy inefficient with energy losses that can sum up to 95%

Electric

Since 1960, several actuator technologies have been developed. Electric actuators can be classified in the following groups:

Electromechanical Actuator (EMA)

It converts the rotational force of an electric rotary motor into a linear movement to generate the requested linear movement through a mechanism; either a belt (Belt Drive axis with stepper or servo), or a screw (either a ball or a lead screw or planetary roller screw).

The main advantages of electromechanical actuators are their relatively good level of accuracy with respect to pneumatics, their possible long lifecycle and the little maintenance effort required (might require grease). It is possible to reach relatively high force, on the order of 100 kN. The main limitation of these actuators are the reachable speed, the important dimensions and weight they require. The main application of such actuators is mainly seen in health care devices and factory automation.

Electrohydraulic Actuator

Another approach is an electrohydraulic actuator, where the electric motor remains the prime mover but provides torque to operate a hydraulic accumulator that is then used to transmit actuation force in much the same way that diesel engine/hydraulics are typically used in heavy equipment. Electrical energy is used to actuate equipment such as multi-turn valves, or electric-powered construction and excavation equipment. When used to control the flow of fluid through a valve, a brake is typically installed above the motor to prevent the fluid pressure from forcing open the valve. If no brake is installed, the actuator gets activated to reclose the valve, which is slowly forced open again. This sets up an oscillation (open, close, open...) and the motor and actuator will eventually become damaged.

Linear Motor

Linear motors are different from electromechanical actuators, they work with the same principle as electric rotary motors, in effect it can be thought as a rotary motor which has been cut and unrolled. Thus, instead of producing a rotational movement, they produce a linear force along their length. Because linear motors cause lower friction losses than other devices, some linear motor products can last over a hundred million cycles.

Linear motors are divided in 3 basic categories: flat linear motor (classic), U-Channel linear motors and Tubular linear motors.

Linear motor technology is the best solution in the context of a low load (up to 30Kgs) because it provides the highest level of speed, control and accuracy.

In fact, it represents the most desired and versatile technology. Due to the limitations of pneumatics, the current electric actuator technology is a viable solution for specific industry applications and it has been successfully introduced in market segments such as the watchmaking, semiconductor and pharmaceutical industries (as high as 60% of the applications. The growing interest for this technology, can be explained by the following characteristics:

- High precision (equal or less than 0,1 mm);
- High cycling rate (greater than 100 cycles/min);
- Possible usage in clean and highly-regulated environments (no leakages of air, humidity or lubricants allowed); and
- Need for programmable motion in the situation of complex operations

The main disadvantages of linear motors are:

- They are expensive respect to pneumatics and other electric technologies.

- They are not easy to integrate in standard machineries due to their important size and high weight.
- Theyhavealowforcedensityrespecttopneumaticandelectromechanical actuators.

Rotary Motor

Rotary motors are actuators that use a piece of energy to form an oscillatory motion at a certain angle of movement. Rotary actuators can have up to a rotation of 360 degrees. This allows it to differ from a linear motor as the linear is bound to a set distance compared to the rotary motor. Rotary motors have the ability to be set at any given degree in a field making the device easier to set up still with durability and a set torque.

Rotary motors can be powered by 3 different techniques such as Electric, Fluid, or Manual. However, Fluid powered rotary actuators have 5 sub-sections of actuators such as Scotch Yoke, Vane, Rack-and-Pinion, Helical, and Electrohydraulic. All forms have their own specific design and use allowing the ability to choose multiple angles of degree.

Applications for the rotary actuators are just about endless but, will more than likely be found dealing with mostly hydraulic pressured devices and industries. Rotary actuators are even used in the robotics field when seeing robotic arms in industry lines. Anything you see that deals with motion control systems to perform a task in technology is a good chance to be a rotary actuator.

Thermal or Magnetic

Actuators which can be actuated by applying thermal or magnetic energy to a solid-state material have been used in commercial applications. Thermal actuators can be triggered by temperature or heating through the Joule effect and tend to be compact, lightweight, economical and with high power density. These actuators use shape memory materials such as shape-memory alloys (SMAs) or magnetic shape-memory alloys (MSMAs).

Mechanical

A mechanical actuator functions to execute movement by converting one kind of motion, such as rotary motion, into another kind, such as linear motion. An example is a rack and pinion. The operation of mechanical actuators is based on combinations of structural components, such as gears and rails, or pulleys and chains.

3D Printed Soft Actuators

The majority of the existing soft actuators are fabricated using multistep low yield processes such as micro-moulding, solid freeform fabrication, and mask lithography. However, these methods require manual fabrication of devices, post processing/assembly, and lengthy iterations until maturity in the fabrication is achieved. To avoid the tedious and time-consuming aspects of the current fabrication processes, researchers are exploring an appropriate manufacturing approach for effective fabrication of soft actuators. Therefore, special soft systems that can be fabricated in a single step by rapid prototyping methods, such as 3D printing, are utilized to narrow the gap between the design and implementation of soft actuators, making the process faster, less expensive, and simpler. They also enable incorporation of all actuator components into a single structure eliminating the need to use external joints, adhesives, and fasteners.

Shape memory polymer (SMP) actuators are the most similar to our muscles, providing a response to a range of stimuli such as light, electrical, magnetic, heat, pH, and moisture changes. They have some deficiencies including fatigue and high response time that have been improved through the introduction of smart materials and combination of different materials by means of advanced fabrication technology. The advent of 3D printers has made a new pathway for fabricating low-cost and fast response SMP actuators.

The process of receiving external stimuli like heat, moisture, electrical input, light or magnetic field by SMP is referred to as shape memory effect (SME). SMP exhibits some rewarding features such a low density, high strain recovery, biocompatibility, and biodegradability.

Photopolymers or light activated polymers (LAP) are another type of SMP that are activated by light stimuli. The LAP actuators can be controlled remotely with instant response and, without any physical contact, only with the variation of light frequency or intensity.

A need for soft, lightweight and biocompatible soft actuators in soft robotics has influenced researchers for devising pneumatic soft actuators because of their intrinsic compliance nature and ability to produce muscle tension.

Polymers such as dielectric elastomers (DE), ionic polymer–metal composites (IPMC), ionic electroactive polymers, polyelectrolyte gels, and gel-metal composites are common materials to form 3D layered structures that can be tailored to work as soft actuators. EAP actuators are categorized as 3D printed soft actuators that respond to electrical excitation as deformation in their shape.

Examples and Applications

In engineering, actuators are frequently used as mechanisms to introduce motion, or to clamp an object so as to prevent motion. In electronic engineering, actuators are a subdivision of transducers. They are devices which transform an input signal (mainly an electrical signal) into some form of motion. Examples of Actuators:

- Comb drive
- Digital micromirror device
- Electric motor
- Electroactive polymer
- Hydraulic cylinder
- Piezoelectric actuator
- Plasma actuator
- Pneumatic actuator
- Screw jack
- Servomechanism
- Solenoid
- Stepper motor
- Shape-memory alloy
- Thermal bimorph
- Hydraulic actuators
- Trim actuator, in aircraft design

Circular to Linear Conversion

Motors are mostly used when circular motions are needed, but can also be used for linear applications by transforming circular to linear motion with a lead screw or similar mechanism. On the other hand, some actuators are intrinsically linear, such as piezoelectric actuators. Conversion between circular and linear motion is commonly made via a few simple types of mechanism including:

- **Screw:** Screw jack, ball screw and roller screw actuators all operate on the principle of the simple machine known as the screw. By rotating the actuator's nut, the screw shaft moves in a line. By moving the screw shaft, the nut rotates.
- **Wheel and Axle:** Hoist, winch, rack and pinion, chain drive, belt drive, rigid chain and rigid belt actuators operate on the principle of the wheel and axle. By rotating a wheel/axle (e.g., drum, gear, pulley or shaft) a linear member (e.g., cable, rack, chain or belt) moves. By moving the linear member, the wheel/axle rotates.

Virtual Instrumentation

In virtual instrumentation, actuators and sensors are the hardware complements of virtual instruments.

Performance Metrics

Performance metrics for actuators include speed, acceleration, and force (alternatively, angular speed, angular acceleration, and torque), as well as energy efficiency and considerations such as mass, volume, operating conditions, and durability, among others.

- **Force:** When considering force in actuators for applications, two main metrics should be considered. These two are static and dynamic loads. Static load is the force capability of the actuator while not in motion. Conversely, the dynamic load of the actuator is the force capability while in motion.
- **Speed:** Speed should be considered primarily at a no-load pace, since the speed will invariably decrease as the load amount increases. The rate the speed will decrease will directly correlate with the amount of force and the initial speed.
- **Operating Conditions:** Actuators are commonly rated using the standard IP Code rating system. Those that are rated for dangerous environments will have a higher IP rating than those for personal or common industrial use.
- **Durability:** This will be determined by each individual manufacturer, depending on usage and quality.

Edge Gateways

An edge gateway, also known as an edge device or edge router, is a networking device that serves as a bridge between different networks. It is typically located at the edge or perimeter of a network, acting as an entry point or gateway for data traffic entering or leaving the network. An edge gateway connects local and external networks, controls network access, filters network traffic, and translates network protocols.

IoT Devices

The Internet of things (IoT) describes devices with sensors, processing ability, software and other technologies that connect and exchange data with other devices and systems over the Internet or other communications networks. The Internet of things encompasses electronics, communication, and computer science engineering. "Internet of things" has been considered a misnomer because devices do not need to be connected to the public internet; they only need to be connected to a network and be individually addressable.

The field has evolved due to the convergence of multiple technologies, including ubiquitous computing, commodity sensors, and increasingly powerful embedded systems, as well as machine learning. Older fields of embedded systems, wireless sensor networks, control systems, automation (including home and building automation), independently and collectively enable the Internet of things. In the consumer market, IoT technology is most synonymous with "smart home" products, including devices and appliances (lighting fixtures, thermostats, home security systems, cameras, and other home appliances) that support one or more common ecosystems and can be controlled via devices associated with that ecosystem, such as smartphones and smart speakers. IoT is also used in healthcare systems.

There are a number of concerns about the risks in the growth of IoT technologies and products, especially in the areas of privacy and security, and consequently there have been industry and government moves to address these concerns, including the development of international and local standards, guidelines, and regulatory frameworks. Because of their interconnected nature, IoT devices are vulnerable to security breaches and privacy concerns. At the same time, the way these devices communicate wirelessly creates regulatory ambiguities, complicating jurisdictional boundaries of the data transfer.

Functions of Edge Devices

- **Data Collection:** Gathering data from the physical environment through sensors and input devices.
- **Data Processing:** Performing computations and analysis on the collected data locally to enable real-time decision-making.
- **Data Storage:** Storing processed data locally for immediate access or temporary holding before transferring to centralized storage.
- **Connectivity:** Enabling communication between devices, gateways, and central systems through various network protocols (e.g., Wi-Fi, Bluetooth, Zigbee, Ethernet).

2.1.2 Endpoints

Endpoints refer to the devices or systems at the outermost layer of a network that interact directly with end users or the environment. In the context of edge computing, endpoints are typically the sources of data generation or the points where data is consumed and acted upon. They can be both input and output devices, providing interaction with the physical world and users.

Examples of Endpoints

- **Smartphones and Tablets:** Mobile devices that serve as endpoints for various applications, collecting data (e.g., GPS, accelerometer) and providing interfaces for user interaction.

- **Laptops and PCs:** Personal computing devices used for accessing and processing data from the edge and cloud.
- **Wearables:** Devices like smartwatches and fitness trackers that monitor health metrics and provide feedback to users.
- **Smart Home Devices:** Gadgets like smart speakers, security cameras, and smart lights that interact with users and their environment to provide automated and intelligent home management.
- **Industrial Machines:** Equipment in manufacturing and industrial settings, such as CNC machines and automated assembly lines, that serve as endpoints for data collection and process control.

Functions of Endpoints

- **User Interaction:** Providing interfaces for users to interact with applications, control devices, and access information.
- **Data Generation:** Collecting data from the physical world through sensors and input mechanisms.
- **Actuation:** Taking actions based on processed data, such as triggering alerts, adjusting settings, or performing mechanical tasks.
- **Communication:** Transmitting data to and receiving instructions from edge devices, gateways, or central systems.

2.1.3 Importance of Edge Devices and Endpoints

- **Real-Time Processing:** Edge devices and endpoints enable real-time data processing and decision-making, essential for applications requiring immediate feedback, such as autonomous vehicles, industrial automation, and smart city infrastructure.
- **Reduced Latency:** By processing data locally, edge devices and endpoints minimize the latency associated with transmitting data to and from centralized cloud servers, enhancing the performance of time-sensitive applications.
- **Bandwidth Optimization:** Localized processing reduces the amount of data sent to the cloud, optimizing bandwidth usage and lowering transmission costs.
- **Enhanced Security and Privacy:** Keeping data processing at the edge limits the exposure of sensitive information to potential breaches during transmission, improving data security and privacy.
- **Scalability and Flexibility:** Edge devices and endpoints provide a scalable and flexible infrastructure that can adapt to varying

workloads and application requirements, supporting the growth of IoT ecosystems.

2.2 EDGE INFRASTRUCTURE AND ARCHITECTURE

Edge computing represents a significant shift from traditional centralized cloud computing to a more distributed approach. By processing data closer to the source, edge computing minimizes latency, optimizes bandwidth, and enhances data security. This shift requires a robust and well-designed infrastructure and architecture. Here's a detailed exploration of edge infrastructure and architecture. Edge infrastructure and architecture represent a critical evolution in the way data is processed and managed.

By decentralizing computing power and bringing it closer to the source of data generation, edge computing addresses the limitations of traditional cloud models, providing reduced latency, optimized bandwidth, and enhanced security. As technology continues to advance, the development and implementation of robust edge infrastructure will be essential for supporting the growing demands of modern applications and industries.

2.2.1 The Basics of Edge Computing

Edge computing involves processing data at or near the point where it is generated, rather than relying solely on a centralized data center. This approach brings computation and data storage closer to the devices that interact with the physical world. Edge computing addresses the limitations of cloud computing, particularly in terms of latency, bandwidth, and data sovereignty.

2.2.2 Components of Edge Infrastructure

Edge infrastructure is a complex ecosystem consisting of various components that work together to facilitate localized data processing. These components include:

Edge Devices

Edge devices are the endpoints where data is generated and initially processed. They include sensors, actuators, and IoT devices.

- **Function:** These devices collect data from their environment, perform initial processing, and may act on the data locally.
- **Examples:** Smart cameras, industrial sensors, wearable health devices, and connected vehicles.

Edge Gateways

Gateways serve as intermediaries between edge devices and the broader network.

- **Function:** They aggregate data from multiple edge devices, perform more complex processing, and ensure secure and efficient data transmission to the cloud or other systems.
- **Examples:** Industrial control systems, smart home hubs, and network routers.

Localized Data Centers

These are smaller data centers located closer to end users compared to traditional centralized cloud data centers.

- **Function:** They provide additional processing power and storage capacity for edge computing tasks.
- **Examples:** Micro data centers in smart buildings, regional data hubs, and mobile edge computing units.

Network Infrastructure

The communication backbone that connects edge devices, gateways, and data centers.

- **Function:** Ensures reliable and secure data transmission across the edge network.
- **Examples:** 5G networks, Wi-Fi, Ethernet, and specialized IoT communication protocols like Zigbee and LoRa.

2.2.3 Edge Computing Architecture

The architecture of an edge computing system is designed to support the specific needs of decentralized processing. It includes several layers and components that ensure efficient data flow and processing.

Device Layer

The layer where data generation and initial processing occur.

- **Components:** Sensors, actuators, IoT devices.
- **Functions:** Data collection, preliminary data processing, and local decision-making.
- **Challenges:** Power consumption, limited processing power, and security vulnerabilities.

Edge Layer

The layer that connects edge devices to the broader network.

- **Components:** Edge gateways, local servers.

- **Functions:** Data aggregation, intermediate processing, protocol translation, and security enforcement.
- **Challenges:** Network reliability, data synchronization, and scalability.

Fog Layer

An intermediate layer between the edge and cloud, often referred to as fog computing.

- **Components:** Fog nodes, localized data centers.
- **Functions:** Additional processing, temporary storage, and data filtering.
- **Challenges:** Resource management, latency optimization, and maintaining consistency.

Cloud Layer

The central data centers where comprehensive data processing and storage occur.

- **Components:** Cloud servers, large-scale data centers.
- **Functions:** Deep analytics, long-term storage, and extensive data processing.
- **Challenges:** Data latency, bandwidth costs, and data privacy concerns.

2.2.4 Key Considerations in Edge Infrastructure Design

Designing an efficient edge infrastructure involves addressing several critical factors:

Scalability

The ability to scale the infrastructure to accommodate increasing amounts of data and devices.

Strategies:

- Modular design,
- Dynamic resource allocation, and
- Automated scaling mechanisms.

Latency

The time delay between data generation and processing.

Strategies:

- Placing processing nodes closer to data sources,
- Optimizing network routes, and
- Using low-latency communication protocols.

Bandwidth

The data transmission capacity of the network.

Strategies:

- Data compression,
- Local data processing, and
- Selective data transmission.

Security

Protecting data and infrastructure from unauthorized access and cyber threats.

Strategies:

- Implementing strong encryption,
- Robust authentication mechanisms, and
- Regular security audits.

Data Privacy and Sovereignty

Ensuring that data handling complies with local regulations and privacy standards.

Strategies:

- Local data processing,
- Data anonymization, and
- Adherence to data governance policies.

Resource Management

Efficiently managing computing, storage, and network resources.

Strategies:

- Dynamic resource allocation,
- Predictive maintenance, and
- Load balancing.

2.2.5 Applications and Use Cases of Edge Infrastructure

Edge infrastructure supports a wide range of applications across various industries, each benefiting from localized processing and reduced latency.

Industrial Automation

Applications:

- Predictive maintenance,
- Real-time monitoring, and
- Automated quality control.

Benefits:

- Increased operational efficiency,
- Reduced downtime, and
- Enhanced safety.

Smart Cities

Applications:

- Traffic management,
- Smart lighting, and
- Waste management.

Benefits:

- Improved urban services,
- Reduced energy consumption, and
- Enhanced quality of life.

Healthcare

Applications:

- Remote patient monitoring,
- Medical imaging, and
- Telemedicine.

Benefits:

- Better patient outcomes,
- Increased access to healthcare, and
- Reduced healthcare costs.

Retail

Applications:

- Personalized shopping experiences,
- Inventory management, and
- Supply chain optimization.

Benefits:

- Improved customer satisfaction,
- Reduced operational costs, and
- Increased sales.

Agriculture

Applications:

- Precision farming,
- Livestock monitoring, and
- Crop management.

Benefits:

- Increased crop yields,
- Reduced resource consumption, and
- Improved farm management.

Autonomous Vehicles

Applications:

- Real-time navigation,
- Vehicle-to-vehicle communication, and
- Safety systems.

Benefits:

- Enhanced safety,
- Improved traffic flow, and
- Reduced emissions.

2.2.6 Future Trends in Edge Infrastructure

The future of edge computing is promising, with several emerging trends poised to enhance its capabilities:

- **5G Integration:** The rollout of 5G networks will provide faster and more reliable connectivity for edge devices, enabling new applications and services.
- **Artificial Intelligence:** AI and machine learning at the edge will enable smarter and more autonomous systems, capable of real-time decision-making and predictive analytics.
- **Enhanced Security Measures:** Advances in security technologies, such as blockchain and quantum cryptography, will further protect edge infrastructure from cyber threats.
- **Edge-to-Cloud Continuum:** Seamless integration between edge and cloud environments will allow for more efficient data processing and resource utilization.

- **Edge-Oriented Development Platforms:** Development platforms tailored for edge computing will simplify the creation and deployment of edge applications.

2.3 EDGE COMPUTING VS. CLOUD COMPUTING

Edge computing and cloud computing are two distinct paradigms in the realm of IT infrastructure and data processing, each with its unique characteristics, advantages, and use cases. Edge computing and cloud computing each offer distinct advantages and serve different needs within the modern IT landscape. Cloud computing excels in providing scalable, cost-effective resources for data storage, big data analytics, and SaaS applications, while edge computing shines in scenarios requiring low latency, bandwidth optimization, and enhanced data privacy. By understanding the strengths and limitations of each approach, organizations can strategically leverage edge and cloud computing to achieve their technological goals and improve operational efficiency. Integrating both paradigms through hybrid solutions can provide the best of both worlds, ensuring optimal performance, scalability, and resilience in a wide range of applications.

2.3.1 Definition and Concept

Cloud Computing

Cloud computing is a model for enabling ubiquitous, convenient, on-demand network access to a shared pool of configurable computing resources (such as networks, servers, storage, applications, and services) that can be rapidly provisioned and released with minimal management effort or service provider interaction. Cloud computing services are typically hosted in large, centralized data centers and delivered over the internet. Examples include Amazon Web Services (AWS), Microsoft Azure, and Google Cloud Platform.

Edge Computing

Edge computing is a distributed computing paradigm that brings computation and data storage closer to the location where it is needed, to improve response times and save bandwidth. Rather than relying on a central cloud, edge computing processes data at the edge of the network, near the source of data generation, such as sensors, IoT devices, and local servers. This approach reduces latency, enhances data privacy, and optimizes bandwidth usage.

2.3.2 Architecture

Cloud Computing Architecture

Cloud computing architecture typically consists of several layers, including the frontend (client devices and user interfaces), the backend (servers, storage systems, and databases), and the network infrastructure that connects them. This centralized model relies on large-scale data centers to provide scalable computing resources.

Edge Computing Architecture

Edge computing architecture decentralizes data processing by distributing it across multiple edge nodes, which can include IoT devices, gateways, and local servers. These nodes are located closer to the data sources and users, allowing for real-time data processing and analysis. The architecture often includes a combination of edge, fog, and cloud layers to ensure seamless data flow and processing.

2.3.3 Key Characteristics

Cloud Computing

- **Scalability:** Cloud computing offers virtually unlimited scalability, allowing businesses to quickly expand or reduce their computing resources based on demand.
- **Cost Efficiency:** With a pay-as-you-go model, cloud computing eliminates the need for significant upfront investment in hardware and infrastructure.
- **Global Accessibility:** Cloud services are accessible from anywhere with an internet connection, supporting remote work and global collaboration.
- **Centralized Management:** Centralized data centers and management simplify IT operations and maintenance.

Edge Computing

- **Low Latency:** By processing data closer to the source, edge computing significantly reduces latency, making it ideal for real-time applications.
- **Bandwidth Optimization:** Edge computing reduces the need to transmit large volumes of data to the cloud, optimizing bandwidth usage.
- **Enhanced Privacy and Security:** Local data processing at the edge can enhance data privacy and security by minimizing data transmission over the internet.
- **Resilience:** Edge computing can continue to operate independently of the cloud, providing greater resilience in case of network failures.

2.3.4 Use Cases

Cloud Computing

- **Data Storage and Backup:** Cloud computing is widely used for storing and backing up large volumes of data, ensuring accessibility and redundancy.

- **Big Data Analytics:** Centralized cloud platforms provide the computational power needed for processing and analyzing big data.
- **Software as a Service (SaaS):** Many applications, such as customer relationship management (CRM) and enterprise resource planning (ERP) systems, are delivered as cloud-based services.
- **Disaster Recovery:** Cloud-based disaster recovery solutions provide robust data protection and quick recovery options.

Edge Computing

- **Autonomous Vehicles:** Edge computing enables real-time data processing and decision-making in autonomous vehicles, reducing latency and improving safety.
- **Industrial IoT:** In industrial settings, edge computing supports real-time monitoring, predictive maintenance, and process automation.
- **Smart Cities:** Edge computing powers smart city applications, such as traffic management, energy optimization, and public safety systems.
- **Healthcare:** Edge computing facilitates remote patient monitoring, medical imaging, and real-time diagnostics in healthcare environments.

2.3.5 Benefits and Challenges

Benefits of Cloud Computing

- **Flexibility:** Cloud computing offers the flexibility to scale resources up or down as needed, accommodating fluctuating workloads.
- **Cost Savings:** The pay-as-you-go pricing model can lead to significant cost savings, especially for businesses with variable resource needs.
- **Access to Advanced Technologies:** Cloud providers offer access to advanced technologies, such as artificial intelligence, machine learning, and big data analytics.
- **Ease of Management:** Centralized management and automated maintenance simplify IT operations.

Challenges of Cloud Computing

- **Latency:** The physical distance between users and cloud data centers can result in higher latency, impacting performance for real-time applications.

- **Bandwidth Costs:** Transmitting large volumes of data to and from the cloud can incur significant bandwidth costs.
- **Data Privacy:** Storing sensitive data in the cloud raises concerns about data privacy and regulatory compliance.
- **Reliance on Internet Connectivity:** Cloud services depend on reliable internet connectivity, which may not be available in all locations.

Benefits of Edge Computing

- **Reduced Latency:** Processing data at the edge minimizes latency, making it ideal for time-sensitive applications.
- **Bandwidth Efficiency:** Local data processing reduces the need for data transmission, optimizing bandwidth usage.
- **Improved Security:** Keeping data closer to its source can enhance security and privacy by limiting exposure to potential breaches.
- **Reliability:** Edge computing can operate independently of central data centers, providing greater resilience in case of network disruptions.

Challenges of Edge Computing

- **Complexity:** Managing a distributed network of edge devices can be complex and require specialized skills.
- **Scalability:** While edge computing improves local processing, scaling across multiple locations can be challenging.
- **Resource Constraints:** Edge devices often have limited processing power and storage compared to centralized cloud resources.
- **Maintenance:** Keeping edge devices updated and secure requires ongoing maintenance and management.

2.3.6 Integration of Edge and Cloud Computing

Hybrid Approaches

Many organizations adopt a hybrid approach, leveraging both edge and cloud computing to optimize their operations.

This integration allows businesses to process time-sensitive data at the edge while utilizing the cloud for long-term storage, deep analytics, and additional computational power.

Examples

- **Smart Retail:** In smart retail environments, edge computing can be used for real-time inventory management and customer analytics, while the cloud handles broader data analysis and integration with other business systems.

- **Telecommunications:** Telecommunications companies use edge computing to deliver low-latency services, such as 5G networks, while relying on the cloud for extensive data processing and storage.
- **Healthcare:** Edge computing enables real-time patient monitoring and diagnostics, with the cloud providing comprehensive data analysis and integration with electronic health records (EHRs).

2.4 FOG COMPUTING: AN EXTENSION OF EDGE COMPUTING

Fog computing or fog networking, also known as fogging, is an architecture that uses edge devices to carry out a substantial amount of computation (edge computing), storage, and communication locally and routed over the Internet backbone.

2.4.1 Concept

In 2011, the need to extend cloud computing with fog computing emerged, in order to cope with huge number of IoT devices and big data volumes for real-time low-latency applications. Fog computing, also called edge computing, is intended for distributed computing where numerous "peripheral" devices connect to a cloud. The word "fog" refers to its cloud-like properties, but closer to the "ground", i.e. IoT devices.

Many of these devices will generate voluminous raw data (e.g., from sensors), and rather than forward all this data to cloud-based servers to be processed, the idea behind fog computing is to do as much processing as possible using computing units co-located with the data-generating devices, so that processed rather than raw data is forwarded, and bandwidth requirements are reduced. An additional benefit is that the processed data is most likely to be needed by the same devices that generated the data, so that by processing locally rather than remotely, the latency between input and response is minimized. This idea is not entirely new: in non-cloud-computing scenarios, special-purpose hardware (e.g., signal-processing chips performing fast Fourier transforms) has long been used to reduce latency and reduce the burden on a CPU.

Fog networking consists of a control plane and a data plane. For example, on the data plane, fog computing enables computing services to reside at the edge of the network as opposed to servers in a data-center. Compared to cloud computing, fog computing emphasizes proximity to end-users and client objectives (e.g., operational costs, security policies, resource exploitation), dense geographical distribution and context-awareness (for what concerns computational and IoT resources), latency reduction and backbone bandwidth savings to achieve better quality of service (QoS) and edge analytics/stream mining, resulting in superior user-experience and redundancy in case of failure while it is also able to be used in Assisted Living scenarios.

Fog networking supports the Internet of Things (IoT) concept, in which most of the devices used by humans on a daily basis will be connected to each other. Examples include phones, wearable health monitoring devices, connected vehicle and augmented reality using devices such as the Google Glass. IoT devices are often resource-constrained and have limited computational abilities to perform cryptography computations. A fog node can provide security for IoT devices by performing these cryptographic computations instead.

SPAWAR, a division of the US Navy, is prototyping and testing a scalable, secure Disruption Tolerant Mesh Network to protect strategic military assets, both stationary and mobile. Machine-control applications, running on the mesh nodes, "take over", when Internet connectivity is lost. Use cases include Internet of Things e.g., smart drone swarms.

The University of Melbourne is addressing the challenges of collecting and processing data from cameras, ECG devices, laptops, smartphones, and IoT devices with its project FogBus 2, which uses edge/fog and Oracle Cloud Infrastructure to process data in real-time.

ISO/IEC 20248 provides a method whereby the data of objects identified by edge computing using Automated Identification Data Carriers (AIDC), a barcode and/or RFID tag, can be read, interpreted, verified and made available into the "Fog" and on the "Edge," even when the AIDC tag has moved on.

2.4.2 History

The term "fog computing" was first developed by Cisco in 2012. November 19, 2015, Cisco Systems, ARM Holdings, Dell, Intel, Microsoft, and Princeton University, founded the OpenFog Consortium to promote interests and development in fog computing. Cisco Sr. Managing-Director Helder Antunes became the consortium's first chairman and Intel's Chief IoT Strategist Jeff Fedders became its first president.

2.4.3 Definition

Both cloud computing and fog computing provide storage, applications, and data to end-users. However, fog computing is closer to end-users and has wider geographical distribution. 'Cloud computing' is the practice of using a network of remote servers hosted on the Internet to store, manage, and process data, rather than a local server or a personal computer. Also known as edge computing or fogging, fog computing facilitates the operation of compute, storage, and networking services between end devices and cloud computing data centers.

National Institute of Standards and Technology in March 2018 released a definition of fog computing adopting much of Cisco's commercial terminology as NIST Special Publication 500-325, *Fog Computing Conceptual Model*, that defines fog computing as a horizontal, physical or virtual resource paradigm that resides between smart end-devices and traditional cloud computing or data center. This paradigm supports vertically-isolated, latency-sensitive applications by providing ubiquitous, scalable, layered, federated, distributed computing, storage, and network connectivity. Thus, fog computing is most distinguished by distance from the edge. In the theoretical model of fog computing, fog computing nodes are physically and functionally operative between edge nodes and centralized cloud. Much of the terminology is undefined, including key architectural terms like "smart", and the distinction between fog computing from edge computing is not generally agreed.

Differences with Edge Computing and Cloud Computing

While edge computing is typically referred to the location where services are instantiated, fog computing implies distribution of the communication, computation, storage resources, and services on or close to devices and systems in the control of end-users. Fog computing is a medium weight and intermediate level of computing power. Rather than a substitute, fog computing often serves as a complement to cloud computing. Fog computing is more energy-efficient than cloud computing.

CHAPTER 3
EDGE COMPUTING TECHNOLOGIES

3.1 EDGE SERVERS AND MICRO DATA CENTERS

As the demand for faster, more efficient data processing continues to grow, traditional centralized data centers are no longer sufficient to meet the needs of modern applications. Edge computing has emerged as a solution, bringing computation and data storage closer to where data is generated. Key components of this paradigm are edge servers and micro data centers, which play a critical role in supporting localized data processing and reducing latency. Edge servers and micro data centers are essential components of the edge computing paradigm, providing localized data processing, storage, and analytics capabilities. They offer numerous benefits, including reduced latency, optimized bandwidth, improved reliability, and enhanced security. However, organizations must address challenges such as management complexity, resource constraints, interoperability, and security to fully realize the potential of edge computing. As technology continues to evolve, the integration of 5G, AI, and machine learning will further enhance the capabilities of edge servers and micro data centers, driving innovation and enabling new applications across various industries.

3.1.1 Edge Servers

Edge servers are computing devices located at the edge of the network, near the data sources and end-users. They perform data processing, storage, and analysis tasks locally, minimizing the need to transmit data to centralized cloud servers. Edge servers are designed to handle real-time data processing and are often used in environments where low latency and high reliability are critical.

Architecture

Edge servers can vary in form and complexity, but they generally consist of high-performance processors, memory, and storage. They are often equipped with specialized hardware for specific tasks, such as GPUs for AI and machine learning workloads. Edge servers are designed to be robust and capable of operating in diverse environments, from industrial settings to remote locations.

Key Features

- **Low Latency:** By processing data locally, edge servers reduce the time it takes for data to travel to and from centralized data centers, providing real-time responses.

- **High Reliability:** Edge servers can continue to operate independently of the central cloud, ensuring continued functionality even during network disruptions.
- **Scalability:** They can be easily deployed and scaled to meet the needs of various applications, from small-scale deployments to large, distributed networks.

3.1.2 Micro Data Centers

Micro data centers are small, self-contained data centers designed to provide localized data processing and storage capabilities. They can be deployed closer to end-users and data sources, supporting edge computing initiatives. Micro data centers offer the benefits of traditional data centers but on a smaller scale, making them suitable for environments with space and power constraints.

Architecture

Micro data centers typically include all the essential components of a traditional data center, such as servers, storage, networking equipment, power supplies, and cooling systems. They are often housed in compact, ruggedized enclosures that can be deployed in a variety of locations, including outdoor and industrial environments. Micro data centers are designed for quick deployment and easy management.

Key Features

- **Compact Size:** Their small footprint allows them to be deployed in space-constrained environments, such as retail stores, manufacturing floors, and remote sites.
- **Ease of Deployment:** Micro data centers are often pre-configured and ready to deploy, reducing installation time and complexity.
- **Enhanced Security:** They provide localized security controls, reducing the risk of data breaches during transmission to centralized data centers.

3.1.3 Benefits of Edge Servers and Micro Data Centers

Reduced Latency

One of the primary benefits of edge servers and micro data centers is the significant reduction in latency. By processing data closer to the source, these components minimize the time it takes for data to travel across the network, enabling real-time applications such as autonomous vehicles, industrial automation, and smart cities.

Bandwidth Optimization

Edge servers and micro data centers help optimize bandwidth usage by processing and filtering data locally. Only the most relevant or aggregated data is sent to centralized data centers, reducing the amount of data transmitted over the network and lowering bandwidth costs.

Improved Reliability and Resilience

By distributing computing resources across multiple edge locations, edge servers and micro data centers enhance the overall reliability and resilience of the network. This distributed approach ensures that localized processing continues even if the central cloud experiences downtime or connectivity issues.

Enhanced Security and Privacy

Localized data processing improves security and privacy by reducing the need to transmit sensitive data over the internet. Edge servers and micro data centers can implement local security measures, such as encryption and access controls, to protect data at the edge.

Scalability and Flexibility

Edge servers and micro data centers provide a scalable and flexible infrastructure that can be tailored to meet the specific needs of various applications. They can be easily added or reconfigured to support changing workloads and business requirements.

3.1.4 Challenges and Considerations

Management and Maintenance

Managing and maintaining a distributed network of edge servers and micro data centers can be complex. Organizations need to implement robust monitoring and management tools to ensure the smooth operation of their edge infrastructure. This includes regular software updates, hardware maintenance, and troubleshooting.

Resource Constraints

Edge servers and micro data centers may have limited resources compared to centralized data centers. Organizations need to carefully plan their deployments to ensure that the available processing power, storage, and network bandwidth are sufficient to meet the demands of their applications.

Interoperability

Ensuring interoperability between edge servers, micro data centers, and centralized cloud infrastructure is crucial for seamless data flow and processing. Organizations need to adopt standardized protocols and interfaces to enable smooth integration and communication between different components.

Security Challenges

While localized processing improves security, edge servers and micro data centers can still be vulnerable to physical and cyber threats.

Organizations need to implement comprehensive security measures, including physical security controls, network security protocols, and regular security audits, to protect their edge infrastructure.

3.1.5 Applications of Edge Servers and Micro Data Centers

Industrial IoT

Edge servers and micro data centers play a crucial role in industrial IoT applications, such as predictive maintenance, real-time monitoring, and process automation. By processing data locally, they enable faster decision-making and reduce downtime in manufacturing and industrial environments.

Smart Cities

Smart city initiatives rely on edge servers and micro data centers to support applications such as traffic management, energy optimization, and public safety.

These components provide the real-time data processing and analytics needed to manage urban infrastructure efficiently.

Healthcare

In healthcare, edge servers and micro data centers enable real-time patient monitoring, medical imaging, and diagnostics. By processing data locally, they improve response times and enhance patient care, particularly in remote and underserved areas.

Retail

Retailers use edge servers and micro data centers to support applications such as personalized shopping experiences, inventory management, and point-of-sale systems.

These components help optimize operations and improve customer satisfaction by providing real-time insights and analytics.

Telecommunications

Telecommunications companies deploy edge servers and micro data centers to support the rollout of 5G networks and deliver low-latency services. These components enable faster data processing and improve the quality of service for mobile users.

3.1.6 Future Trends

5G Integration

The rollout of 5G networks will further enhance the capabilities of edge servers and micro data centers. The increased speed and lower latency of 5G will enable new applications and services, driving greater adoption of edge computing.

AI and Machine Learning

Integrating AI and machine learning capabilities into edge servers and micro data centers will enable more intelligent and autonomous systems. These technologies will enhance real-time data processing, predictive analytics, and decision-making at the edge.

Standardization

As edge computing continues to grow, there will be a push towards standardization of protocols and interfaces to ensure interoperability and seamless integration between different components. Standardization will simplify the deployment and management of edge infrastructure.

Edge-to-Cloud Continuum

The concept of an edge-to-cloud continuum will become more prevalent, where data processing and storage seamlessly transition between edge, fog, and cloud environments. This approach will optimize resource utilization and provide greater flexibility for organizations.

3.2 EDGE GATEWAYS AND EDGE ROUTERS

3.2.1 Edge Gateways

Edge gateways are a pivotal component of edge computing, acting as intermediaries between edge devices and the broader network. They facilitate the local processing of data, ensure secure and efficient data transmission, and enable the integration of various devices and systems.

Edge gateways are essential components of the edge computing paradigm, providing localized data processing, protocol translation, and secure data transmission. They offer numerous benefits, including reduced latency, optimized bandwidth, enhanced security, and improved scalability. However, organizations must address challenges such as complex management, resource constraints, interoperability issues, and security risks to fully leverage the potential of edge gateways. As technology continues to evolve, the integration of 5G, AI, and machine learning will further enhance the capabilities of edge gateways, driving innovation and enabling new applications across various industries.

Definition and Concept of Edge Gateways

Edge Gateways

Edge gateways are specialized devices or software platforms located at the network's edge. They serve as bridges between local edge devices (such as sensors, IoT devices, and actuators) and centralized cloud or data center infrastructure.

Edge gateways perform data aggregation, initial processing, protocol translation, and secure data transmission, playing a crucial role in the edge computing ecosystem.

Role in Edge Computing

Edge gateways enhance the efficiency and effectiveness of edge computing by handling data closer to its source. This reduces the need for constant communication with centralized cloud servers, minimizing latency and bandwidth usage while ensuring timely and secure data processing.

Architecture of Edge Gateways

Hardware Components

Edge gateways typically consist of robust hardware designed to operate in diverse and sometimes harsh environments. Key hardware components include:

- **Processors:** High-performance CPUs or specialized processors (such as GPUs and TPUs) for handling complex data processing tasks.
- **Memory:** Sufficient RAM and storage capacity to manage and temporarily store data from multiple edge devices.
- **Networking Interfaces:** Multiple communication interfaces, including Ethernet, Wi-Fi, cellular, and specialized IoT protocols like Zigbee, LoRa, and Bluetooth.
- **Power Supply:** Reliable power sources, including battery backup, to ensure uninterrupted operation.

Software Components

The software architecture of edge gateways includes several layers and modules to facilitate data processing, management, and communication:

- **Operating System:** A lightweight and optimized operating system that supports real-time processing and efficient resource management.
- **Middleware:** Software layers that provide services such as data aggregation, filtering, and protocol translation.
- **Security Modules:** Tools and protocols for ensuring data integrity, encryption, and secure communication.

- **Management Tools:** Interfaces for remote monitoring, configuration, and maintenance of the gateway and connected devices.

Functions of Edge Gateways

Data Aggregation and Filtering

Edge gateways collect data from multiple edge devices and aggregate it for initial processing. They filter and preprocess the data to reduce the volume of information that needs to be transmitted to centralized systems. This helps in optimizing bandwidth and ensures that only relevant data is sent for further analysis.

Protocol Translation

Edge gateways enable communication between devices using different protocols by performing protocol translation. They act as intermediaries, converting data from one format to another to ensure seamless integration and interoperability between heterogeneous devices and systems.

Local Data Processing

By processing data locally, edge gateways reduce latency and enable real-time decision-making. They can execute algorithms and perform analytics on the aggregated data, providing immediate insights and actions without relying on remote cloud servers.

Secure Data Transmission

Edge gateways ensure secure data transmission between edge devices and centralized infrastructure. They implement encryption, authentication, and other security measures to protect data integrity and prevent unauthorized access.

Benefits of Edge Gateways

Reduced Latency

One of the primary benefits of edge gateways is the significant reduction in latency. By processing data locally and minimizing the need for long-distance communication, edge gateways enable real-time responses and actions, which are crucial for applications like autonomous vehicles, industrial automation, and smart cities.

Bandwidth Optimization

Edge gateways optimize bandwidth usage by filtering and preprocessing data before transmitting it to the cloud. This reduces the volume of data that needs to be sent over the network, lowering bandwidth costs and preventing network congestion.

Enhanced Security and Privacy

Edge gateways enhance data security and privacy by implementing local security measures and reducing the exposure of sensitive data during transmission. They provide a secure environment for data processing and communication, mitigating the risk of data breaches and cyber threats.

Scalability and Flexibility

Edge gateways offer scalable and flexible solutions for managing diverse and distributed edge devices. They can be easily deployed and configured to support various applications and workloads, allowing organizations to scale their edge infrastructure as needed.

Challenges of Edge Gateways

Complex Management

Managing and maintaining edge gateways can be complex, especially in large-scale deployments with numerous devices. Organizations need robust tools and strategies for monitoring, updating, and troubleshooting edge gateways to ensure their optimal performance and reliability.

Resource Constraints

Edge gateways may have limited processing power, memory, and storage compared to centralized cloud servers. This can constrain their ability to handle large volumes of data and complex analytics, requiring careful planning and optimization of workloads.

Interoperability Issues

Ensuring interoperability between different devices, protocols, and systems is a significant challenge for edge gateways. Organizations need to adopt standardized protocols and interfaces to enable seamless communication and integration between heterogeneous components.

Security Risks

While edge gateways enhance security, they can also be vulnerable to physical and cyber threats. Organizations must implement comprehensive security measures, including physical security controls, network security protocols, and regular security audits, to protect their edge infrastructure.

Applications of Edge Gateways

Industrial Automation

In industrial settings, edge gateways support applications such as predictive maintenance, real-time monitoring, and process automation. They enable local data processing and analytics, improving operational efficiency and reducing downtime.

Smart Cities

Edge gateways play a crucial role in smart city initiatives, supporting applications like traffic management, energy optimization, and public safety. They provide the real-time data processing and communication needed to manage urban infrastructure effectively.

Healthcare

In healthcare, edge gateways facilitate remote patient monitoring, medical imaging, and diagnostics. By processing data locally, they enable real-time insights and actions, enhancing patient care and outcomes.

Retail

Retailers use edge gateways to support applications like personalized shopping experiences, inventory management, and point-of-sale systems. Edge gateways help optimize operations and improve customer satisfaction by providing real-time insights and analytics.

Telecommunications

Telecommunications companies deploy edge gateways to support the rollout of 5G networks and deliver low-latency services. Edge gateways enable faster data processing and improve the quality of service for mobile users.

Future Trends

5G Integration

The integration of edge gateways with 5G networks will enhance their capabilities, providing faster and more reliable connectivity for edge devices. This will enable new applications and services, driving greater adoption of edge computing.

AI and Machine Learning

Incorporating AI and machine learning capabilities into edge gateways will enable more intelligent and autonomous systems. These technologies will enhance real-time data processing, predictive analytics, and decision-making at the edge.

Standardization

As edge computing continues to grow, there will be a push towards standardization of protocols and interfaces to ensure interoperability and seamless integration between different components. Standardization will simplify the deployment and management of edge gateways.

3.2.2 Edge Routers

Edge routers are a critical component in the architecture of edge computing, playing a vital role in connecting local networks with external networks, ensuring data flows efficiently and securely. They act as intermediaries between different network segments, providing routing capabilities, security, and management of data traffic at the edge of the network.

Edge routers are essential components of the edge computing paradigm, providing connectivity, routing, security, and traffic management at the network's edge. They offer numerous benefits, including improved network performance, enhanced security, scalability, efficient bandwidth utilization, and reliability. However, organizations must address challenges such as complex management, high costs, interoperability issues, and security risks to fully leverage the potential of edge routers. As technology continues to evolve, the integration of 5G, AI, and machine learning will further enhance the capabilities of edge routers, driving innovation and enabling new applications across various industries.

Definition and Concept of Edge Routers

Edge Routers

Edge routers are networking devices located at the boundary of a network that connects local area networks (LANs) to external wide area networks (WANs) or the internet.

They manage data traffic between internal networks and external networks, providing essential services such as routing, security, and quality of service (QoS) management. Edge routers are designed to handle high volumes of data traffic and ensure efficient and secure communication between different network segments.

Role in Edge Computing

In edge computing, edge routers play a crucial role by providing connectivity between edge devices, local data centers, and cloud infrastructure.

They facilitate the flow of data from the edge to the cloud and vice versa, ensuring low latency, high security, and reliable communication.

Architecture of Edge Routers

Hardware Components

Edge routers consist of robust hardware designed to handle high-speed data processing and routing. Key hardware components include:

- **Processors**: High-performance CPUs capable of managing complex routing tasks and processing large volumes of data traffic.
- **Memory**: Sufficient RAM and storage capacity to handle routing tables, data caching, and temporary storage.
- **Network Interfaces**: Multiple interfaces for connecting to different

network segments, including Ethernet, fiber optics, and wireless interfaces.

- **Power Supply**: Reliable power sources, often with redundancy and battery backup, to ensure continuous operation.
- **Software Components**: The software architecture of edge routers includes various layers and modules to support routing, security, and management functions:
- **Operating System**: A specialized operating system designed for networking, such as Cisco IOS, Juniper Junos, or open-source alternatives like VyOS.
- **Routing Protocols**: Implementation of various routing protocols, such as OSPF, BGP, and EIGRP, to manage data traffic and routing decisions.
- **Security Modules**: Tools and protocols for ensuring data integrity, encryption, firewalling, and intrusion detection/prevention.
- **Management Tools**: Interfaces for remote monitoring, configuration, and management of the router and network traffic.

Functions of Edge Routers

Routing

The primary function of edge routers is to manage the routing of data packets between different networks. They use routing tables and protocols to determine the best path for data to travel from the source to the destination. Edge routers ensure efficient data traffic management, optimizing network performance and minimizing latency.

Security

Edge routers provide essential security functions to protect the network from external threats. They implement firewall rules, VPNs, and encryption to secure data transmission. Edge routers also include intrusion detection and prevention systems (IDS/IPS) to identify and mitigate potential security breaches.

Quality of Service (QoS) Management

Edge routers manage the quality of service (QoS) for data traffic, ensuring that critical applications receive the necessary bandwidth and low latency. QoS management helps prioritize traffic based on application requirements, preventing congestion and ensuring optimal network performance.

Traffic Management and Load Balancing

Edge routers handle traffic management and load balancing to distribute data traffic evenly across the network. They help prevent network bottlenecks and ensure that resources are utilized efficiently. Load balancing also enhances network reliability by providing redundancy and failover capabilities.

Benefits of Edge Routers

Improved Network Performance

Edge routers enhance network performance by efficiently managing data traffic and reducing latency. They ensure that data packets are routed through the most optimal paths, minimizing delays and improving the overall user experience.

Enhanced Security

By implementing robust security measures, edge routers protect the network from external threats. They provide a first line of defense against cyberattacks, ensuring that sensitive data remains secure during transmission.

Scalability and Flexibility

Edge routers offer scalability and flexibility, allowing organizations to expand their networks as needed. They can support various network configurations and integrate with different devices and systems, providing a versatile solution for diverse networking requirements.

Efficient Bandwidth Utilization

Edge routers optimize bandwidth utilization by managing data traffic and prioritizing critical applications. This ensures that available bandwidth is used efficiently, preventing congestion and ensuring smooth network operations.

Reliability and Redundancy

Edge routers provide reliability and redundancy, ensuring continuous network operation even in the event of hardware failures or network disruptions. They support failover mechanisms and load balancing to maintain network availability and performance.

Challenges of Edge Routers

Complex Management

Managing and maintaining edge routers can be complex, especially in large-scale deployments with numerous devices. Organizations need robust tools and strategies for monitoring, updating, and troubleshooting edge routers to ensure their optimal performance and reliability.

High Costs

Edge routers can be expensive to purchase and maintain, particularly for small and medium-sized businesses. The costs of hardware, software, and ongoing management can be significant, requiring careful budget planning and resource allocation.

Interoperability Issues

Ensuring interoperability between different devices, protocols, and systems can be challenging for edge routers. Organizations need to adopt standardized protocols and interfaces to enable seamless communication and integration between heterogeneous components.

Security Risks

While edge routers enhance security, they can also be vulnerable to physical and cyber threats. Organizations must implement comprehensive security measures, including physical security controls, network security protocols, and regular security audits, to protect their edge infrastructure.

Applications of Edge Routers

Industrial IoT

In industrial settings, edge routers support applications such as predictive maintenance, real-time monitoring, and process automation. They enable efficient data routing and secure communication between IoT devices, improving operational efficiency and reducing downtime.

Smart Cities

Edge routers play a crucial role in smart city initiatives, supporting applications like traffic management, energy optimization, and public safety. They provide the necessary connectivity and data routing for managing urban infrastructure effectively.

Healthcare

In healthcare, edge routers facilitate remote patient monitoring, medical imaging, and diagnostics. By ensuring secure and efficient data transmission, they enhance patient care and outcomes, particularly in remote and underserved areas.

Retail

Retailers use edge routers to support applications like personalized shopping experiences, inventory management, and point-of-sale systems. Edge routers help optimize operations and improve customer satisfaction by providing reliable connectivity and data routing.

Telecommunications

Telecommunications companies deploy edge routers to support the rollout of 5G networks and deliver low-latency services. Edge routers enable faster data processing and improve the quality of service for mobile users, ensuring seamless connectivity.

Future Trends

5G Integration

The integration of edge routers with 5G networks will enhance their capabilities, providing faster and more reliable connectivity for edge devices. This will enable new applications and services, driving greater adoption of edge computing.

AI and Machine Learning

Incorporating AI and machine learning capabilities into edge routers will enable more intelligent and autonomous systems. These technologies will enhance real-time data processing, predictive analytics, and decision-making at the edge.

Standardization

As edge computing continues to grow, there will be a push towards standardization of protocols and interfaces to ensure interoperability and seamless integration between different components. Standardization will simplify the deployment and management of edge routers.

3.3 EDGE OPERATING SYSTEMS

"Edge Operating Systems" typically refers to operating systems designed to run on edge computing devices. These devices are located closer to the data source or user, reducing latency and improving performance for applications that require real-time processing or low-latency communication.

Some examples of Edge Operating Systems include:

3.3.1 Linux-based OS

Linux is both an open-source Unix-like kernel and a generic name for a family of open-source Unix-like operating systems based on the Linux kernel, an operating system kernel first released on September 17, 1991, by Linus Torvalds. Linux is typically packaged as a Linux distribution (distro), which includes the kernel and supporting system software and libraries, many of which are provided by the GNU Project.

Popular Linux distributions include Debian, Fedora Linux, Arch Linux, and Ubuntu. Commercial distributions include Red Hat Enterprise Linux and SUSE Linux Enterprise. Desktop Linux distributions include a windowing system such as X11 or Wayland and a desktop environment such as GNOME or KDE Plasma. Distributions intended for servers may not have a graphical user interface at all, or include a solution stack such as LAMP. Because Linux is freely redistributable, anyone may create a distribution for any purpose.

Linux was originally developed for personal computers based on the Intel x86 architecture, but has since been ported to more platforms than any other operating system. Because of the dominance of Linux-based Android on smartphones, Linux, including Android, has the largest installed base of all general-purpose operating systems as of May 2022. Linux is, as of March 2024, used by around 4 percent of desktop computers. The Chromebook, which runs the Linux kernel-based ChromeOS, dominates the US K–12 education market and represents nearly 20 percent of sub-$300 notebook sales in the US. Linux is the leading operating system on servers (over 96.4% of the top one million web servers' operating systems are Linux), leads other big iron systems such as mainframe computers, and is used on all of the world's 500 fastest supercomputers (as of November 2017, having gradually displaced all competitors).

Linux also runs on embedded systems, i.e., devices whose operating system is typically built into the firmware and is highly tailored to the system. This includes routers, automation controls, smart home devices, video game consoles, televisions (Samsung and LG Smart TVs), automobiles (Tesla, Audi, Mercedes-Benz, Hyundai, and Toyota), and spacecraft (Falcon 9 rocket, Dragon crew capsule, and the *Perseverance* rover).

Linux is one of the most prominent examples of free and open-source software collaboration. The source code may be used, modified, and distributed commercially or non-commercially by anyone under the terms of its respective licenses, such as the GNU General Public License (GPL). The Linux kernel, for example, is licensed under the GPLv2, with an exception for system calls that allows code that calls the kernel via system calls not to be licensed under the GPL.

History

Precursors

The Unix operating system was conceived and implemented in 1969, at AT&T's Bell Labs, in the United States by Ken Thompson, Dennis Ritchie, Douglas McIlroy, and Joe Ossanna. First released in 1971, Unix was written entirely in assembly language, as was common practice at the time. In 1973, in a key pioneering approach, it was rewritten in the C programming language by Dennis Ritchie (except for some hardware and I/O routines). The availability of a high-level language implementation of Unix made its porting to different computer platforms easier.

Due to an earlier antitrust case forbidding it from entering the computer business, AT&T licensed the operating system's source code as a trade secret to anyone who asked. As a result, Unix grew quickly and became widely adopted by academic institutions and businesses. In 1984, AT&T divested itself of its regional operating companies, and was released from its obligation not to enter the computer business;

freed of that obligation, Bell Labs began selling Unix as a proprietary product, where users were not legally allowed to modify it.

Onyx Systems began selling early microcomputer-based Unix workstations in 1980. Later, Sun Microsystems, founded as a spin-off of a student project at Stanford University, also began selling Unix-based desktop workstations in 1982. While Sun workstations did not use commodity PC hardware, for which Linux was later originally developed, it represented the first successful commercial attempt at distributing a primarily single-user microcomputer that ran a Unix operating system.

With Unix increasingly "locked in" as a proprietary product, the GNU Project, started in 1983 by Richard Stallman, had the goal of creating a "complete Unix-compatible software system" composed entirely of free software. Work began in 1984. Later, in 1985, Stallman started the Free Software Foundation and wrote the GNU General Public License (GNU GPL) in 1989. By the early 1990s, many of the programs required in an operating system (such as libraries, compilers, text editors, a command-line shell, and a windowing system) were completed, although low-level elements such as device drivers, daemons, and the kernel, called GNU Hurd, were stalled and incomplete.

Minix was created by Andrew S. Tanenbaum, a computer science professor, and released in 1987 as a minimal Unix-like operating system targeted at students and others who wanted to learn operating system principles. Although the complete source code of Minix was freely available, the licensing terms prevented it from being free software until the licensing changed in April 2000.

Although not released until 1992, due to legal complications, the development of 386BSD, from which NetBSD, OpenBSD and FreeBSD descended, predated that of Linux. Linus Torvalds has stated on separate occasions that if the GNU kernel or 386BSD had been available at the time (1991), he probably would not have created Linux.

Creation

While attending the University of Helsinki in the fall of 1990, Torvalds enrolled in a Unix course. The course used a MicroVAX minicomputer running Ultrix, and one of the required texts was *Operating Systems: Design and Implementation* by Andrew S. Tanenbaum. This textbook included a copy of Tanenbaum's Minix operating system. It was with this course that Torvalds first became exposed to Unix. In 1991, he became curious about operating systems. Frustrated by the licensing of Minix, which at the time limited it to educational use only, he began to work on his operating system kernel, which eventually became the Linux kernel.

On July 3, 1991, to implement Unix system calls, Linus Torvalds attempted unsuccessfully to obtain a digital copy of the POSIX standards documentation with a request to the *comp.os.minix* newsgroup. After not finding the POSIX documentation, Torvalds initially resorted to determining system calls from SunOS documentation owned by the university for use in operating its Sun Microsystems server. He also learned some system calls from Tanenbaum's Minix text.

Torvalds began the development of the Linux kernel on Minix and applications written for Minix were also used on Linux. Later, Linux matured and further Linux kernel development took place on Linux systems. GNU applications also replaced all Minix components, because it was advantageous to use the freely available code from the GNU Project with the fledgling operating system; code licensed under the GNU GPL can be reused in other computer programs as long as they also are released under the same or a compatible license. Torvalds initiated a switch from his original license, which prohibited commercial redistribution, to the GNU GPL. Developers worked to integrate GNU components with the Linux kernel, creating a fully functional and free operating system.

Naming

Linus Torvalds had wanted to call his invention "Freax", a portmanteau of "free", "freak", and "x" (as an allusion to Unix). During the start of his work on the system, some of the project's makefiles included the name "Freax" for about half a year. Initially, Torvalds considered the name "Linux" but dismissed it as too egotistical.

To facilitate development, the files were uploaded to the FTP server of FUNET in September 1991. Ari Lemmke, Torvalds' coworker at the Helsinki University of Technology (HUT) who was one of the volunteer administrators for the FTP server at the time, did not think that "Freax" was a good name, so he named the project "Linux" on the server without consulting Torvalds. Later, however, Torvalds consented to "Linux".

According to a newsgroup post by Torvalds, the word "Linux" should be pronounced with a short 'i' as in 'print' and 'u' as in 'put'. To further demonstrate how the word "Linux" should be pronounced, he included an audio guide with the kernel source code. However, in this recording, he pronounces Linux as */□linʊks/* (*LEEN-uuks*) with a short but close front unrounded vowel, instead of a near-close near-front unrounded vowel as in his newsgroup post.

Commercial and Popular Uptake

The adoption of Linux in production environments, rather than being used only by hobbyists, started to take off first in the mid-1990s in the supercomputing community, where organizations such as NASA started to replace their increasingly expensive machines with clusters of inexpensive commodity computers running Linux. Commercial use began when Dell and IBM, followed by Hewlett-Packard, started offering Linux support to escape Microsoft's monopoly in the desktop operating system market.

Today, Linux systems are used throughout computing, from embedded systems to virtually all supercomputers, and have secured a place in server installations such as the popular LAMP application stack. The use of Linux distributions in home and enterprise desktops has been growing. Linux distributions have also become popular in the netbook market, with many devices shipping with customized Linux distributions installed, and Google releasing their own ChromeOS designed for netbooks.

Linux's greatest success in the consumer market is perhaps the mobile device market, with Android being the dominant operating system on smartphones and very popular on tablets and, more recently, on wearables. Linux gaming is also on the rise with Valve showing its support for Linux and rolling out SteamOS, its own gaming-oriented Linux distribution, which was later implemented in their Steam Deck platform. Linux distributions have also gained popularity with various local and national governments, such as the federal government of Brazil.

Current Development

Linus Torvalds is the lead maintainer for the Linux kernel and guides its development, while Greg Kroah-Hartman is the lead maintainer for the stable branch. Zoë Kooyman is the executive director of the Free Software Foundation, which in turn supports the GNU components. Finally, individuals and corporations develop third-party non-GNU components. These third-party components comprise a vast body of work and may include both kernel modules and user applications and libraries. Linux vendors and communities combine and distribute the kernel, GNU components, and non-GNU components, with additional package management software in the form of Linux distributions.

Design

Many developers of open-source software agree that the Linux kernel was not designed but rather evolved through natural selection. Torvalds considers that although the design of Unix served as a scaffolding, "Linux grew with a lot of mutations – and because the mutations were less than random, they were faster and more directed than alpha-particles in DNA." Eric S. Raymond considers Linux's revolutionary aspects to be social, not technical: before Linux, complex software was designed carefully by small groups, but "Linux evolved in a completely different way. From nearly the beginning, it was rather casually hacked on by huge numbers of volunteers coordinating only through the Internet. Quality was maintained not by rigid standards or autocracy but by the naively simple strategy of releasing every week and getting feedback from hundreds of users within days, creating a sort of rapid Darwinian selection on the mutations introduced by developers." Bryan Cantrill, an engineer of a competing OS, agrees that "Linux wasn't designed, it evolved", but considers this to be a limitation, proposing that some features, especially those related to security, cannot be evolved into, "this is not a biological system at the end of the day, it's a software system."

A Linux-based system is a modular Unix-like operating system, deriving much of its basic design from principles established in Unix during the 1970s and 1980s. Such a system uses a monolithic kernel, the Linux kernel, which handles process control, networking, access to the peripherals, and file systems. Device drivers are either integrated directly with the kernel or added as modules that are loaded while the system is running.

The GNU userland is a key part of most systems based on the Linux kernel, with Android being the notable exception. The GNU C library, an implementation of the C standard library, works as a wrapper for the system calls of the Linux kernel necessary to the kernel-userspace interface, the toolchain is a broad collection of programming tools vital to Linux development (including the compilers used to build the Linux kernel itself), and the coreutils implement many basic Unix tools. The GNU Project also develops Bash, a popular CLI shell. The graphical user interface (or GUI) used by most Linux systems is built on top of an implementation of the X Window System. More recently, the Linux community has sought to advance to Wayland as the new display server protocol, in place of X11. Many other open-source software projects contribute to Linux systems.

Installed components of a Linux system include the following:

- A bootloader, for example GNU GRUB, LILO, SYSLINUX or systemd-boot. This is a program that loads the Linux kernel into the computer's main memory, by being executed by the computer when it is turned on and after the firmware initialization is performed.
- An init program, such as the traditional sysvinit and the newer systemd, OpenRC and Upstart. This is the first process launched by the Linux kernel, and is at the root of the process tree. It starts processes such as system services and login prompts (whether graphical or in terminal mode).
- Software libraries, which contain code that can be used by running processes. On Linux systems using ELF-format executable files, the dynamic linker that manages the use of dynamic libraries is known as ld-linux.so. If the system is set up for the user to compile software themselves, header files will also be included to describe the programming interface of installed libraries. Besides the most

commonly used software library on Linux systems, the GNU C Library (glibc), there are numerous other libraries, such as SDL and Mesa.

  - The C standard library is the library necessary to run programs written in C on a computer system, with the GNU C Library being the standard. It provides an implementation of the POSIX API, as well as extensions to that API. For embedded systems, alternatives such as musl, EGLIBC (a glibc fork once used by Debian) and uClibc (which was designed for uClinux) have been developed, although the last two are no longer maintained. Android uses its own C library, Bionic. However, musl can additionally be used as a replacement for glibc on desktop and laptop systems, as seen on certain Linux distributions like Void Linux.

- Basic Unix commands, with GNU coreutils being the standard implementation. Alternatives exist for embedded systems, such as the copyleft BusyBox, and the BSD-licensed Toybox.
- Widget toolkits are the libraries used to build graphical user interfaces (GUIs) for software applications. Numerous widget toolkits are available, including GTK and Clutter developed by the GNOME Project, Qt developed by the Qt Project and led by The Qt Company, and Enlightenment Foundation Libraries (EFL) developed primarily by the Enlightenment team.
- A package management system, such as dpkg and RPM. Alternatively packages can be compiled from binary or source tarballs.
- User interface programs such as command shells or windowing environments.

User Interface

The user interface, also known as the shell, is either a command-line interface (CLI), a graphical user interface (GUI), or controls attached to the associated hardware, which is common for embedded systems. For desktop systems, the default user interface is usually graphical, although the CLI is commonly available through terminal emulator windows or on a separate virtual console.

CLI shells are text-based user interfaces, which use text for both input and output. The dominant shell used in Linux is the Bourne-Again Shell (bash), originally developed for the GNU Project. Most low-level Linux components, including various parts of the userland, use the CLI exclusively. The CLI is particularly suited for automation of repetitive or delayed tasks and provides very simple inter-process communication. On desktop systems, the most popular user interfaces are the GUI shells, packaged together with extensive desktop environments, such as KDE Plasma, GNOME, MATE, Cinnamon, LXDE, Pantheon, and Xfce, though a variety of additional user interfaces exist. Most popular user interfaces are based on the X

Window System, often simply called "X". It provides network transparency and permits a graphical application running on one system to be displayed on another where a user may interact with the application; however, certain extensions of the X Window System are not capable of working over the network. Several X display servers exist, with the reference implementation, X.Org Server, being the most popular.

Server distributions might provide a command-line interface for developers and administrators, but provide a custom interface for end-users, designed for the use case of the system. This custom interface is accessed through a client that resides on another system, not necessarily Linux-based.

Several types of window managers exist for X11, including tiling, dynamic, stacking, and compositing. Window managers provide means to control the placement and appearance of individual application windows, and interact with the X Window System. Simpler X window managers such as dwm, ratpoison, or i3wm provide a minimalist functionality, while more elaborate window managers such as FVWM, Enlightenment, or Window Maker provide more features such as a built-in taskbar and themes, but are still lightweight when compared to desktop environments. Desktop environments include window managers as part of their standard installations, such as Mutter (GNOME), KWin (KDE), or Xfwm (xfce), although users may choose to use a different window manager if preferred.

Wayland is a display server protocol intended as a replacement for the X11 protocol; as of 2022, it has received relatively wide adoption. Unlike X11, Wayland does not need an external window manager and compositing manager. Therefore, a Wayland compositor takes the role of the display server, window manager, and compositing manager. Weston is the reference implementation of Wayland, while GNOME's Mutter and KDE's KWin are being ported to Wayland as standalone display servers. Enlightenment has already been successfully ported since version 19. Additionally, many window managers have been made for Wayland, such as Sway or Hyprland, as well as other graphical utilities such as Waybar or Rofi.

Video Input Infrastructure

Linux currently has two modern kernel-userspace APIs for handling video input devices: V4L2 API for video streams and radio, and DVB API for digital TV reception. Due to the complexity and diversity of different devices, and due to the large number of formats and standards handled by those APIs, this infrastructure needs to evolve to better fit other devices. Also, a good userspace device library is the key to the success of having userspace applications to be able to work with all formats supported by those devices.

Development

The primary difference between Linux and many other popular contemporary operating systems is that the Linux kernel and other components are free and open-source software. Linux is not the only such operating system, although it is by far the most widely used. Some free and open-source software licenses are based on the principle of copyleft, a kind of reciprocity: any work derived from a copyleft piece of software must also be copyleft itself. The most common free software license, the GNU General Public License (GPL), is a form of copyleft and is used for the Linux kernel and many of the components from the GNU Project.

Linux-based distributions are intended by developers for interoperability with other operating systems and established computing standards. Linux systems adhere to POSIX, SUS, LSB, ISO, and ANSI standards where possible, although to date only one Linux distribution has been POSIX.1 certified, Linux-FT.

Free software projects, although developed through collaboration, are often produced independently of each other. The fact that the software licenses explicitly permit redistribution, however, provides a basis for larger-scale projects that collect the software produced by stand-alone projects and make it available all at once in the form of a Linux distribution.

Many Linux distributions manage a remote collection of system software and application software packages available for download and installation through a network connection. This allows users to adapt the operating system to their specific needs. Distributions are maintained by individuals, loose-knit teams, volunteer organizations, and commercial entities. A distribution is responsible for the default configuration of the installed Linux kernel, general system security, and more generally integration of the different software packages into a coherent whole. Distributions typically use a package manager such as apt, yum, zypper, pacman or portage to install, remove, and update all of a system's software from one central location.

Community

A distribution is largely driven by its developer and user communities. Some vendors develop and fund their distributions on a volunteer basis, Debian being a well-known example. Others maintain a community version of their commercial distributions, as Red Hat does with Fedora, and SUSE does with openSUSE.

In many cities and regions, local associations known as Linux User Groups (LUGs) seek to promote their preferred distribution and by extension free software. They hold meetings and provide free demonstrations, training, technical support, and operating system installation to new users. Many Internet communities also provide support to Linux users and developers. Most distributions and free software / open-source projects have IRC chatrooms or newsgroups. Online forums are another means of support, with notable examples being LinuxQuestions.org and the various distribution-specific support and community forums, such as ones for Ubuntu, Fedora, Arch Linux, Gentoo, etc. Linux distributions host mailing lists; commonly there will be a specific topic such as usage or development for a given list.

There are several technology websites with a Linux focus. Print magazines on Linux often bundle cover disks that carry software or even complete Linux distributions.

Although Linux distributions are generally available without charge, several large corporations sell, support, and contribute to the development of the components of the system and free software. An analysis of the Linux kernel in 2017 showed that well over 85% of the code was developed by programmers who are being paid for their work, leaving about 8.2% to unpaid developers and 4.1% unclassified. Some of the major corporations that provide contributions include Intel, Samsung, Google, AMD, Oracle, and Facebook. Several corporations, notably Red Hat, Canonical, and SUSE have built a significant business around Linux distributions.

The free software licenses, on which the various software packages of a distribution built on the Linux kernel are based, explicitly accommodate and encourage commercialization; the relationship between a Linux distribution as a whole and individual vendors may be seen as symbiotic. One common business model of commercial suppliers is charging for support, especially for business users. A number of companies also offer a specialized business version of their distribution, which adds proprietary support packages and tools to administer higher numbers of installations or to simplify administrative tasks.

Another business model is to give away the software to sell hardware. This used to be the norm in the computer industry, with operating systems such as CP/M, Apple DOS, and versions of the classic Mac OS before 7.6 freely copyable (but not modifiable). As computer hardware standardized throughout the 1980s, it became more difficult for hardware manufacturers to profit from this tactic, as the OS would run on any manufacturer's computer that shared the same architecture.

Programming on Linux

Most programming languages support Linux either directly or through third-party community based ports. The original development tools used for building both Linux applications and operating system programs are found within the GNU toolchain, which includes the GNU Compiler Collection (GCC) and the GNU Build System. Amongst others, GCC provides compilers for Ada, C, C++, Go and Fortran. Many programming languages have a cross-platform reference implementation that supports Linux, for example PHP, Perl, Ruby, Python, Java, Go, Rust and Haskell.

First released in 2003, the LLVM project provides an alternative cross-platform open-source compiler for many languages. Proprietary compilers for Linux include the Intel C++ Compiler, Sun Studio, and IBM XL C/C++ Compiler. BASIC is available in procedural form from QB64, PureBasic, Yabasic, GLBasic, Basic4GL, XBasic, wxBasic, SdlBasic, and Basic-256, as well as object oriented through Gambas, FreeBASIC, B4X, Basic for Qt, Phoenix Object Basic, NS Basic, ProvideX, Chipmunk Basic, RapidQ and Xojo. Pascal is implemented through GNU Pascal, Free Pascal, and Virtual Pascal, as well as graphically via Lazarus, PascalABC.NET, or Delphi using FireMonkey (previously through Borland Kylix).

A common feature of Unix-like systems, Linux includes traditional specific-purpose programming languages targeted at scripting, text processing and system configuration and management in general. Linux distributions support shell scripts, awk, sed and make. Many programs also have an embedded programming language to support configuring or programming themselves. For example, regular expressions are supported in programs like grep and locate, the traditional Unix message transfer agent Sendmail contains its own Turing complete scripting system, and the advanced text editor GNU Emacs is built around a general purpose Lisp interpreter.

Most distributions also include support for PHP, Perl, Ruby, Python and other dynamic languages. While not as common, Linux also supports C# and other CLI languages (via Mono), Vala, and Scheme. Guile Scheme acts as an extension language targeting the GNU system utilities, seeking to make the conventionally small, static, compiled C programs of Unix design rapidly and dynamically extensible via an elegant, functional high-level scripting system; many GNU programs can be compiled with optional Guile bindings to this end. A number of Java virtual machines and development kits run on Linux, including the original Sun Microsystems JVM (HotSpot), and IBM's J2SE RE, as well as many open-source projects like Kaffe and Jikes RVM; Kotlin, Scala, Groovy and other JVM languages are also available.

GNOME and KDE are popular desktop environments and provide a framework for developing applications. These projects are based on the GTK and Qt widget toolkits, respectively, which can also be used independently of the larger framework. Both support a wide variety of languages. There are a number of Integrated development environments available including Anjuta, Code::Blocks, CodeLite, Eclipse, Geany, ActiveState Komodo, KDevelop, Lazarus, MonoDevelop, NetBeans, and Qt Creator, while the long-established editors Vim, nano and Emacs remain popular.

Hardware Support

The Linux kernel is a widely ported operating system kernel, available for devices ranging from mobile phones to supercomputers; it runs on a highly diverse range of computer architectures, including ARM-based Android smartphones and the IBM Z mainframes. Specialized distributions and kernel forks exist for less mainstream architectures; for example, the ELKS kernel fork can run on Intel 8086 or Intel 80286 16-bit microprocessors, while the µClinux kernel fork may run on systems without a memory management unit. The kernel also runs on architectures that were only ever intended to use a proprietary manufacturer-created operating system, such as Macintosh computers (with PowerPC, Intel, and Apple silicon processors), PDAs, video game consoles, portable music players, and mobile phones.

Linux has a reputation for supporting old hardware very well by maintaining standardized drivers for a long time. There are several industry associations and hardware conferences devoted to maintaining and improving support for diverse hardware under Linux, such as FreedomHEC. Over time, support for different hardware has improved in Linux, resulting in any off-the-shelf purchase having a "good chance" of being compatible.

In 2014, a new initiative was launched to automatically collect a database of all tested hardware configurations.

Market Share and Uptake

Many quantitative studies of free/open-source software focus on topics including market share and reliability, with numerous studies specifically examining Linux. The Linux market is growing, and the Linux operating system market size is expected to see a growth of 19.2% by 2027, reaching $15.64 billion, compared to $3.89 billion in 2019. Analysts project a Compound Annual Growth Rate (CAGR) of 13.7% between 2024 and 2032, culminating in a market size of USD 34.90 billion by the latter year. Analysts and proponents attribute the relative success of Linux to its security, reliability, low cost, and freedom from vendor lock-in.

Desktops and Laptops

According to web server statistics (that is, based on the numbers recorded from visits to websites by client devices), as of February 2024, the estimated market share of Linux on desktop computers is around 3.7%. In comparison, Microsoft Windows has a market share of around 72.9%, while macOS covers around 16.13%.

Web Servers

W3Cook publishes stats that use the top 1,000,000 Alexa domains, which as of May 2015 estimate that 96.55% of web servers run Linux, 1.73% run Windows, and 1.72% run FreeBSD.

W3Techs publishes stats that use the top 10,000,000 Alexa domains and the top 1,000,000 Tranco domains, updated monthly and as of November 2020 estimate that Linux is used by 39% of the web servers, versus 21.9% being used by Microsoft Windows. 40.1% used other types of Unix.

IDC's Q1 2007 report indicated that Linux held 12.7% of the overall server market at that time; this estimate was based on the number of Linux servers sold by various companies, and did not include server hardware purchased separately that had Linux installed on it later.

Mobile Devices

Android, which is based on the Linux kernel, has become the dominant operating system for smartphones. In April 2023, 68.61% of mobile devices accessing websites using StatCounter were from Android. Android is also a popular operating system for tablets, being responsible for more than 60% of tablet sales as of 2013. According to web server statistics, as of October 2021 Android has a market share of about 71%, with iOS holding 28%, and the remaining 1% attributed to various niche platforms.

Film Production

For years, Linux has been the platform of choice in the film industry. The first major film produced on Linux servers was 1997's *Titanic*. Since then major studios including DreamWorks Animation, Pixar, Weta Digital, and Industrial Light & Magic have migrated to Linux. According to the Linux Movies Group, more than 95% of the servers and desktops at large animation and visual effects companies use Linux.

Use in Government

Linux distributions have also gained popularity with various local and national governments. News of the Russian military creating its own Linux distribution has also surfaced, and has come to fruition as the G.H.ost Project. The Indian state of Kerala has gone to the extent of mandating that all state high schools run Linux on their computers. China uses Linux exclusively as the operating system for its Loongson processor family to achieve technology independence. In Spain, some regions have developed their own Linux distributions, which are widely used in education and official institutions, like gnuLinEx in Extremadura and Guadalinex in Andalusia. France and Germany have also taken steps toward the adoption of Linux. North Korea's Red Star OS, developed as of 2002, is based on a version of Fedora Linux.

Copyright, Trademark, and Naming

The Linux kernel is licensed under the GNU General Public License (GPL), version 2. The GPL requires that anyone who distributes software based on source code under this license must make the originating source code (and any modifications) available to the recipient under the same terms. Other key components of a typical Linux distribution are also mainly licensed under the GPL, but they may use other licenses; many libraries use the GNU Lesser General Public License (LGPL), a more permissive variant of the GPL, and the X.Org implementation of the X Window System uses the MIT License.

Torvalds states that the Linux kernel will not move from version 2 of the GPL to version 3. He specifically dislikes some provisions in the new license which prohibit the use of the software in digital rights management. It would also be impractical to obtain permission from all the copyright holders, who number in the thousands.

A 2001 study of Red Hat Linux 7.1 found that this distribution contained 30 million source lines of code. Using the Constructive Cost Model, the study estimated that this distribution required about eight thousand person-years of development time. According to the study, if all this software had been developed by conventional proprietary means, it would have cost about US$1.82 billion to develop in 2023 in the United States. Most of the source code (71%) was written in the C programming language, but many other languages were used, including C++, Lisp, assembly language, Perl, Python, Fortran, and various shell scripting languages. Slightly over half of all lines of code were licensed under the GPL. The Linux kernel itself was 2.4 million lines of code, or 8% of the total.

In a later study, the same analysis was performed for Debian version 4.0 (etch, which was released in 2007). This distribution contained close to 283 million source lines of code, and the study estimated that it would have required about seventy three thousand man-years and cost US$10.2 billion (in 2023 dollars) to develop by conventional means.

In the United States, the name *Linux* is a trademark registered to Linus Torvalds. Initially, nobody registered it. However, on August 15, 1994, William R. Della Croce Jr. filed for the trademark *Linux*, and then demanded royalties from Linux distributors. In 1996, Torvalds and some affected organizations sued him to have the trademark assigned to Torvalds, and, in 1997, the case was settled. The licensing of the trademark has since been handled by the Linux Mark Institute (LMI). Torvalds has stated that he trademarked the name only to prevent someone else from using it. LMI originally charged a nominal sublicensing fee for use of the Linux name as part of trademarks, but later changed this in favor of offering a free, perpetual worldwide sublicense.

The Free Software Foundation (FSF) prefers *GNU/Linux* as the name when referring to the operating system as a whole, because it considers Linux distributions to be variants of the GNU operating system initiated in 1983 by Richard Stallman, president of the FSF. The foundation explicitly takes no issue over the name Android for the Android OS, which is also an operating system based on the Linux kernel, as GNU is not a part of it.

A minority of public figures and software projects other than Stallman and the FSF, notably distributions consisting of only free software, such as Debian (which had been sponsored by the FSF up to 1996), also use *GNU/Linux* when referring to the operating system as a whole. Most media and common usage, however, refers to this family of operating systems simply as *Linux*, as do many large Linux distributions (for example, SUSE Linux and Red Hat Enterprise Linux).

As of May 2011, about 8% to 13% of the lines of code of the Linux distribution Ubuntu (version "Natty") is made of GNU components (the range depending on whether GNOME is considered part of GNU); meanwhile, 6% is taken by the Linux kernel, increased to 9% when including its direct dependencies.

3.3.2 Windows IoT

Windows IoT, short for Windows Internet of Things and formerly known as Windows Embedded, is a family of operating systems from Microsoft designed for use in embedded systems. Microsoft has three different subfamilies of operating systems for embedded devices targeting a wide market, ranging from small-footprint, real-time devices to point of sale (POS) devices like kiosks. Windows Embedded operating systems are available to original equipment manufacturers (OEMs), who make it available to end users preloaded with their hardware, in addition to volume license customers in some cases.

In April 2018, Microsoft released Azure Sphere, another operating system designed for IoT applications running on the Linux kernel.

The IoT Family

Microsoft rebranded "Windows Embedded" to "Windows IoT" starting with the release of embedded editions of Windows 10.

Enterprise

Windows IoT Enterprise branded editions, version 1809 and older, are binary identical to their respective Windows 10 Enterprise editions – Long-Term Servicing Branch (LTSB), Current Branch for Business (CBB), Semi-Annual Channel (SAC), and Long-Term Servicing Channel (LTSC) – but are licensed exclusively for use in embedded devices. This brand replaces the Embedded Industry, Embedded Standard, and "For Embedded Systems" (FES) brands/subfamilies. Plain unlabeled, Retail/Thin Client, Tablet, and Small Tablet SKUs are available, again differing only in licensing.

It now contains a minor change that allows the use of smaller storage devices, with the possibility of more changes being made in the future. In addition, starting with the LTSC edition of version 21H2, Windows 10 IoT Enterprise LTSC will gain an extra five years of support compared to Windows 10 Enterprise LTSC.

- **Windows 10 IoT Enterprise 2015 (value-based pricing):**
  - SKU 6EU-00124 – Windows 10 IoT Enterprise 2015 LTSB – High End Edition (Intel Core i7 | Intel Xeon | AMD FX)
  - SKU 6EU-00125 – Windows 10 IoT Enterprise 2015 LTSB – Value Edition (Intel Core i3/i5 | AMD R-Series, A10, A8)
  - SKU 6EU-00126 – Windows 10 IoT Enterprise 2015 LTSB – Entry Edition (Intel Atom/Celeron | AMD E1, E2, A4, A6)
- **Windows 10 IoT Enterprise 2016 (value-based pricing):**
  - SKU 6EU-00034 – Windows 10 IoT Enterprise 2016 LTSB – High End Edition (Intel Core i7 | Intel Xeon | AMD FX)
  - SKU 6EU-00035 – Windows 10 IoT Enterprise 2016 LTSB – Value Edition (Intel Core i3/i5 | AMD R-Series, A10, A8)
  - SKU 6EU-00036 – Windows 10 IoT Enterprise 2016 LTSB – Entry Edition (Intel Atom/Celeron | AMD E1, E2, A4, A6)
- **Windows 10 IoT Enterprise 2016 (category-based pricing):**
  - SKU 6F6-00036 – Windows 10 IoT Enterprise 2016 CBB – High End Edition (Intel Core i7 | Intel Xeon | AMD FX)
  - SKU 6F6-00037 – Windows 10 IoT Enterprise 2016 CBB – Value Edition (Intel Core i3/i5 | AMD R-Series, A10, A8)
  - SKU 6F6-00038 – Windows 10 IoT Enterprise 2016 CBB – Entry Edition (Intel Atom/Celeron | AMD E1, E2, A4, A6)
  - SKU 6F6-00036 – Windows 10 IoT Enterprise 2016 SAC – High End Edition (Intel Core i7 | Intel Xeon | AMD FX)
  - SKU 6F6-00037 – Windows 10 IoT Enterprise 2016 SAC – Value Edition (Intel Core i3/i5 | AMD R-Series, A10, A8)
  - SKU 6F6-00038 – Windows 10 IoT Enterprise 2016 SAC – Entry Edition (Intel Atom/Celeron | AMD E1, E2, A4, A6)
- **Windows 10 IoT Enterprise 2019 (value-based pricing):**
  - SKU MUT-00013 – Windows 10 IoT Enterprise 2019 LTSC – High End Edition (Intel Core i7 | Intel Xeon | AMD FX)
  - SKU MUU-00005 – Windows 10 IoT Enterprise 2019 LTSC – Value Edition (Intel Core i3/i5 | AMD R-Series, A10, A8)
  - SKU MUV-00005 – Windows 10 IoT Enterprise 2019 LTSC – Entry Edition (Intel Atom/Celeron | AMD E1, E2, A4, A6)
- **Windows 10 IoT Enterprise 2019 (category-based pricing):**
  - SKU 6F6-00036 – Windows 10 IoT Enterprise 2019 SAC – High End Edition (Intel Core i7 | Intel Xeon | AMD FX)
  - SKU 6F6-00037 – Windows 10 IoT Enterprise 2019 SAC – Value Edition (Intel Core i3/i5 | AMD R-Series, A10, A8)
  - SKU 6F6-00038 – Windows 10 IoT Enterprise 2019 SAC – Entry Edition (Intel Atom/Celeron | AMD E1, E2, A4, A6)

- **Windows 10 IoT Enterprise 2021 (value-based pricing):**
    - Windows 10 IoT Enterprise 2021 LTSC – High End Edition (Intel Core i7 | Intel Xeon | AMD FX)
    - Windows 10 IoT Enterprise 2021 LTSC – Value Edition (Intel Core i3/i5 | AMD R-Series, A10, A8)
    - Windows 10 IoT Enterprise 2021 LTSC – Entry Edition (Intel Atom/Celeron | AMD E1, E2, A4, A6)
- **Windows 10 IoT Enterprise 2021 (category-based pricing):**
    - Windows 10 IoT Enterprise 2021 SAC – High End Edition (Intel Core i7 | Intel Xeon | AMD FX)
    - Windows 10 IoT Enterprise 2021 SAC – Value Edition (Intel Core i3/i5 | AMD R-Series, A10, A8)
    - Windows 10 IoT Enterprise 2021 SAC – Entry Edition (Intel Atom/Celeron | AMD E1, E2, A4, A6)
- **Windows 11 IoT Enterprise 2021:**
    - Windows 11 IoT Enterprise 2021 – High End Edition (Intel Core i7 | Intel Xeon | AMD Ryzen | AMD EPYC)
    - Windows 11 IoT Enterprise 2021 – Value Edition (Intel Core i3/i5 | AMD RYZEN)
    - Windows 11 IoT Enterprise 2021 – Entry Edition (Intel Atom/Celeron | AMD Athlon)
- **Windows 11 IoT Enterprise 2022:**
    - Windows 11 IoT Enterprise 2022 – High End Edition (Intel Core i7 | Intel Xeon | AMD Ryzen | AMD EPYC)
    - Windows 11 IoT Enterprise 2022 – Value Edition (Intel Core i3/i5 | AMD Ryzen)
    - Windows 11 IoT Enterprise 2022 – Entry Edition (Intel Atom/Celeron | AMD Athlon)

Mobile

Windows 10 IoT Mobile, also known as Windows 10 IoT Mobile Enterprise, is a binary equivalent of Windows 10 Mobile Enterprise licensed for IoT applications. Unsupported as of January 14, 2020.

Core

Windows 10 IoT Core is considered by some to be the successor to Windows Embedded Compact, although it maintains very little compatibility with it. Optimized for smaller and lower-cost industry devices, it is also provided free of charge for use in devices like the Raspberry Pi for hobbyist use.

- **Core Pro:** Windows 10 IoT Core Pro provides the ability to defer and control updates and is licensed only via distributors; it is otherwise identical to the normal IoT Core edition.

Server

Windows Server IoT 2019 is a full, binary equivalent version of Windows Server 2019, intended to aggregate data from many 'things'. Like the IoT Enterprise variants, it remains identical in behavior to its regularly licensed counterpart, but differs only in licensing terms. It also is offered in both LTSC and SAC options.

Embedded Family

Embedded Compact

Windows Embedded Compact is the variant of Windows Embedded for very small computers and embedded systems, including consumer electronics devices like set-top boxes and video game consoles. Windows Embedded Compact is a modular real-time operating system with a specialized kernel that can run in under 1 MB of memory. It comes with the *Platform Builder* tool that can be used to add modules to the installation image to create a custom installation, depending on the device used. Windows Embedded Compact is available for ARM, MIPS, SuperH and x86 processor architectures.

Microsoft made available a specialized variant of Windows Embedded Compact, known as Windows Mobile, for use in mobile phones. It is a customized image of Windows Embedded Compact along with specialized modules for use in Mobile phones. Windows Mobile was available in four editions: *Windows Mobile Classic* (for Pocket PC), *Windows Mobile Standard* (for smartphones) and *Windows Mobile Professional* (for PDA/Pocket PC Phone Edition) and *Windows Mobile for Automotive* (for communication/entertainment/information systems used in automobiles). Modified variants of Windows Mobile were used for Portable Media Centers. In 2010, *Windows Mobile* was replaced by *Windows Phone 7*, which was also based on Windows Embedded Compact, but was not compatible with any previous products.

Windows Embedded Compact 2013 is a real-time operating system which runs on ARM, x86, SH, and derivatives of those architectures. It included.NET Framework, UI framework, and various open source drivers and services as 'modules'.

Embedded Standard

Windows Embedded Standard is the brand of Windows Embedded operating systems designed to provide enterprises and device manufacturers the freedom to choose which capabilities will be part of their industry devices and intelligent system solutions, intended to build ATMs and devices for the healthcare and manufacturing industries, creating industry-specific devices. This brand consists of Windows NT

4.0 Embedded, Windows XP Embedded, Windows Embedded Standard 2009 (WES09), Windows Embedded Standard 7 (WES7, known as Windows Embedded Standard 2011 prior to release), and Windows Embedded 8 Standard. It provides the full Win32 API. Windows Embedded Standard 2009 includes Silverlight,.NET Framework 3.5, Internet Explorer 7, Windows Media Player 11, RDP 6.1, Network Access Protection, Microsoft Baseline Security Analyzer and support for being managed by Windows Server Update Services and System Center Configuration Manager.

Windows Embedded Standard 7 is based on Windows 7 and was previously codenamed Windows Embedded 'Quebec'. Windows Embedded Standard 7 includes Windows Vista and Windows 7 features such as Aero, SuperFetch, ReadyBoost, Windows Firewall, Windows Defender, address space layout randomization, Windows Presentation Foundation, Silverlight 2, Windows Media Center among several other packages. It is available in IA-32 and x64 variants and was released in 2010. It has a larger minimum footprint (~300 MB) compared to 40 MB of XPe and also requires product activation. Windows Embedded Standard 7 was released on April 27, 2010. Windows Embedded 8 Standard was released on March 20, 2013. IE11 for this edition of Windows 8 was released in April 2019, with support for IE10 ending on January 31, 2020.

For Embedded Systems (FES)

Binary identical variants of the editions as are available in retail, but licensed exclusively for use in embedded devices. They are available for both IA-32 as well as x64 processors. Subfamily is known to include Windows for Workgroups 3.11, Windows 95 to 98, Windows NT Workstation, Windows 2000 Professional, Windows ME, Windows XP Professional, Windows Vista Business and Ultimate, Windows 7 Professional and Ultimate, Windows 8 Pro and Enterprise, and Windows 8.1 Pro and Enterprise.

This subfamily originally simply had Embedded tacked onto the end of the SKU name until sometime around the release of Windows XP when the naming scheme changed to FES. Examples of this include Windows NT Workstation Embedded, Windows 2000 Pro Embedded, and Windows ME Embedded. Microsoft changed the moniker for FES products again starting with some Windows 8/8.1 based SKUs, simply labeling them Windows Embedded before the Windows version and edition. Two examples of this are Windows Embedded 8 Pro and Windows Embedded 8.1 Enterprise.

- **Server:** Windows Embedded Server FES products include Server, Home Server, SQL Server, Storage Server, DPM Server, ISA Server, UAG Server, TMG Server, and Unified Data Storage Server etc. of various years including 2000, 2003, 2003 R2, 2004, 2005, 2006, 2007, 2008, 2008 R2, 2012, and 2012 R2 etc.

Embedded Industry

Windows Embedded Industry is the brand of Windows Embedded operating systems for industry devices and once only for point of sale systems. This brand was originally limited to the Windows Embedded for Point of Service operating system released in 2006, which is based on Windows XP with SP2. Since, Microsoft has released an updated version of Windows Embedded for Point of Service named Windows Embedded POSReady 2009, this time based on Windows XP with SP3. In 2011 Windows Embedded 7 POSReady based on Windows 7 SP1 was released, which succeeded POSReady 2009. Microsoft has since changed the name of this product from "Windows Embedded POSReady" to "Windows Embedded Industry". Microsoft released Windows Embedded 8 Industry in April 2013, followed by 8.1 Industry in October 2013.

Embedded NAVReady

Windows Embedded NAVReady, also known as Navigation Ready, is a plug-in component for Windows CE 5.0. It is intended to be useful for building portable handheld navigation devices.

Embedded Automotive

Windows Embedded Automotive, formerly Microsoft Auto, Windows CE for Automotive, Windows Automotive, and Windows Mobile for Automotive, is an embedded operating system based on Windows CE for use on computer systems in automobiles. The latest release, Windows Embedded Automotive 7 was announced on October 19, 2010.

3.3.3 Google Cloud IoT Edge

Google Cloud Platform (GCP), offered by Google, is a suite of cloud computing services that provides a series of modular cloud services including computing, data storage, data analytics, and machine learning, alongside a set of management tools. It runs on the same infrastructure that Google uses internally for its end-user products, such as Google Search, Gmail, and Google Docs, according to Verma, et.al. Registration requires a credit card or bank account details.

Google Cloud Platform provides infrastructure as a service, platform as a service, and serverless computing environments. In April 2008, Google announced App Engine, a platform for developing and hosting web applications in Google-managed data centers, which was the first cloud computing service from the company. The service became generally available in November 2011. Since the announcement of App Engine, Google added multiple cloud services to the platform.

Google Cloud Platform is a part of Google Cloud, which includes the Google Cloud Platform public cloud infrastructure, as well as Google Workspace (G Suite), enterprise versions of Android and ChromeOS, and application programming interfaces (APIs) for machine learning and enterprise mapping services.

Products

Google lists over 100 products under the Google Cloud brand. Some of the key services are listed below.

Compute

- **App Engine:** Platform as a Service to deploy applications developed with Java, PHP, Node.js, Python, C#,.Net, Ruby and Go programming languages.
- **Compute Engine:** Infrastructure as a Service to run Microsoft Windows and Linux virtual machines.
- **Google Kubernetes Engine (GKE) or GKE on-Prem Offered as Part of Anthos Platform:** Containers as a Service based on Kubernetes.
- **Cloud Functions:** Functions as a Service to run event-driven code written in Node.js, Java, Python, or Go.
- **Cloud Run:** Compute execution environment based on Knative. Offered as Cloud Run (fully managed) or as Cloud Run for Anthos. Currently supports GCP, AWS and VMware management.

Storage and Databases

- **Cloud Storage:** Object storage with integrated edge caching to store unstructured data.
- **Cloud SQL:** Database as a Service based on MySQL, PostgreSQL and Microsoft SQL Server.
- **Cloud Bigtable:** Managed NoSQL database service.
- **Cloud Spanner:** Horizontally scalable, strongly consistent, relational database service.
- **Cloud Datastore:** NoSQL database for web and mobile applications.
- **Persistent Disk:** Block storage for Compute Engine virtual machines.
- **Cloud Memorystore:** Managed in-memory data store based on Redis and Memcached.
- **Local SSD:** High-performance, transient, local block storage.
- **Filestore:** High-performance file storage for Google Cloud users.
- **AlloyDB:** Fully managed PostgreSQL database service.

Networking

- **VPC:** Virtual Private Cloud for managing the software defined network of cloud resources.
- **Cloud Load Balancing:** Software-defined, managed service for load balancing the traffic.
- **Cloud Armor:** Web application firewall to protect workloads from DDoS attacks.
- **Cloud CDN:** Content Delivery Network based on Google's globally distributed edge points of presence.
- **Cloud Interconnect:** Service to connect a data center with Google Cloud Platform
- **Cloud DNS:** Managed, authoritative DNS hosting service running on the same infrastructure as Google.
- **Network Service Tiers:** Option to choose Premium vs Standard network tier for higher-performing network.

Big Data

- **BigQuery:** Scalable, managed enterprise data warehouse for analytics.
- **Cloud Dataflow:** Managed service based on Apache Beam for stream and batch data processing.
- **Cloud Data Fusion:** A managed ETL service based on the Open Source Cask Data Application Platform.
- **Dataproc:** Big data platform for running Apache Hadoop and Apache Spark jobs.
- **Cloud Composer:** Managed workflow orchestration service built on Apache Airflow.
- **Cloud Datalab:** Tool for data exploration, analysis, visualization and machine learning. This is a fully managed Jupyter Notebook service.
- **Cloud Dataprep:** Data service based on Trifacta to visually explore, clean, and prepare data for analysis.
- **Cloud Pub/Sub:** Scalable event ingestion service based on message queues.
- **Looker Studio:** Business intelligence tool to visualize data through dashboards and reports.
- **Looker:** Business intelligence platform.

Cloud AI

- **Cloud AutoML:** Service to train and deploy custom machine learning models. As of September 2018, the service is in Beta.
- **Cloud TPU:** Accelerators used by Google to train machine learning models.
- **Cloud Machine Learning Engine:** Managed service for training and building machine learning models based on mainstream frameworks.
- **Cloud Talent Solution (Formerly Cloud Job Discovery):** Service based on Google's search and machine learning capabilities for the recruiting ecosystem.
- **Dialogflow Enterprise:** Development environment based on Google's machine learning for building conversational interfaces.
- **Cloud Natural Language:** Text analysis service based on Google Deep Learning models.
- **Cloud Speech-to-Text:** Speech to text conversion service based on machine learning.
- **Cloud Text-to-Speech:** Text to speech conversion service based on machine learning.
- **Cloud Translation API:** Service to dynamically translate between thousands of available language pairs.
- **Cloud Vision API:** Image analysis service based on machine learning.
- **Cloud Video Intelligence:** Video analysis service based on machine learning.

Management Tools

- **Operations Suite (Formerly Stackdriver):** Monitoring, logging, tracing, and diagnostics for applications on Google Cloud Platform.
- **Cloud Deployment Manager:** Tool to deploy Google Cloud Platform resources defined in templates created in YAML, Python or Jinja2.
- **Cloud Console:** Web interface to manage Google Cloud Platform resources.
- **Cloud Shell:** Browser-based shell command-line access to manage Google Cloud Platform resources.
- **Cloud Console Mobile App:** Android and iOS application to manage Google Cloud Platform resources.
- **Cloud APIs:** APIs to programmatically access Google Cloud Platform resources

Identity and Security

- **Cloud Identity:** Single sign-on (SSO) service based on SAML 2.0 and OpenID.
- **Cloud IAM:** Identity & Access Management (IAM) service for defining policies based on role-based access control.
- **Cloud Identity-Aware Proxy:** Service to control access to cloud applications running on Google Cloud Platform without using a VPN.
- **Cloud Data Loss Prevention API:** Service to automatically discover, classify, and redact sensitive data.
- **Security Key Enforcement:** Two-step verification service based on a security key.
- **Cloud Key Management Service:** Cloud-hosted key management service integrated with IAM and audit logging.
- **Cloud Resource Manager:** Service to manage resources by project, folder, and organization based on the hierarchy.
- **Cloud Security Command Center:** Security and data risk platform for data and services running in Google Cloud Platform.
- **Cloud Security Scanner:** Automated vulnerability scanning service for applications deployed in App Engine.
- **Access Transparency:** Near real-time audit logs providing visibility to Google Cloud Platform administrators.
- **VPC Service Controls:** Service to manage security perimeters for sensitive data in Google Cloud Platform services.

Internet of Things (IoT)

- **Cloud IoT Core:** Secure device connection and management service for Internet of Things.
- **Edge TPU:** Purpose-built ASIC designed to run inference at the edge. As of September 2018, this product is in private beta.
- **Cloud IoT Edge:** Brings AI to the edge computing layer.

API Platform

- **Maps Platform:** APIs for maps, routes, and places based on Google Maps.
- **Apigee API Platform:** Lifecycle management platform to design, secure, deploy, monitor, and scale APIs.

- **API Monetization:** Tool for API providers to create revenue models, reports, payment gateways, and developer portal integrations.
- **Developer Portal:** Self-service platform for developers to publish and manage APIs.
- **API Analytics:** Service to analyze API-driven programs through monitoring, measuring, and managing APIs.
- **Apigee Sense:** Enables API security by identifying and alerting administrators to suspicious API behaviors.
- **Cloud Endpoints:** An NGINX-based proxy to deploy and manage APIs.
- **Service Infrastructure:** A set of foundational services for building Google Cloud products.

Regions and Zones

A region is a specific geographical location where users can deploy cloud resources. Each region is an independent geographic area that consists of zones. A zone is a deployment area for Google Cloud Platform resources within a region. Zones should be considered a single failure domain within a region. Most regions have three zones.

3.4 EDGE ANALYTICS AND MACHINE LEARNING AT THE EDGE

Edge analytics and machine learning at the edge represent a paradigm shift in how data is processed and insights are derived in modern computing environments. Traditionally, data processing has been centralized, with large amounts of data being transmitted to cloud servers for analysis.

However, with the proliferation of Internet of Things (IoT) devices and the need for real-time decision-making, edge computing has emerged as a powerful solution. Edge analytics and machine learning bring data processing capabilities closer to the data source or edge devices, enabling faster response times, reduced latency, and improved efficiency in various applications.

Edge analytics and machine learning represent transformative technologies that empower organizations to extract valuable insights and drive actionable outcomes at the edge of the network.

By combining real-time data processing with intelligent decision-making capabilities, these technologies enable faster response times, reduced operational costs, and enhanced user experiences across a wide range of applications. As the ecosystem continues to evolve, addressing challenges related to resource constraints, security, and integration will be critical to realizing the full potential of edge computing in the era of digital transformation.

3.4.1 Understanding Edge Computing

Edge computing refers to the practice of processing data near the edge of the network, where the data is generated, instead of relying solely on centralized data centers. This approach minimizes the need to transmit large volumes of data to distant servers, thereby reducing network congestion and latency. Edge devices can range from sensors and actuators in industrial settings to smartphones and smart appliances in consumer applications. By performing data processing tasks locally, edge computing enhances real-time decision-making capabilities and supports applications that require low-latency responses, such as autonomous vehicles, remote monitoring, and augmented reality.

3.4.2 The Role of Analytics at the Edge

Analytics at the edge involves processing and analyzing data locally on edge devices or gateways before transmitting relevant insights to centralized servers or the cloud. This approach is particularly advantageous in scenarios where immediate action is required based on incoming data. For example, in manufacturing environments, edge analytics can monitor equipment performance in real-time, detect anomalies, and trigger maintenance actions without relying on cloud connectivity. Similarly, in healthcare, wearable devices equipped with edge analytics can monitor vital signs and alert medical professionals to critical conditions promptly.

3.4.3 Benefits of Edge Analytics

- **Reduced Latency**: By processing data locally, edge analytics minimizes the time it takes to receive insights and make decisions, making it ideal for applications requiring real-time responsiveness.
- **Bandwidth Efficiency**: Edge analytics reduces the volume of data that needs to be transmitted to centralized servers, optimizing bandwidth usage and lowering operational costs.
- **Improved Data Privacy and Security**: Keeping sensitive data within the edge environment can enhance privacy and security by reducing exposure to potential cyber threats during data transmission.
- **Scalability**: Edge analytics supports scalable deployments by distributing computational tasks across multiple edge devices, accommodating growing data volumes and diverse application requirements.

3.4.4 Machine Learning Capabilities at the Edge

Machine learning (ML) at the edge extends traditional analytics by enabling edge devices to learn from data locally and make intelligent decisions autonomously. This capability is critical in environments where continuous learning and adaptation to changing conditions are necessary. Edge ML models are typically lightweight and optimized for deployment on resource-constrained devices, such as IoT sensors and edge gateways. They leverage techniques like transfer learning and model compression to achieve efficient inference without compromising accuracy.

3.4.5 Applications of Machine Learning at the Edge

- **Predictive Maintenance:** Edge ML models can analyze sensor data in real-time to predict equipment failures or maintenance needs, optimizing asset uptime and reducing operational costs.
- **Anomaly Detection:** By detecting anomalies locally, edge ML models can promptly identify unusual patterns or events, such as security breaches or equipment malfunctions, and trigger appropriate responses.
- **Personalized Services:** In retail and consumer electronics, edge ML enables personalized recommendations and user experiences based on local data analysis, enhancing customer satisfaction and engagement.
- **Autonomous Systems:** Edge ML supports autonomous decision-making in systems like autonomous vehicles and drones, enabling them to navigate and respond to dynamic environments without constant reliance on cloud connectivity.

3.4.6 Challenges and Considerations

Despite its benefits, deploying analytics and machine learning at the edge presents several challenges that organizations must address:

- **Resource Constraints:** Edge devices often have limited computational power, memory, and storage capacity, requiring optimization techniques to ensure efficient execution of analytics and ML tasks.
- **Data Quality and Integration:** Ensuring the accuracy and reliability of data collected at the edge is crucial for maintaining the effectiveness of analytics and ML models. Integration with existing data systems and protocols can also be complex.
- **Security Concerns:** Securing edge devices against unauthorized access and data breaches is paramount, especially when handling sensitive information locally.
- **Lifecycle Management:** Managing and updating edge analytics and ML models across distributed devices can be challenging, requiring robust deployment and version control strategies.

3.4.7 Future Directions

The evolution of edge analytics and machine learning continues to drive innovation across various industries, with ongoing advancements in hardware capabilities, software frameworks, and deployment strategies. Future trends include:

- **Edge-to-Cloud Synergy**: Enhanced integration between edge and cloud environments to leverage complementary strengths in data processing, storage, and scalability.
- **AIoT (Artificial Intelligence of Things)**: The convergence of AI and IoT technologies to enable intelligent edge devices capable of autonomous decision-making and adaptive behavior.
- **Edge-native ML Models**: Development of specialized ML models optimized for edge deployment, incorporating techniques such as federated learning and differential privacy to address privacy and scalability challenges.
- **Edge-as-a-Service**: Emergence of managed service offerings that simplify the deployment and management of edge analytics and ML solutions, catering to diverse industry needs.

CHAPTER 4
EDGE COMPUTING IN IOT

4.1 INTEGRATION OF EDGE COMPUTING AND IOT

The integration of edge computing and the Internet of Things (IoT) represents a pivotal advancement in modern computing architectures, enabling enhanced data processing capabilities and real-time decision-making at the edge of the network. IoT devices generate vast amounts of data from sensors and actuators, which traditionally has been transmitted to centralized cloud servers for processing and analysis. However, with the proliferation of connected devices and the need for low-latency applications, edge computing has emerged as a complementary solution.

The integration of edge computing with IoT represents a transformative approach to leveraging distributed computing resources, enhancing data processing capabilities, and enabling real-time decision-making at the edge of the network. By deploying edge servers or gateways near IoT devices, organizations can unlock new opportunities for innovation, efficiency, and responsiveness across diverse industry sectors. Addressing challenges related to resource constraints, interoperability, security, and data governance is crucial to realizing the full potential of edge computing in driving digital transformation and shaping the future of connected ecosystems.

4.1.1 Understanding Edge Computing in the Context of IoT

Edge computing extends traditional cloud computing by decentralizing data processing and storage capabilities to the edge of the network, where data is generated and consumed. IoT devices, ranging from smart sensors in industrial settings to wearable devices in healthcare and consumer electronics, benefit from edge computing's ability to handle data-intensive tasks locally. By deploying edge servers or gateways near IoT devices, organizations can streamline data flows, enhance real-time analytics, and support applications that require immediate insights and actions, such as autonomous vehicles, smart cities, and industrial automation.

4.1.2 Benefits of Integrating Edge Computing with IoT

- **Reduced Latency:** Edge computing minimizes the time it takes to transmit data to centralized servers for processing, enabling faster response times and real-time decision-making in IoT applications. This is critical for scenarios where milliseconds can impact operational efficiency or safety, such as in autonomous vehicles or remote medical monitoring.

- **Bandwidth Optimization**: By processing data locally, edge computing reduces the volume of data that needs to be transmitted over the network to the cloud, optimizing bandwidth usage and alleviating network congestion. This is particularly advantageous in environments with limited or unreliable connectivity.
- **Improved Data Privacy and Security**: Edge computing enhances data privacy and security by keeping sensitive information within the local network environment, reducing exposure to potential cyber threats during data transmission to centralized servers. This is crucial for industries like healthcare and finance, where data confidentiality is paramount.
- **Scalability**: The integration of edge computing and IoT supports scalable deployments by distributing computational tasks across a network of edge devices and gateways. This flexibility accommodates growing data volumes, diverse application requirements, and dynamic operational environments without overburdening centralized infrastructure.

4.1.3 Use Cases of Edge Computing and IoT Integration

- **Smart Manufacturing**: In manufacturing environments, edge computing enables real-time monitoring and optimization of production processes by analyzing sensor data locally. This improves operational efficiency, reduces downtime through predictive maintenance, and facilitates agile decision-making based on current production conditions.
- **Smart Cities**: Edge computing supports smart city initiatives by deploying sensors and edge devices throughout urban infrastructure to monitor traffic flow, air quality, and public safety in real-time. Local data processing enables faster incident response, adaptive traffic management, and efficient resource allocation for sustainable urban development.
- **Healthcare**: IoT devices equipped with edge computing capabilities enhance patient monitoring and healthcare delivery by analyzing vital signs, detecting anomalies, and providing timely alerts to medical professionals. Edge-based health monitoring systems ensure continuous data availability and immediate intervention, improving patient outcomes and reducing hospitalization risks.

- **Retail and Consumer Electronics**: Edge computing enhances personalized customer experiences in retail by analyzing customer behavior data from IoT devices, such as smart shelves or wearable devices. Local data processing enables retailers to offer targeted promotions, optimize inventory management, and improve customer engagement through real-time insights and recommendations.

4.1.4 Challenges and Considerations

Despite its benefits, integrating edge computing with IoT presents several challenges that organizations must address:

- **Resource Constraints**: Edge devices often have limited computational power, memory, and storage capacity, requiring optimization techniques to ensure efficient execution of data processing tasks and applications.
- **Interoperability**: Ensuring compatibility and seamless integration between diverse IoT devices, edge platforms, and cloud services is essential for achieving a unified and cohesive IoT ecosystem. Standardization efforts and open-source frameworks play a crucial role in promoting interoperability across heterogeneous environments.
- **Data Governance**: Managing data governance policies, regulatory compliance, and data sovereignty issues becomes complex when processing sensitive information locally on edge devices. Clear guidelines and secure data management practices are necessary to protect privacy and maintain compliance with global data protection regulations.
- **Security**: Securing edge devices against potential cyber threats, unauthorized access, and data breaches is paramount. Implementing robust security measures, such as encryption, authentication, and intrusion detection systems, helps mitigate risks and safeguard sensitive data within the edge environment.

4.1.5 Future Directions

The convergence of edge computing and IoT is poised to drive continued innovation across various industries, with ongoing advancements in technology, infrastructure, and application development. Future trends include:

- **Edge AI**: Integration of artificial intelligence (AI) capabilities at the edge to enable autonomous decision-making, predictive analytics, and adaptive learning in IoT applications.

- **5G and Edge Computing:** Leveraging 5G networks to enhance edge computing capabilities, enabling ultra-low latency, high bandwidth connectivity, and supporting mission-critical IoT applications, such as autonomous vehicles and remote surgery.

4.2 REAL-TIME DATA PROCESSING AT THE EDGE

Real-time data processing at the edge refers to the capability of processing data as soon as it is generated, near the source of data creation, rather than transmitting it to centralized cloud servers for analysis. This approach minimizes latency, improves response times, and enables immediate decision-making in various applications across industries. With the proliferation of Internet of Things (IoT) devices and the need for real-time insights, edge computing has become instrumental in supporting critical use cases such as autonomous vehicles, industrial automation, healthcare monitoring, and smart city deployments. Real-time data processing at the edge represents a transformative approach to leveraging distributed computing resources, enabling faster decision-making, and supporting latency-sensitive applications across diverse industry sectors. By deploying edge computing solutions, organizations can harness the power of local data processing, optimize network performance, and enhance system reliability while addressing challenges related to resource constraints, security, and scalability. As the ecosystem continues to evolve, addressing these challenges and embracing emerging technologies will be essential to realizing the full potential of real-time data processing at the edge in driving digital transformation and shaping the future of connected environments.

4.2.1 Understanding Edge Computing in Real-Time Data Processing

Edge computing extends traditional cloud computing by decentralizing computational tasks to edge devices or gateways located closer to where data is produced. IoT devices equipped with sensors and actuators generate continuous streams of data, which can overwhelm centralized servers if processed entirely in the cloud. By deploying edge computing solutions, organizations can analyze data locally, filter relevant information, and transmit actionable insights to centralized systems or end-users in real-time. This distributed architecture optimizes network bandwidth, reduces operational costs, and enhances scalability for applications requiring immediate data processing and decision-making capabilities.

4.2.2 Benefits of Real-Time Data Processing at the Edge

- **Low Latency and Faster Response Times:** Processing data locally at the edge minimizes the time it takes to analyze and act upon incoming data, enabling real-time responses to events and reducing latency-sensitive application delays.

- **Bandwidth Optimization**: Edge computing reduces the volume of data that needs to be transmitted to centralized servers, optimizing network bandwidth and alleviating congestion. This is particularly beneficial in environments with limited or intermittent connectivity.
- **Improved Reliability and Resilience:** Local data processing at the edge enhances system reliability by reducing dependency on continuous cloud connectivity. Edge devices can continue to operate autonomously and make decisions even when disconnected from the cloud, ensuring uninterrupted service delivery.
- **Enhanced Privacy and Security**: Keeping sensitive data within the local edge environment minimizes exposure to potential cyber threats during data transmission. This approach enhances data privacy and compliance with regulatory requirements, particularly in industries such as healthcare and finance.

4.2.3 Applications of Real-Time Data Processing at the Edge

- **Industrial IoT and Automation:** Edge computing enables predictive maintenance, real-time monitoring of equipment performance, and process optimization in industrial settings. By analyzing sensor data locally, organizations can detect anomalies, prevent downtime, and improve operational efficiency.
- **Autonomous Vehicles**: Real-time data processing at the edge is crucial for autonomous vehicles to make split-second decisions based on sensor data from their surroundings. Edge computing ensures rapid detection of obstacles, traffic signals, and road conditions, enhancing vehicle safety and navigation accuracy.
- **Healthcare Monitoring**: Edge devices equipped with healthcare sensors can monitor patient vital signs, detect abnormalities, and alert medical professionals in real-time. This capability improves patient outcomes by enabling timely intervention and reducing response times during emergencies.
- **Smart Cities:** Edge computing supports smart city initiatives by analyzing data from IoT sensors deployed throughout urban infrastructure. Real-time insights enable efficient management of traffic flow, public safety monitoring, and resource allocation for sustainable urban development.

4.2.4 Challenges and Considerations

Despite its benefits, implementing real-time data processing at the edge presents several challenges that organizations must address:

- **Resource Constraints:** Edge devices often have limited computational power, memory, and storage capacity, requiring optimization techniques to efficiently execute data processing tasks and support real-time applications.
- **Data Quality and Integration:** Ensuring the accuracy, reliability, and consistency of data collected and processed at the edge is critical for maintaining the effectiveness of real-time analytics and decision-making. Integration with existing data systems and protocols can be complex, requiring standardized approaches and interoperable solutions.
- **Security and Privacy:** Securing edge devices against potential cyber threats, unauthorized access, and data breaches is paramount. Implementing robust security measures, such as encryption, authentication, and intrusion detection systems, helps mitigate risks and safeguard sensitive information within the edge environment.
- **Scalability and Management:** Managing a distributed network of edge devices and gateways requires effective scalability and lifecycle management strategies. Organizations must ensure seamless deployment, monitoring, and updates of edge computing solutions to accommodate growing data volumes and evolving application requirements.

4.2.5 Future Directions

The evolution of real-time data processing at the edge continues to drive innovation across various industries, with ongoing advancements in technology, infrastructure, and application development. Future trends include:

- **Edge AI and Machine Learning:** Integration of artificial intelligence (AI) and machine learning (ML) capabilities at the edge to enable autonomous decision-making, predictive analytics, and adaptive learning in real-time applications.
- **5G and Edge Computing:** Leveraging 5G networks to enhance edge computing capabilities, enabling ultra-low latency, high bandwidth connectivity, and supporting mission-critical IoT applications such as remote surgery and augmented reality.

4.3 EDGE SECURITY AND PRIVACY CONCERNS IN IOT

Edge computing has revolutionized the Internet of Things (IoT) landscape by decentralizing data processing and enabling real-time decision-making closer to where data is generated. While edge computing offers numerous benefits, including reduced latency and improved operational efficiency, it also introduces unique security and privacy challenges. Edge devices, such as IoT sensors and gateways, often operate in distributed and dynamic environments, making them vulnerable to various cyber threats and privacy breaches. Edge computing offers unprecedented opportunities for enhancing operational efficiency, real-time decision-making, and user experiences across diverse IoT applications. However, the integration of edge devices into IoT ecosystems introduces significant security and privacy challenges that must be addressed to mitigate risks and ensure trustworthiness.

By implementing robust security measures, privacy-enhancing technologies, and regulatory compliance strategies, organizations can safeguard sensitive data, protect user privacy rights, and foster a secure and resilient edge computing environment. As edge computing continues to evolve, collaboration among industry stakeholders, academia, and regulatory bodies is essential to address emerging threats, promote best practices, and achieve a balanced approach to security and privacy in IoT deployments.

4.3.1 Security Challenges in Edge Computing

Device Vulnerabilities

Edge devices typically have limited computational resources and may lack robust security features, making them susceptible to malware, unauthorized access, and physical tampering. Vulnerabilities in firmware or operating systems can be exploited to compromise device integrity and compromise sensitive data.

Network Security

Edge networks may operate in heterogeneous environments with diverse communication protocols and connectivity options. Securing data transmission between edge devices, gateways, and cloud servers is essential to prevent interception, eavesdropping, or man-in-the-middle attacks.

Authentication and Access Control

Ensuring secure authentication and access control mechanisms for edge devices is critical to prevent unauthorized entities from gaining access to sensitive data or manipulating device operations.

Weak or default credentials pose significant risks and should be replaced with strong authentication protocols.

Data Encryption

Encrypting data at rest and in transit between edge devices and cloud servers safeguards data confidentiality and mitigates the risk of data interception or unauthorized access. Implementing strong encryption algorithms and key management practices is essential for protecting sensitive information.

4.3.2 Privacy Concerns in Edge Computing

Data Localization and Sovereignty

Edge computing involves processing and storing data locally on edge devices or gateways, raising concerns about data localization and compliance with regional privacy regulations. Ensuring adherence to data sovereignty laws and regulations is essential to protect user privacy and avoid legal consequences.

Data Minimization and Consent

Collecting and processing only necessary data at the edge minimizes privacy risks and complies with principles of data minimization. Obtaining explicit consent from users for data collection, processing, and sharing activities is crucial for respecting individual privacy rights and building trust.

Contextual Awareness

Edge devices may collect sensitive contextual information, such as location data or biometric identifiers, which require enhanced privacy safeguards. Implementing privacy-enhancing technologies, such as anonymization and pseudonymization, helps mitigate privacy risks associated with sensitive data processing.

Transparency and Accountability

Providing transparency regarding data processing practices and establishing accountability frameworks enhances user trust and compliance with privacy regulations. Organizations should disclose information about data collection, storage, and sharing practices to empower users to make informed decisions about their personal data.

4.3.3 Mitigation Strategies and Best Practices

Security-by-Design

Incorporating security principles into the design and development of edge devices and applications enhances resilience against cyber threats. Implementing secure coding practices, conducting regular security assessments, and maintaining firmware updates mitigate vulnerabilities and strengthen device security.

Network Segmentation

Segregating edge networks from enterprise networks and implementing firewall rules and access controls minimize the impact of security breaches and unauthorized access attempts. Network segmentation isolates critical assets and restricts lateral movement of malicious actors within the network.

Edge Intelligence and Threat Detection

Deploying edge intelligence and threat detection mechanisms, such as intrusion detection systems (IDS) and anomaly detection algorithms, enhances early detection and response to security incidents. Real-time monitoring of edge environments enables proactive threat mitigation and reduces potential damage from cyber attacks.

Data Governance and Compliance

Establishing comprehensive data governance frameworks and compliance programs ensures adherence to privacy regulations and industry standards. Conducting privacy impact assessments (PIAs), maintaining data inventories, and implementing data retention policies protect user privacy and support regulatory compliance efforts.

4.3.4 Emerging Technologies and Future Trends

Blockchain Technology

Leveraging blockchain technology for decentralized data storage and transaction verification enhances data integrity, transparency, and auditability in edge computing environments. Blockchain-based solutions provide tamper-resistant mechanisms for securely managing and sharing data across distributed networks.

Privacy-Preserving Technologies

Advancements in privacy-preserving technologies, such as homomorphic encryption and differential privacy, enable secure data processing and analysis while preserving individual privacy rights. These technologies mitigate privacy risks associated with sensitive data handling at the edge.

Edge AI for Security

Integrating artificial intelligence (AI) and machine learning (ML) capabilities at the edge enables autonomous threat detection, anomaly detection, and adaptive security measures. Edge AI enhances real-time decision-making and improves responsiveness to evolving cyber threats in dynamic edge environments.

Regulatory Developments

Evolving regulatory frameworks and standards, such as the General Data Protection Regulation (GDPR) and California Consumer Privacy Act (CCPA), influence data protection practices in edge computing. Compliance with regulatory requirements is essential for minimizing legal liabilities and building trust with stakeholders.

4.4 CASE STUDIES IN IOT EDGE COMPUTING

IoT edge computing represents a transformative approach to data processing and decision-making by decentralizing computational tasks and analytics closer to where data is generated. This section explores notable case studies across various industries, highlighting how organizations leverage edge computing to enhance operational efficiency, improve real-time responsiveness, and drive innovation in IoT applications. IoT edge computing represents a paradigm shift in data processing and analytics, enabling organizations to leverage real-time insights, enhance operational efficiency, and drive innovation across diverse industry sectors. By deploying edge computing solutions, organizations can unlock new opportunities for improving customer experiences, optimizing resource utilization, and achieving sustainable growth in the digital era. Addressing challenges related to resource constraints, security, interoperability, and data governance is essential to realizing the full potential of IoT edge computing and shaping the future of connected ecosystems. As technology continues to evolve, collaboration among industry stakeholders, academia, and regulatory bodies will be crucial in advancing edge computing innovations and fostering a secure, resilient, and scalable IoT landscape.

4.4.1 Smart Manufacturing: Predictive Maintenance with Edge Analytics

In smart manufacturing, edge computing plays a crucial role in optimizing equipment performance and reducing downtime through predictive maintenance strategies. A notable case study involves a global automotive manufacturer that deployed IoT sensors on production equipment to monitor operational metrics, such as temperature, vibration, and pressure. Edge computing solutions installed on local gateways analyze sensor data in real-time, using machine learning algorithms to detect anomalies indicative of potential equipment failures. By predicting maintenance needs before issues escalate, the manufacturer can schedule proactive repairs, minimize unplanned downtime, and optimize production efficiency.

4.4.2 Healthcare: Real-Time Patient Monitoring and Analytics

Edge computing transforms healthcare delivery by enabling real-time monitoring and analytics of patient health data, enhancing clinical decision-making and patient care outcomes. A leading hospital network implemented IoT-enabled medical devices, such as wearable biosensors and bedside monitors, connected to edge computing platforms within hospital premises. These devices continuously collect and analyze patient vital signs, ECG readings, and other medical data locally, leveraging edge AI algorithms to detect abnormal patterns or critical events. Healthcare providers receive timely alerts and actionable insights, enabling prompt intervention and personalized treatment plans tailored to each patient's condition, thereby improving patient outcomes and hospital operational efficiency.

4.4.3 Smart Cities: Traffic Management and Environmental Monitoring

In smart city initiatives, edge computing supports dynamic traffic management and environmental monitoring systems, enhancing urban sustainability and public safety. A metropolitan city deployed IoT sensors across traffic intersections, streetlights, and air quality monitoring stations equipped with edge computing capabilities. Local edge devices process sensor data in real-time to analyze traffic flow patterns, optimize signal timings, and alleviate congestion. Additionally, environmental sensors measure air quality parameters, such as particulate matter and pollution levels, to inform timely interventions for improving urban air quality and public health. Edge computing enhances city resilience by enabling adaptive responses to real-time data insights, supporting efficient resource allocation and sustainable urban development.

4.4.4 Retail: Personalized Customer Experiences and Inventory Management

In retail environments, edge computing enhances customer engagement through personalized experiences and operational efficiency in inventory management. A global retail chain implemented IoT-enabled smart shelves and customer tracking systems integrated with edge computing platforms in stores. Smart shelves equipped with RFID tags and sensors automatically monitor product inventory levels and expiration dates, triggering real-time updates to inventory databases. Concurrently, edge computing analyzes customer behavior data, such as browsing patterns and purchase history, to generate personalized recommendations and promotional offers in real-time. By delivering targeted marketing campaigns and ensuring product availability, the retailer enhances customer satisfaction, increases sales conversion rates, and optimizes store operations through streamlined inventory management.

4.4.5 Agriculture: Precision Farming and Crop Monitoring

Edge computing revolutionizes agriculture practices through precision farming techniques and real-time crop monitoring solutions, optimizing agricultural productivity and resource efficiency.

A large-scale farm deployed IoT sensors and drones equipped with edge computing capabilities to monitor soil moisture levels, nutrient content, and crop health indicators across expansive fields. Edge analytics processes sensor data locally, generating actionable insights for farmers to adjust irrigation schedules, apply fertilizers, and detect early signs of crop diseases or pest infestations. By enabling data-driven decision-making and proactive agricultural management practices, edge computing empowers farmers to maximize crop yields, conserve water resources, and sustainably enhance farm profitability.

4.4.6 Challenges and Considerations

While these case studies demonstrate the transformative impact of IoT edge computing across diverse industries, several challenges must be addressed for successful deployment and scalability:

- **Resource Constraints**: Edge devices often have limited computational power, memory, and storage capacity, necessitating optimization techniques for efficient data processing and analytics.
- **Security and Privacy**: Safeguarding edge devices against cyber threats, ensuring data confidentiality, and complying with regulatory requirements remain critical concerns in IoT deployments.
- **Interoperability**: Ensuring seamless integration and compatibility between diverse IoT devices, edge computing platforms, and cloud services to facilitate data interoperability and system scalability.
- **Data Governance**: Establishing robust data governance frameworks, including data quality management, privacy protection, and regulatory compliance, to maintain trust and transparency in data-driven decision-making.

4.4.7 Future Directions

Looking ahead, advancements in edge computing technologies and emerging trends are poised to further accelerate innovation and adoption across IoT applications:

5G and Edge Computing

Leveraging 5G networks to enhance edge computing capabilities, enabling ultra-low latency, high bandwidth connectivity, and supporting mission-critical IoT applications such as autonomous vehicles and remote healthcare.

Edge-as-a-Service (EaaS)

Evolution of managed service offerings that simplify deployment, management, and scaling of edge computing solutions, enabling organizations to focus on innovation and business outcomes.

CHAPTER 5
EDGE COMPUTING IN TELECOMMUNICATIONS

5.1 MOBILE EDGE COMPUTING (MEC)

Multi-access edge computing (MEC), formerly mobile edge computing, is an ETSI-defined network architecture concept that enables cloud computing capabilities and an IT service environment at the edge of the cellular network and, more in general at the edge of any network.

The basic idea behind MEC is that by running applications and performing related processing tasks closer to the cellular customer, network congestion is reduced and applications perform better. MEC technology is designed to be implemented at the cellular base stations or other edge nodes, and enables flexible and rapid deployment of new applications and services for customers. Combining elements of information technology and telecommunications networking, MEC also allows cellular operators to open their radio access network (RAN) to authorized third parties, such as application developers and content providers. Technical standards for MEC are being developed by the European Telecommunications Standards Institute, which has produced a technical white paper about the concept.

5.1.1 Distributed Computing in the RAN

MEC provides a distributed computing environment for application and service hosting. It also has the ability to store and process content close to cellular subscribers, for faster response time. Applications can also be exposed to real-time radio access network (RAN) information.

The key element is the MEC application server, which is integrated at the RAN element. This server provides computing resources, storage capacity, connectivity and access to RAN information. It supports a multitenancy run-time and hosting environment for applications.

The virtual appliance applications are delivered as packaged operating system virtual machine (VM) images or containers incorporating operating systems and applications. The platform also provides a set of middleware application and infrastructure services. Application software can be provided from equipment vendors, service providers and third-parties.

5.1.2 Deployment

The MEC application server can be deployed at the macro base station EnodeB that is part of an LTE cellular network, or at the Radio Network Controller (RNC) that is part of a 3G cellular network and at a multi-technology cell aggregation site. The multi-technology cell aggregation site can be located indoors or outdoors.

5.1.3 Business and Technical Benefits

By using mobile edge computing technology, a cellular operator can efficiently deploy new services for specific customers or classes of customers. The technology also reduces the signal load of the core network, and can host applications and services in a less costly way. It also collects data about storage, network bandwidth, CPU utilization, etc., for each application or service deployed by a third party. Application developers and content providers can take advantage of close proximity to cellular subscribers and real-time RAN information.

MEC has been created using open standards and application programming interfaces (APIs), using common programming models, relevant tool chains and software development kits to encourage and expedite the development of new applications for the new MEC environment.

5.1.4 Applications

Since MEC architecture has only recently been proposed, there are as yet very few applications that have adopted this architecture. However, many case studies have been proposed in recent articles. Some of the notable applications in mobile edge computing are computational offloading, content delivery, mobile big data analytics, edge video caching, collaborative computing, connected cars, smart venues, smart enterprises, healthcare, smartgrids, service function chaining, indoor positioning, etc.

5.1.5 Current Uses

Some applications which incorporate MEC were made available in 2015. For example, active device location tracking allows operators to track active terminal equipment, independent of Global Positioning System devices.

This is based on third-party geolocation algorithms within an application hosted on the MEC application server.

Another use is distributed content and Domain Name System (DNS) caching, which reduces server load and speeds up delivery of data to customers. The first commercial product available at a bigger scale is AWS Wavelength. Customers are able to run their applications on AWS services in the edge of a 4G/5G network of a specific telco.

5.1.6 Technical Standards

Technical standards for MEC are being developed by the European Telecommunications Standards Institute (ETSI), which created a new Industry Specification Group in 2014 for this purpose. The participating companies are: Allot Communications Systems Ltd, ASTRI, AT&T, B-Com, Cadzow Communications Consulting, Ceragon Networks, Cisco Systems Belgium, ETRI, Eurecom, Fujitsu Laboratories of Europe, Hewlett-Packard France, Huawei TechnologiesFrance, Huawei Technologies(UK) Co. Ltd, IBM Europe, Intel Corporation, ISMB, InterDigital Communication, ITRI, JCP-Connect, Juniper, Motorola Mobility Ltd, National Technique Assistance Centre, NEC Europe Ltd, Nokia Solutions and Networks, NTT Corporation, NTT Docomo, Orange, PoLTE, PeerApp Ltd, PT Portugal SGPS SA, Quortus Limited, Red Hat Ltd, Saguna Networks, Samsung Electronics R&D Institute UK Ltd, Sony Europe Ltd, Sony Mobile Communications, Telecom Italia, Telefonica, Telekom Austria AG, Turk Telekom, Vasona Networks, Verizon, Viavi Solutions, Vodafone Group Services plc, Xilinx Inc., YAANA Ltd, and ZTE Corporation.

5.2 NETWORK SLICING AND EDGE SYNERGIES

Network slicing and edge computing represent complementary technologies that are revolutionizing the telecommunications and computing landscapes, respectively. Together, they enable dynamic and customizable network architectures that support diverse use cases, ranging from ultra-low latency applications to massive IoT deployments.

Network slicing and edge computing represent transformative technologies that converge to enhance network flexibility, efficiency, and service delivery across diverse IoT applications. By leveraging network slicing to create customizable network architectures and integrating edge computing for real-time data processing and analytics, organizations can unlock new opportunities for innovation, responsiveness, and operational excellence. Addressing challenges related to interoperability, resource management, security, and regulatory compliance is essential to realizing the full potential of network slicing and edge computing synergies in shaping the future of connected ecosystems. As technology continues to evolve, collaborative efforts among industry stakeholders, standardization bodies, and regulatory authorities will be crucial in driving forward the adoption and advancement of network slicing and edge computing innovations.

5.2.1 Understanding Network Slicing

5G network slicing is a network architecture that enables the multiplexing of virtualized and independent logical networks on the same physical network infrastructure. Each network slice is an isolated end-to-end network tailored to fulfill diverse requirements requested by a particular application.

For this reason, this technology assumes a central role to support 5G mobile networks that are designed to efficiently embrace a plethora of services with very different service level requirements (SLR). The realization of this service-oriented view of the network leverages on the concepts of software-defined networking (SDN) and network function virtualization (NFV) that allow the implementation of flexible and scalable network slices on top of a common network infrastructure.

From a business model perspective, each network slice is administrated by a mobile virtual network operator (MVNO). The infrastructure provider (the owner of the telecommunication infrastructure) leases its physical resources to the MVNOs that share the underlying physical network. According to the availability of the assigned resources, a MVNO can autonomously deploy multiple network slices that are customized to the various applications provided to its own users.

History

The history of network slicing can be tracked back to the late 80s with the introduction of the concept of "slice" in the networking field. Overlay networks provided the first form of network slicing since heterogeneous network resources were combined to create virtual networks over a common infrastructure. However, they lacked a mechanism that could enable their programmability.

In the early 2000s, PlanetLab introduced a virtualization framework that allowed groups of users to program network functions in order to obtain isolated and application-specific slices. The advent of SDN technologies in 2009 further extended the programmability capabilities via open interfaces that enabled the realization of fully configurable and scalable network slices.

In the context of mobile networks, network slicing evolved from the concept of RAN sharing that was initially introduced in LTE standard. Examples of such technology are multi-operator radio access networks (MORAN) and multi-operator core networks (MOCN), which allow network operators to share common LTE resources within the same radio access network (RAN).

Key Concepts

The "one-size-fits-all" network paradigm employed in the past mobile networks (2G, 3G and 4G) is no longer suited to efficiently address a market model composed of very different applications like *machine-type communication*, *ultra reliable low latency communication* and *enhanced mobile broadband* content delivery.

Network slicing emerges as an essential technique in 5G networks to accommodate such different and possibly contrasting quality of service (QoS) requirements exploiting a single physical network infrastructure. The basic idea of network slicing is to "slice" the original network architecture in multiple logical and independent networks that are configured to effectively meet the various services requirements. To quantitatively realize such concept, several techniques are employed:

- **Network Functions:** They express elementary network functionalities that are used as "building blocks" to create every network slice.
- **Virtualization:** It provides an abstract representation of the physical resources under a unified and homogeneous scheme. In addition, it enables a scalable slice deployment relying on NFV that allows the decoupling of each network function instance from the network hardware it runs on.
- **Orchestration:** It is a process that allows coordination of all the different network components that are involved in the life-cycle of each network slice. In this context, SDN is employed to enable a dynamic and flexible slice configuration.

Impact and Applications

In commercial terms, network slicing allows a mobile operator to create specific virtual networks that cater to particular clients and use cases. Certain applications - such as mobile broadband, machine-to-machine communications (e.g., in manufacturing or logistics), or smart cars - will benefit from leveraging different aspects of 5G technology. One might require higher speeds, another low latency, and yet another access to edge computing resources. By creating separate slices that prioritise specific resources a 5G operator can offer tailored solutions to particular industries. Some sources insist this will revolutionise industries like marketing, augmented reality, or mobile gaming, while others are more cautious, pointing to unevenness in network coverage and poor reach of advantages beyond increased speed.

Slicing will be very useful to MVNOs as different use cases can be supported in a layer based on parameters like low latency high speed for video streaming for OTT focused MVNOs, similarly telemetry operations could have lower speed parameter and as on.

Slicing can also enhance service continuity via improved roaming across networks, by creating a virtual network running on physical infrastructure that spans multiple local or national networks; or by allowing a host network to create an optimised virtual network which replicates the one offered by a roaming device's home network.

Architecture Overview

Although there are different proposals of network slice architectures, it is possible to define a general architecture that maps the common elements of each solution into a general and unified framework. From a high-level perspective, the network slicing architecture can be considered as composed of two mains blocks, one dedicated to the actual slice implementation and the other dedicated to the slice management and configuration.

The first block is designed as a multi-tier architecture composed by three layers (service layer, network function layer, infrastructure layer), where each one contributes to the slice definition and deployment with distinct tasks. The second block is designed as a centralized network entity, generically denoted as *network slice controller*, that monitors and manages the functionalities between the three layers in order to efficiently coordinate the coexistence of multiple slices.

Service Layer

The service layer interfaces directly with the network business entities (e.g., MVNOs and 3rd party service providers) that share the underlying physical network and it provides a unified vision of the service requirements. Each service is formally represented as *service instance*, which embeds all the network characteristics in the form of SLA requirements that are expected to be fully satisfied by a suitable slice creation.

Network Function Layer

The network function layer is in charge of the creation of each network slice according to service instance requests coming from the upper layer. It is composed of a set of *network functions* that embody well-defined behaviors and interfaces. Multiple network functions are placed over the virtual network infrastructure and chained together to create an end-to-end network slice instance that reflects the network characteristics requested by the service. The configuration of the network functions are performed by means of a set of *network operations* that allow management of their full lifecycle (from their placement when a slice is created to their de-allocation when the function provided is no longer needed).

To increase resource usage efficiency, the same network function can be simultaneously shared by different slices at the cost of an increase in the complexity of operations management. Conversely, a one-to-one mapping between each network function and each slice eases the configuration procedures, but can lead to poor and inefficient resource usage.

Infrastructure Layer

The infrastructure layer represents the actual physical network topology (radio access network, transport network and core network) upon which every network slice is multiplexed and it provides the physical network resources to host the several network functions composing each slice.

The network domain of the available resources includes a heterogeneous set of infrastructure components like data centers (storage and computation capacity resources), devices enabling network connectivity such as routers (networking resources) and base stations (radio bandwidth resources).

Network Slice Controller

The network slice controller is defined as a network orchestrator, which interfaces with the various functionalities performed by each layer to coherently manage each slice request.

The benefit of such network element is that it enables an efficient and flexible slice creation that can be reconfigured during its life-cycle. Operationally, the network slice controller oversees several tasks that provide more effective coordination between the aforementioned layers:

- **End-to-End Service Management:** Mapping of the various service instances expressed in terms of SLA requirements with suitable network functions capable of satisfying the service constraints.
- **Virtual Resources Definition:** Virtualization of the physical network resources in order to simplify the resources management operations performed to allocate network functions.
- **Slice Life-Cycle Management:** Slice performance monitoring across all the three layers in order to dynamically reconfigure each slice to accommodate possible SLA requirements modifications.

Due to the complexity of the performed tasks which address different purposes, the network slice controller can be composed by multiple orchestrators that independently manage a subset of functionalities of each layer. To fulfill the service requirements, the various orchestration entities need to coordinate with each other by exchanging high-level information about the state of the operations involved in the slice creation and deployment.

Slice Isolation

Slice isolation is an important requirement that allows enforcing the core concept of network slicing about the simultaneous coexistence of multiple slices sharing the same infrastructure. This property is achieved by imposing that each slice's performance must not have any impact on the other slice's performance. The benefit of this design choice is that enhances the network slice architecture in two main aspects:

- **Slice Security:** Cyber-attacks or faults occurrences affect only the target slice and have limited impact on the life-cycle of other existing slices.

- **Slice Privacy:** Private information related to each slice (e.g., user statistics, MVNO business model) are not shared among other slices.

Guaranteeing QoS

Slicing has become an important part of 5G networks, but we don't have to forget to guarantee the QoS. Some studies have demonstrated that formulating the problem with the QoS as a stochastic problem, permit us to maximize the average throughput of the AP, while satisfying the constraints related to the QoS.

Monetizing 5G Network Slicing

Monetizing 5G services faster is one of the topics that interests network operators the most because the costs of building and maintaining 5G networks are high, and it's difficult to predict the demand for 5G services. 5G network slicing is one of the effective ways to offer customized services for different industries such as manufacturing, transportation, and healthcare. Combined with AIOps, ML/AI-driven automation and 5G lifecycle optimization, it can reduce OpEx and increase revenues for network operators.

5G Core Network Slicing

In the 3GPP 5G core architecture, the user plane and control plane functions are separated. Control plane capabilities, for instance, session management, access authentication, policy management, and user data storage are independent of the user plane functionality. The user plane handles packet forwarding, encapsulation or de-capsulation, and associated transport level specifics. This separation leads to the distribution of the user plane functions close to the edge of network slices (e.g., so as to reduce latency) and to be independent of the control plane. The main 5G core network entities are the Authentication server function (AUSF), Unstructured data storage network function (UDSF), Network exposure function (NEF), NF repository function (NRF), Policy control function (PCF), Unified data management (UDM), Network Slice Selection Function (NSSF), Communication Service Management Function (CSMF), AMF, SMF, and UPF. The AMF (as a function of the CP) controls UEs that have been authenticated to use the services of the operator and manages the mobility of the UEs across the gNBs. The SMF (again part of the CP) manages the sessions of UEs, while AMF transmits the session management messages between the UEs and SMF. UPF (as part of the UP) performs the processing and forwarding of the user data. NSSF (as a function of the CP) is responsible for the management and orchestration of network slices. CSMF (as a function of the CP) translates the requirements of services to requirements relating to network slices. 5G Core network functions can be sliced to support specific services for different UEs. Thanks to the modular nature of the 5G core, the network functions of the 5G core can be split and shared between different network slices to reduce management complexity. In general, we can perform 5G core network slicing in two ways. We can implement dedicated core network functions per network slice. In this architecture, each network slice has a set of completely dedicated core network functions (e.g., AUSF, AMF, SMF, and UDM). The UEs can access various services from network slices and different core networks. Alternatively, we can share some control plane functions between the network slices while others such as user plane functions are slice specific (e.g., UPF). AMF is usually shared by several network slices, while SMF and UPF are usually dedicated to specific network slices. The AMF function will be shared between different network slices in order to reduce the mobility management signaling when the UE uses the services of different network slices simultaneously. For example, UE location management or the control signaling between the UE and the old AMF will be reduced when it will be connected to the new AMF of another network slice. Also, UDM and NSSF are typically shared by all network slices to reduce the management complexity of network slices.

Network Slicing Security

The emergence of network slicing also exposes novel security and privacy challenges, primarily related to aspects such as network slicing life-cycle security, inter-slice security, intra-slice security, slice broker security, zero-touch network and management security, and blockchain security. Therefore, enhancing the security, privacy, and trust of network slicing has become a key research area toward realizing the true capabilities of 5G. Various security solutions are proposed for resolving the security threats, challenges, and issues of network slicing. These solutions include artificial intelligence based solutions, security orchestration, blockchain based solutions, Security Service Level Agreement (SSLA) and policy based solutions, security monitoring based solutions, slice isolation, security-by-design and privacy-by-design, and offering security as a service.

5.2.2 Role of Edge Computing in Network Slicing

Edge computing extends network slicing capabilities by decentralizing computational tasks and data processing closer to the network edge, where data is generated and consumed. Edge computing infrastructure, comprising edge servers, gateways, and IoT devices, facilitates real-time data analytics, content delivery, and application processing within proximity to end-users. By integrating with network slicing, edge computing enhances service agility, reduces latency, and optimizes resource utilization across distributed edge environments.

5.2.3 Benefits of Network Slicing and Edge Synergies

Customized Service Offerings

Network slicing enables service providers to offer customized service-level agreements (SLAs) tailored to specific user requirements, such as enhanced mobile broadband (eMBB), ultra-reliable low-latency communications (URLLC), and massive machine-type communications (mMTC). Edge computing enhances service personalization by delivering localized content, real-time analytics, and responsive applications based on user proximity and context.

Optimized Resource Allocation

Network slices allocate dedicated network resources, including spectrum, bandwidth, and computing resources, to efficiently support diverse applications and traffic patterns. Edge computing optimizes resource allocation by dynamically provisioning edge resources based on workload demands, ensuring efficient utilization and scalability across distributed edge environments.

Low Latency and High Performance

Combining edge computing with network slicing reduces data transit times and processing delays by minimizing round-trip latency between edge devices and centralized cloud servers. Real-time data analytics and decision-making at the edge enable ultra-low latency applications, such as autonomous vehicles, augmented reality (AR), and industrial automation, to operate seamlessly and responsively.

Enhanced Security and Privacy

Network slicing enhances security by isolating traffic and data flows within dedicated slices, mitigating risks of cross-slice interference and unauthorized access. Edge computing enhances data privacy by processing sensitive information locally, reducing exposure to potential cyber threats during data transmission and storage.

5.2.4 Applications of Network Slicing and Edge Synergies

Smart Manufacturing

Network slicing and edge computing support real-time monitoring of industrial IoT devices, predictive maintenance, and process automation in smart factories. Dedicated network slices ensure reliable connectivity and low-latency communication between production equipment, while edge computing enables local data processing and analytics to optimize operational efficiency and minimize downtime.

Telemedicine and Healthcare

In telemedicine applications, network slicing provides secure and reliable connectivity for remote consultations, medical diagnostics, and patient monitoring. Edge computing supports real-time analysis of medical data, enabling healthcare providers to deliver timely interventions, personalized treatments, and continuous health monitoring services without compromising data privacy or regulatory compliance.

Smart Cities

Network slicing and edge computing facilitate smart city initiatives by supporting intelligent transportation systems, environmental monitoring, and public safety applications.

Dedicated network slices ensure robust connectivity and prioritized data transmission for emergency services, while edge computing enables real-time data processing, adaptive traffic management, and responsive city infrastructure.

Augmented Reality (AR) and Gaming

Network slicing optimizes network performance for AR applications and multiplayer gaming experiences by prioritizing low-latency communications and high-bandwidth data transmission. Edge computing enhances AR capabilities by delivering immersive content, real-time interaction, and personalized user experiences based on location-aware data processing and edge analytics.

5.2.5 Challenges and Considerations

Despite their transformative potential, network slicing and edge computing face several challenges that require careful consideration and mitigation strategies:

Interoperability

Ensuring compatibility and seamless integration between diverse network slices, edge computing platforms, and legacy systems to facilitate interoperable service delivery and data exchange.

Resource Management

Efficiently managing network resources, including spectrum allocation, bandwidth utilization, and computing capacity, to optimize performance and scalability across dynamic edge environments.

Security and Privacy

Implementing robust security measures, such as encryption, authentication, and access controls, to protect data integrity and privacy within network slices and edge computing deployments.

Regulatory Compliance

Addressing regulatory requirements and compliance standards, such as data localization and privacy regulations, to ensure lawful and ethical use of network slicing and edge computing technologies.

5.2.6 Future Directions

Looking ahead, ongoing advancements and emerging trends are expected to further enhance the integration of network slicing and edge computing:

AI-driven Network Management

Integration of artificial intelligence (AI) and machine learning (ML) algorithms to automate network slice orchestration, optimize resource allocation, and predict network performance based on real-time data analytics.

Edge-as-a-Service (EaaS)

Evolution of managed service offerings that simplify deployment, management, and scaling of network slicing and edge computing solutions, enabling organizations to leverage on-demand services for innovative applications and business outcomes.

5G Evolution and Beyond

Continued evolution of 5G networks and beyond, including advancements in network slicing capabilities, edge computing infrastructure, and IoT connectivity, to support emerging use cases such as smart cities, autonomous systems, and immersive digital experiences.

5.3 5G AND EDGE COMPUTING SYNERGIES

The convergence of 5G and edge computing represents a transformative paradigm shift in telecommunications and computing, promising to revolutionize digital experiences, industrial automation, smart city initiatives, and more.

5G and edge computing synergies represent a transformative convergence that empowers organizations to deliver high-performance, low-latency applications and services across diverse industries. By leveraging 5G networks for high-speed connectivity and edge computing for localized data processing and analytics, organizations can unlock new opportunities for innovation, operational efficiency, and customer engagement in the digital era. Addressing challenges related to infrastructure deployment, interoperability, security, and regulatory compliance is essential to realizing the full potential of 5G and edge computing synergies and driving forward the future of connected ecosystems. As technology continues to evolve, collaborative efforts among industry stakeholders, standardization bodies, and regulatory authorities will be crucial in fostering a secure, resilient, and scalable 5G-powered edge computing landscape.

5.3.1 Understanding 5G Networks

5G is the fifth-generation technology standard for cellular networks, which cellular phone companies began deploying worldwide in 2019, and is the successor to 4G technology that provides connectivity to most current mobile phones.

Like its predecessors, 5G networks are cellular networks, in which the service area is divided into small geographical areas called *cells*. All 5G wireless devices in a cell are connected to the Internet and the telephone network by radio waves through a basestation and antennae in the cell. The new networks have higher download speeds, with a peak speed of 10 gigabits per second (Gbit/s) when there is only one user in the network. 5G has higher bandwidth to deliver faster speeds than 4G and can connect more devices, improving the quality of Internet services in crowded areas. Due to the increased bandwidth, it is expected the 5G networks will increasingly be used as general internet service providers (ISPs), competing with existing ISPs such as cable internet, and also will make possible new applications in internet-of-things (IoT) and machine-to-machine areas. Cellphones with only 4G capability are not able to use the 5G networks.

5G networks are cellular networks, in which the service area is divided into small geographical areas called *cells*. All 5G wireless devices in a cell communicate by radio waves with a cellular base station via fixed antennas, over frequencies assigned by the base station. The base stations, termed nodes, are connected to switching centers in the telephone network and routers for Internet access by high-bandwidth optical fiber or wireless backhaul connections. As in other cellular networks, a mobile device moving from one cell to another is automatically handed off seamlessly.

The industry consortium setting standards for 5G, the 3rd Generation Partnership Project (3GPP), defines "5G" as any system using 5G NR (5G New Radio) software — a definition that came into general use by late 2018. 5G continues to use OFDM encoding.

Several network operators use millimeter waves called FR2 in 5G terminology, for additional capacity and higher throughputs. Millimeter waves have a shorter range than the lower frequency microwaves, therefore the cells are of a smaller size. Millimeter waves also have more trouble passing through building walls and humans. Millimeter-wave antennas are smaller than the large antennas used in previous cellular networks.

The increased data rate is achieved partly by using additional higher-frequency radio waves in addition to the low- and medium-band frequencies used in previous cellular networks. For providing a wide range of services, 5G networks can operate in three frequency bands — low, medium, and high.

5G can be implemented in low-band, mid-band or high-band millimeter-wave. Low-band 5G uses a similar frequency range to 4G cellphones, 600–900 MHz, which can potentially offer higher download speeds than 4G: 5–250 megabits per second (Mbit/s). Low-band cell towers have a range and coverage area similar to 4G towers. Mid-band 5G uses microwaves of 1.7–4.7 GHz, allowing speeds of 100–900 Mbit/s, with each cell tower providing service up to several kilometers in radius. This level of service is the most widely deployed, and was deployed in many metropolitan areas in 2020. Some regions are not implementing the low band, making Mid-band the minimum service level. High-band 5G uses frequencies of 24–47 GHz, near the bottom of the millimeter wave band, although higher frequencies may be used in the future. It often achieves download speeds in the gigabit-per-second (Gbit/s) range, comparable to co-axial cable Internet service. However, millimeter waves (mmWave or mmW) have a more limited range, requiring many small cells. They can be impeded or blocked by materials in walls or windows or pedestrians. Due to their higher cost, plans are to deploy these cells only in dense urban environments and areas where crowds of people congregate such as sports stadiums and convention centers. The above speeds are those achieved in actual tests in 2020, and speeds are expected to increase during rollout. The spectrum ranging from 24.25 to 29.5 GHz has been the most licensed and deployed 5G mmWave spectrum range in the world.

Rollout of 5G technology has led to debate over its security and relationship with Chinese vendors. It has also been the subject of health concerns and misinformation, including discredited conspiracy theories linking it to the COVID-19 pandemic.

The ITU-R has defined three main application areas for the enhanced capabilities of 5G. They are Enhanced Mobile Broadband (eMBB), Ultra Reliable Low Latency Communications (URLLC), and Massive Machine Type Communications (mMTC). Only eMBB is deployed in 2020; URLLC and mMTC are several years away in most locations.

Enhanced Mobile Broadband (eMBB) uses 5G as a progression from 4G LTE mobile broadband services, with faster connections, higher throughput, and more capacity. This will benefit areas of higher traffic such as stadiums, cities, and concert venues.

'Ultra-Reliable Low-Latency Communications' (URLLC) refers to using the network for mission-critical applications that require uninterrupted and robust data exchange. Short-packet data transmission is used to meet both reliability and latency requirements of the wireless communication networks.

Massive Machine-Type Communications (mMTC) would be used to connect to a large number of devices. 5G technology will connect some of the 50 billion connected IoT devices. Most will use the less expensive Wi-Fi. Drones, transmitting via 4G or 5G, will aid in disaster recovery efforts, providing real-time data for emergency responders. Most cars will have a 4G or 5G cellular connection for many services. Autonomous cars do not require 5G, as they have to be able to operate where they do not have a network connection. However, most autonomous vehicles also feature tele-operations for mission accomplishment, and these greatly benefit from 5G technology.

History

In April 2008, NASA partnered with Geoff Brown and Machine-to-Machine Intelligence (M2Mi) Corp to develop a fifth generation communications technology approach, though largely concerned with working with nanosats. That same year, the South Korean IT R&D program of "5G mobile communication systems based on beam-division multiple access and relays with group cooperation" was formed.

In August 2012, New York University founded NYU Wireless, a multi-disciplinary academic research centre that has conducted pioneering work in 5G wireless communications. On October 8, 2012, the UK's University of Surrey secured £35M for a new 5G research centre, jointly funded by the British government's UK Research Partnership Investment Fund (UKRPIF) and a consortium of key international mobile operators and infrastructure providers, including Huawei, Samsung, Telefónica Europe, Fujitsu Laboratories Europe, Rohde & Schwarz, and Aircom International. It will offer testing facilities to mobile operators keen to develop a mobile standard that uses less energy and less radio spectrum, while delivering speeds higher than current 4G with aspirations for the new technology to be ready within a decade. On November 1, 2012, the EU project "Mobile and wireless communications Enablers for the Twenty-twenty Information Society" (METIS) starts its activity toward the definition of 5G. METIS achieved an early global consensus on these systems. In this sense, METIS played an important role of building consensus among other external major stakeholders prior to global standardization activities. This was done by initiating and addressing work in relevant global fora (e.g. ITU-R), as well as in national and regional regulatory bodies. That same month, the iJOIN EU project was launched, focusing on "small cell" technology, which is of key importance for taking advantage of limited and strategic resources, such as the radio wave spectrum. According to Günther Oettinger, the European Commissioner for Digital Economy and Society (2014–2019), "an innovative utilization of spectrum" is one of the key factors at the heart of 5G success. Oettinger further described it as "the essential resource for the wireless connectivity of which 5G will be the main driver". iJOIN was selected by the European Commission as one of the pioneering 5G research projects to showcase early results on this technology at the Mobile World Congress 2015 (Barcelona, Spain).

In February 2013, ITU-R Working Party 5D (WP 5D) started two study items: (1) Study on IMT Vision for 2020 and beyond, and; (2) Study on future technology trends for terrestrial IMT systems. Both aiming at having a better understanding of future technical aspects of mobile communications toward the definition of the next generation mobile. On May 12, 2013, Samsung Electronics stated that they had developed a "5G" system. The core technology has a maximum speed of tens of Gbit/s (gigabits per second). In testing, the transfer speeds for the "5G" network sent data at 1.056 Gbit/s to a distance of up to 2 kilometers with the use of an 8*8 MIMO. In July 2013, India and Israel agreed to work jointly on development of fifth generation (5G) telecom technologies. On October 1, 2013, NTT (Nippon Telegraph and Telephone), the same company to launch world's first 5G network in Japan, wins Minister of Internal Affairs and Communications Award at CEATEC for 5G R&D efforts. On November 6, 2013, Huawei announced plans to invest a minimum of $600 million into R&D for next generation 5G networks capable of speeds 100 times higher than modern LTE networks.

On April 3, 2019, South Korea became the first country to adopt 5G. Just hours later, Verizon launched its 5G services in the United States, and disputed South Korea's claim of becoming the world's first country with a 5G network, because allegedly, South Korea's 5G service was launched initially for just six South Korean celebrities so that South Korea could claim the title of having the world's first 5G network. In fact, the three main South Korean telecommunication companies (SK Telecom, KT, and LG Uplus) added more than 40,000 users to their 5G network on the launch day. In June 2019, the Philippines became the first country in Southeast Asia to roll out a 5G broadband network after Globe Telecom commercially launched its 5G data plans to customers. AT&T brings 5G service to consumers and businesses in December 2019 ahead of plans to offer 5G throughout the United States in the first half of 2020.

In 2020, AIS and TrueMove H launched 5G services in Thailand, making it the first country in Southeast Asia to have commercial 5G. A functional mockup of a Russian 5G base station, developed by domestic specialists as part of Rostec's digital division Rostec.digital, was presented in Nizhny Novgorod at the annual conference "Digital Industry of Industrial Russia". 5G speeds have declined in many countries since 2022, which has driven the development of 5.5G to increase connection speeds.

Performance

Speed

5G is capable of delivering significantly faster data rates than 4G, with peak data rates of up to 20 gigabits per second (Gbps). Furthermore, average 5G download speeds have been recorded at 186.3 Mbit/s in the U.S. by T-Mobile, while South Korea leads globally with average speeds of 432 megabits per second (Mbps). 5G networks are also designed to provide significantly more capacity than 4G networks, with a projected 100-fold increase in network capacity and efficiency.

The most widely used form of 5G, sub-6 GHz 5G (mid-band), is capable of delivering data rates ranging from 10 to 1,000 megabits per second (Mbps), with a much greater reach than mmWave bands. C-Band (n77/n78) was deployed by various U.S. operators in 2022 in the sub-6 bands, although its deployment by Verizon and

AT&T was delayed until early January 2022 due to safety concerns raised by the Federal Aviation Administration. The record for 5G speed in a deployed network is 5.9 Gbps as of 2023, but this was tested before the network was launched. Low-band frequencies (such as n5) offer a greater coverage area for a given cell, but their data rates are lower than those of mid and high bands in the range of 5–250 megabits per second (Mbps).

Latency

In 5G, the ideal "air latency" is of the order of 8 to 12 milliseconds i.e., excluding delays due to HARQ retransmissions, handovers, etc. Retransmission latency and backhaul latency to the server must be added to the "air latency" for correct comparisons. Verizon reported the latency on its 5G early deployment is 30 ms. Edge Servers close to the towers can probably reduce latency to between 10 and 15 milliseconds. Latency is much higher during handovers; ranging from 50 to 500 milliseconds depending on the type of handover. Reducing handover interruption time is an ongoing area of research and development; options include modifying the handover margin (offset) and the time-to-trigger (TTT).

Error Rate

5G uses an adaptive modulation and coding scheme (MCS) to keep the block error rate (BLER) extremely low. Whenever the error rate crosses a (very low) threshold the transmitter will switch to a lower MCS, which will be less error-prone. This way speed is sacrificed to ensure an almost zero error rate.

Range

The range of 5G depends on many factors: transmit power, frequency, and interference. For example, mmWave (e.g.: band n258) will have a lower range than mid-band (e.g.: band n78) which will have a lower range than low-band (e.g.: band n5) Given the marketing hype on what 5G can offer, simulators and drive tests are used by cellular service providers for the precise measurement of 5G performance.

Standards

Initially, the term was associated with the International Telecommunication Union's IMT-2020 standard, which required a theoretical peak download speed of 20 gigabits per second and 10 gigabits per second upload speed, along with other requirements. Then, the industry standards group 3GPP chose the 5G NR (New Radio) standard together with LTE as their proposal for submission to the IMT-2020 standard.

5G NR can include lower frequencies (FR1), below 6 GHz, and higher frequencies (FR2), above 24 GHz. However, the speed and latency in early FR1 deployments, using 5G NR software on 4G hardware (non-standalone), are only slightly better than new 4G systems, estimated at 15 to 50% better.

The standard documents are organized by 3rd Generation Partnership Project (3GPP), with its system architecture defined in TS 23.501. The packet protocol for mobility management (establishing connection and moving between base stations) and session management (connecting to networks and network slices) is described in TS 24.501. Specifications of key data structures are found in TS 23.003.

Fronthaul Network

IEEE covers several areas of 5G with a core focus on wireline sections between the Remote Radio Head (RRH) and Base Band Unit (BBU). The 1914.1 standards focus on network architecture and dividing the connection between the RRU and BBU into two key sections. Radio Unit (RU) to the Distributor Unit (DU) being the NGFI-I (Next Generation Fronthaul Interface) and the DU to the Central Unit (CU) being the NGFI-II interface allowing a more diverse and cost-effective network. NGFI-I and NGFI-II have defined performance values which should be compiled to ensure different traffic types defined by the ITU are capable of being carried. The IEEE 1914.3 standard is creating a new Ethernet frame format capable of carrying IQ data in a much more efficient way depending on the functional split utilized. This is based on the 3GPP definition of functional splits.

5G NR

5G NR (New Radio) is the de facto air interface developed for 5G networks. It is the global standard for 3GPP 5G networks. The study of NR within 3GPP started in 2015, and the first specification was made available by the end of 2017. While the 3GPP standardization process was ongoing, the industry had already begun efforts to implement infrastructure compliant with the draft standard, with the first large-scale commercial launch of 5G NR having occurred at the end of 2018. Since 2019, many operators have deployed 5G NR networks and handset manufacturers have developed 5G NR enabled handsets.

5Gi

5Gi is an alternative 5G variant developed in India. It was developed in a joint collaboration between IIT Madras, IIT Hyderabad, TSDSI, and the Centre of Excellence in Wireless Technology (CEWiT). 5Gi is designed to improve 5G coverage in rural and remote areas over varying geographical terrains. 5Gi uses Low Mobility Large Cell (LMLC) to extend 5G connectivity and the range of a base station. In April 2022, 5Gi was merged with the global 5G NR standard in the 3GPP Release 17 specifications.

Pre-Standard Implementations

- **5G TF:** American carrier Verizon used a pre-standard variation of 5G known as 5G TF (Verizon 5G Technical Forum) for Fixed Wireless

Access in 2018. The 5G service provided to customers in this standard is incompatible with 5G NR. Verizon has since migrated to 5G NR.

- **5G-SIG:** KT Corporation had a pre-standard variation of 5G developed called 5G-SIG. This was deployed at the Pyeongchang 2018 Winter Olympics.

Internet of Things

In the Internet of things (IoT), 3GPP is going to submit the evolution of NB-IoT and eMTC (LTE-M) as 5G technologies for the LPWA (Low Power Wide Area) use case.

Non-Terrestrial Network

Standards are being developed by 3GPP to provide access to end devices via non-terrestrial networks (NTN), i.e. satellite or airborne telecommunication equipment to allow for better coverage outside of populated or otherwise hard to reach locations. The enhanced communication quality relies on the unique properties of Air to Ground channel. Several manufacturers have announced and released hardware that integrates 5G with satellite networks:

- Samsung Electronics introduced a standardized 5G NTN modem technology in Korea in February 2023, simulated on their Exynos Modem 5300, facilitating smartphone-satellite communication.
- MediaTek launched the world's first commercially available 5G IoT-NTN chipset, MT6825, capable of automatic satellite message receipt and extensive power efficiency.
- Qualcomm, in collaboration with Skylo, announced new satellite IoT solutions on June 22, 2023, including the Qualcomm 212S and 9205S modems, supporting the Qualcomm Aware platform for real-time asset tracking and device management.
- Motorola's Defy Satellite Link hotspot, powered by MediaTek's MT6825, became available in June 2023, providing a portable satellite messaging solution with robust battery life and built-in GPS.
- Rakuten Symphony, in collaboration with Supermicro, announced high-performing Open RAN technologies and storage systems for operators of cloud-based mobile services.

Deployment

Beyond mobile operator networks, 5G is also expected to be used for private networks with applications in industrial IoT, enterprise networking, and critical communications, in what being described as NR-U (5G NR in Unlicensed Spectrum) and Non-Public Networks (NPNs) operating in licensed spectrum. By the mid-to-late

2020s, standalone private 5G networks are expected to become the predominant wireless communications medium to support the ongoing Industry 4.0 revolution for the digitization and automation of manufacturing and process industries. 5G was expected to increase phone sales. Initial 5G NR launches depended on pairing with existing LTE (4G) infrastructure in non-standalone (NSA) mode (5G NR radio with 4G core), before maturation of the standalone (SA) mode with the 5G core network.

As of April 2019, the Global Mobile Suppliers Association had identified 224 operators in 88 countries that have demonstrated, are testing or trialing, or have been licensed to conduct field trials of 5G technologies, are deploying 5G networks or have announced service launches. The equivalent numbers in November 2018 were 192 operators in 81 countries. The first country to adopt 5G on a large scale was South Korea, in April 2019. Swedish telecoms giant Ericsson predicted that 5G internet will cover up to 65% of the world's population by the end of 2025. Also, it plans to invest 1 billion reals ($238.30 million) in Brazil to add a new assembly line dedicated to fifth-generation technology (5G) for its Latin American operations.

When South Korea launched its 5G network, all carriers used Samsung, Ericsson, and Nokia base stations and equipment, except for LG U Plus, who also used Huawei equipment. Samsung was the largest supplier for 5G base stations in South Korea at launch, having shipped 53,000 base stations at the time, out of 86,000 base stations installed across the country at the time.

The first fairly substantial deployments were in April 2019. In South Korea, SK Telecom claimed 38,000 base stations, KT Corporation 30,000 and LG U Plus 18,000; of which 85% are in six major cities. They are using 3.5 GHz (sub-6) spectrum in non-standalone (NSA) mode and tested speeds were from 193 to 430 Mbit/s down. 260,000 signed up in the first month and 4.7 million by the end of 2019. T-Mobile US was the first company in the world to launch a commercially available 5G NR Standalone network.

Nine companies sell 5G radio hardware and 5G systems for carriers: Altiostar, Cisco Systems, Datang Telecom/Fiberhome, Ericsson, Huawei, Nokia, Qualcomm, Samsung, and ZTE. As of 2023, Huawei is the leading 5G equipment manufacturer and has the greatest market share of 5G equipment and has built approximately 70% of worldwide 5G base stations.

Spectrum

Large quantities of new radio spectrum (5G NR frequency bands) have been allocated to 5G. For example, in July 2016, the U.S. Federal Communications Commission (FCC) freed up vast amounts of bandwidth in underused high-band spectrum for 5G. The Spectrum Frontiers Proposal (SFP) doubled the amount of millimeter-wave unlicensed spectrum to 14 GHz and created four times the amount of flexible, mobile-use spectrum the FCC had licensed to date. In March 2018, European Union lawmakers agreed to open up the 3.6 and 26 GHz bands by 2020.

As of March 2019, there are reportedly 52 countries, territories, special administrative regions, disputed territories and dependencies that are formally considering introducing certain spectrum bands for terrestrial 5G services, are holding consultations regarding suitable spectrum allocations for 5G, have reserved spectrum for 5G, have announced plans to auction frequencies or have already allocated spectrum for 5G use.

5G Devices

In March 2019, the Global Mobile Suppliers Association released the industry's first database tracking worldwide 5G device launches. In it, the GSA identified 23 vendors who have confirmed the availability of forthcoming 5G devices with 33 different devices including regional variants. There were seven announced 5G device form factors: (telephones (×12 devices), hotspots (×4), indoor and outdoor customer-premises equipment (×8), modules (×5), Snap-on dongles and adapters (×2), and USB terminals (×1)). By October 2019, the number of announced 5G devices had risen to 129, across 15 form factors, from 56 vendors.

In the 5G IoT chipset arena, as of April 2019 there were four commercial 5G modem chipsets and one commercial processor/platform, with more launches expected in the near future. On March 4, 2019, the first-ever all-5G smartphone Samsung Galaxy S10 5G was released. According to *Business Insider*, the 5G feature was showcased as more expensive in comparison with the 4G Samsung Galaxy S10e. On March 19, 2020, HMD Global, the current maker of Nokia-branded phones, announced the Nokia 8.3 5G, which it claimed as having a wider range of 5G compatibility than any other phone released to that time. The mid-range model is claimed to support all 5G bands from 600 MHz to 3.8 GHz. Many phone manufacturers support 5G. Google Pixel devices support 5G, starting with the 4a 5G and Pixel 5. Apple devices also support 5G, starting with the iPhone 12 and later models.

Technology

New Radio Frequencies

The air interface defined by 3GPP for 5G is known as New Radio (NR), and the specification is subdivided into two frequency bands, FR1 (below 6 GHz) and FR2 (24–54 GHz)

Frequency Range 1 (< 6 GHz):

- Otherwise known as sub-6, the maximum channel bandwidth defined for FR1 is 100 MHz, due to the scarcity of continuous spectrum in this crowded frequency range. The band most widely being used for 5G in this range is 3.3–4.2 GHz. The Korean carriers use the n78 band at 3.5 GHz.

- Some parties used the term "mid-band" frequency to refer to higher part of this frequency range that was not used in previous generations of mobile communication.

Frequency Range 2 (24–71 GHz):

- The minimum channel bandwidth defined for FR2 is 50 MHz and the maximum is 400 MHz, with two-channel aggregation supported in 3GPP Release 15. Signals in this frequency range with wavelengths between 4 and 12 mm are called millimeter waves. The higher the carrier frequency, the greater the ability to support high data-transfer speeds. This is because a given channel bandwidth takes up a lower fraction of the carrier frequency, so high-bandwidth channels are easier to realize at higher carrier frequencies.

Massive MIMO

MIMO systems use multiple antennas at the transmitter and receiver ends of a wireless communication system. Multiple antennas use the spatial dimension for multiplexing in addition to the time and frequency ones, without changing the bandwidth requirements of the system. Massive MIMO (multiple-input and multiple-output) antennas increases sector throughput and capacity density using large numbers of antennas. This includes Single User MIMO and Multi-user MIMO (MU-MIMO). Each antenna is individually-controlled and may embed radio transceiver components.

Edge Computing

Edge computing is delivered by computing servers closer to the ultimate user. It reduces latency, data traffic congestion and can improve service availability.

Small Cell

Small cells are low-powered cellular radio access nodes that operate in licensed and unlicensed spectrum that have a range of 10 meters to a few kilometers. Small cells are critical to 5G networks, as 5G's radio waves can't travel long distances, because of 5G's higher frequencies.

Beamforming

There are two kinds of beamforming (BF): digital and analog. Digital beamforming involves sending the data across multiple streams (layers), while analog beamforming shaping the radio waves to point in a specific direction. The analog BF technique combines the power from elements of the antenna array in such a way that signals at particular angles experience constructive interference, while other signals pointing to other angles experience destructive interference. This improves signal quality in the specific direction, as well as data transfer speeds. 5G uses both digital and analog beamforming to improve the system capacity.

Convergence of Wi-Fi and Cellular

One expected benefit of the transition to 5G is the convergence of multiple networking functions to achieve cost, power, and complexity reductions. LTE has targeted convergence with Wi-Fi band/technology via various efforts, such as License Assisted Access (LAA; 5G signal in unlicensed frequency bands that are also used by Wi-Fi) and LTE-WLAN Aggregation (LWA; convergence with Wi-Fi Radio), but the differing capabilities of cellular and Wi-Fi have limited the scope of convergence. However, significant improvement in cellular performance specifications in 5G, combined with migration from Distributed Radio Access Network (D-RAN) to Cloud- or Centralized-RAN (C-RAN) and rollout of cellular small cells can potentially narrow the gap between Wi-Fi and cellular networks in dense and indoor deployments. Radio convergence could result in sharing ranging from the aggregation of cellular and Wi-Fi channels to the use of a single silicon device for multiple radio access technologies.

NOMA (Non-Orthogonal Multiple Access)

NOMA (non-orthogonal multiple access) is a proposed multiple-access technique for future cellular systems via allocation of power.

SDN/NFV

Initially, cellular mobile communications technologies were designed in the context of providing voice services and Internet access. Today a new era of innovative tools and technologies is inclined towards developing a new pool of applications. This pool of applications consists of different domains such as the Internet of Things (IoT), web of connected autonomous vehicles, remotely controlled robots, and heterogeneous sensors connected to serve versatile applications. In this context, network slicing has emerged as a key technology to efficiently embrace this new market model.

Channel Coding

The channel coding techniques for 5G NR have changed from Turbo codes in 4G to polar codes for the control channels and LDPC (low-density parity check codes) for the data channels.

Operation in Unlicensed Spectrum

In December 2018, 3GPP began working on unlicensed spectrum specifications known as 5G NR-U, targeting 3GPP Release 16. Qualcomm has made a similar proposal for LTE in unlicensed spectrum.

5G Wireless Power

5G wireless power is a technology based on 5G standards that transfers wireless power. It adheres to technical standards set by the 3rd Generation Partnership Project, the International Telecommunication Union, and the Institute of Electrical and Electronics Engineers. It utilizes extremely high frequency radio waves with wavelengths from one to ten millimeters, also known as mmWaves. Up to 6μW of power has been demonstrated being captured from 5G signals at a distance of 180m by researchers at Georgia Tech. Internet of things devices could benefit from 5G wireless power technology, given their low power requirements that are within the range of what has been achieved using 5G power capture.

Future Evolution

5G-Advanced

5G-Advanced (also known as 5.5G) is a name for 3GPP release 18, which as of 2021 is under conceptual development. 5G-Advanced is expected to appear in commercial products in mid-2024.

Concerns

Security Concerns

A report published by the European Commission and European Agency for Cybersecurity details the security issues surrounding 5G. The report warns against using a single supplier for a carrier's 5G infrastructure, especially those based outside the European Union; Nokia and Ericsson are the only European manufacturers of 5G equipment.

On October 18, 2018, a team of researchers from ETH Zurich, the University of Lorraine and the University of Dundee released a paper entitled, "A Formal Analysis of 5G Authentication". It alerted that 5G technology could open ground for a new era of security threats. The paper described the technology as "immature and insufficiently tested," and one that "enables the movement and access of vastly higher quantities of data, and thus broadens attack surfaces". Simultaneously, network security companies such as Fortinet, Arbor Networks, A10 Networks, and Voxility advised on personalized and mixed security deployments against massive DDoS attacks foreseen after 5G deployment.

IoT Analytics estimated an increase in the number of IoT devices, enabled by 5G technology, from 7 billion in 2018 to 21.5 billion by 2025. This can raise the attack surface for these devices to a substantial scale, and the capacity for DDoS attacks, cryptojacking, and other cyberattacks could boost proportionally. In addition, the EPS solution for 5G networks has identified a design vulnerability. The vulnerability affects the operation of the device during cellular network switching.

Due to fears of potential espionage of users of Chinese equipment vendors, several countries (including the United States, Australia and the United Kingdom as of early 2019) have taken actions to restrict or eliminate the use of Chinese equipment in their respective 5G networks. A 2012 U.S. House Permanent Select Committee on Intelligence report concluded that using equipment made by Huawei and ZTE, another Chinese telecommunications company, could "undermine core U.S. national security interests". In 2018, six U.S. intelligence chiefs, including the directors of the CIA and FBI, cautioned Americans against using Huawei products, warning that the company could conduct "undetected espionage". Further, a 2017 investigation by the FBI determined that Chinese-made Huawei equipment could disrupt U.S. nuclear arsenal communications. Chinese vendors and the Chinese government have denied claims of espionage, but experts have pointed out that Huawei would have no choice but to hand over network data to the Chinese government if Beijing asked for it because of Chinese National Security Law.

In August, 2020, the U.S. State Department launched "The Clean Network" as a U.S. government-led, bi-partisan effort to address what it described as "the long-term threat to data privacy, security, human rights and principled collaboration posed to the free world from authoritarian malign actors". Promoters of the initiative have stated that it has resulted in an "alliance of democracies and companies", "based on democratic values". On October 7, 2020, the UK Parliament's Defence Committee released a report claiming that there was clear evidence of collusion between Huawei and Chinese state and the Chinese Communist Party. The UK Parliament's Defence Committee said that the government should consider removal of all Huawei equipment from its 5G networks earlier than planned. In December 2020, the United States announced that more than 60 nations, representing more than two thirds of the world's gross domestic product, and 200 telecom companies, had publicly committed to the principles of The Clean Network. This alliance of democracies included 27 of the 30 NATO members; 26 of the 27 EU members, 31 of the 37 OECD nations, 11 of the 12 Three Seas nations as well as Japan, Israel, Australia, Singapore, Taiwan, Canada, Vietnam, and India.

Weather Forecasting

The spectrum used by various 5G proposals, especially the n258 band centered at 26 GHz, will be near that of passive remote sensing such as by weather and Earth observation satellites, particularly for water vapor monitoring at 23.8 GHz. Interference is expected to occur due to such proximity and its effect could be significant without effective controls. An increase in interference already occurred with some other prior proximate band usages. Interference to satellite operations impairs numerical weather prediction performance with substantially deleterious economic and public safety impacts in areas such as commercial aviation.

The concerns prompted U.S. Secretary of Commerce Wilbur Ross and NASA Administrator Jim Bridenstine in February 2019 to urge the FCC to delay some spectrum auction proposals, which was rejected. The chairs of the House Appropriations Committee and House Science Committee wrote separate letters to FCC chairman Ajit Pai asking for further review and consultation with NOAA, NASA, and DoD, and warning of harmful impacts to national security. Acting NOAA director Neil Jacobs testified before the House Committee in May 2019 that 5G out-of-band emissions could produce a 30% reduction in weather forecast accuracy and that the resulting degradation in ECMWF model performance would have resulted in failure to predict the track and thus the impact of Superstorm Sandy in 2012. The United States Navy in March 2019 wrote a memorandum warning of deterioration and made technical suggestions to control band bleed-over limits, for testing and fielding, and for coordination of the wireless industry and regulators with weather forecasting organizations.

At the 2019 quadrennial World Radiocommunication Conference (WRC), atmospheric scientists advocated for a strong buffer of -55 dBW, European regulators agreed on a recommendation of -42 dBW, and US regulators (the FCC) recommended a restriction of -20 dBW, which would permit signals 150 times stronger than the European proposal. The ITU decided on an intermediate -33 dBW until September 1, 2027, and after that a standard of -39 dBW. This is closer to the European recommendation but even the delayed higher standard is much weaker than that requested by atmospheric scientists, triggering warnings from the World Meteorological Organization (WMO) that the ITU standard, at 10 times less stringent than its recommendation, brings the "potential to significantly degrade the accuracy of data collected". A representative of the American Meteorological Society (AMS) also warned of interference, and the European Centre for Medium-Range Weather Forecasts (ECMWF), sternly warned, saying that society risks "history repeat[ing] itself" by ignoring atmospheric scientists' warnings (referencing global warming, monitoring of which could be imperiled). In December 2019, a bipartisan request was sent from the US House Science Committee to the Government Accountability Office (GAO) to investigate why there is such a discrepancy between recommendations of US civilian and military science agencies and the regulator, the FCC.

Aviation

The United States FAA has warned that radar altimeters on aircraft, which operate between 4.2 and 4.4 GHz, might be affected by 5G operations between 3.7 and 3.98 GHz. This is particularly an issue with older altimeters using RF filters which lack protection from neighboring bands. This is not as much of an issue in Europe, where 5G uses lower frequencies between 3.4 and 3.8 GHz. Nonetheless, the DGAC in France has also expressed similar worries and recommended 5G phones be turned off or be put in airplane mode during flights.

On December 31, 2021, U.S. Transportation Secretary Pete Buttigieg and Steve Dickinson, administrator of the Federal Aviation Administration asked the chief executives of AT&T and Verizon to delay 5G implementation over aviation concerns. The government officials asked for a two-week delay starting on January 5, 2022, while investigations are conducted on the effects on radar altimeters. The government transportation officials also asked the cellular providers to hold off their new 5G service near 50 priority airports, to minimize disruption to air traffic that would be caused by some planes being disallowed from landing in poor visibility. After coming to an agreement with government officials the day before, Verizon and AT&T activated their 5G networks on January 19, 2022, except for certain towers near 50 airports. AT&T scaled back its deployment even further than its agreement with the FAA required.

The FAA rushed to test and certify radar altimeters for interference so that planes could be allowed to perform instrument landings (e.g., at night and in low visibility) at affected airports. By January 16, it had certified equipment on 45% of the U.S. fleet, and 78% by January 20. Airlines complained about the avoidable impact on their operations, and commentators said the affair called into question the competence of the FAA. Several international airlines substituted different planes so they could avoid problems landing at scheduled airports, and about 2% of flights (320) were cancelled by the evening of January 19.

Satellite

A number of 5G networks deployed on the radio frequency band of 3.3–3.6 GHz are expected to cause interference with C-Band satellite stations, which operate by receiving satellite signals at 3.4–4.2 GHz frequency. This interference can be mitigated with low-noise block downconverters and waveguide filters.

Wi-Fi

In regions like the US and EU, the 6 GHz band is to be opened up for unlicensed applications, which would permit the deployment of 5G-NR Unlicensed, 5G version of LTE in unlicensed spectrum, as well as Wi-Fi 6e. However, interference could occur with the co-existence of different standards in the frequency band.

Overhype

There have been concerns surrounding the promotion of 5G, questioning whether the technology is overhyped. There are questions on whether 5G will truly change the customer experience, ability for 5G's mmWave signal to provide significant coverage, overstating what 5G can achieve or misattributing continuous technological improvement to "5G", lack of new use case for carriers to profit from, wrong focus on emphasizing direct benefits on individual consumers instead of for internet of things devices or solving the last mile problem, and overshadowing the possibility that in some aspects there might be other more appropriate technologies. Such sort of concerns have also led to consumers not trusting information provided by cellular providers on the topic.

Misinformation

Health

There is a long history of fear and anxiety surrounding wireless signals that predates 5G technology. The fears about 5G are similar to those that have persisted throughout the 1990s and 2000s. They center on fringe claims that non-ionizing radiation poses dangers to human health. Unlike ionizing radiation, non-ionizing radiation cannot remove electrons from atoms. According to the US Centers for Disease Control and Prevention (CDC) "exposure to intense, direct amounts of non-ionizing radiation may result in damage to tissue due to heat. This is not common and mainly of concern in the workplace for those who work on large sources of non-ionizing radiation devices and instruments." Some advocates of fringe health claim the regulatory standards are too low and influenced by lobbying groups.

There have been rumors that 5G mobile phone use can cause cancer, but this is a myth. Many popular books of dubious merit have been published on the subject including one by Joseph Mercola alleging that wireless technologies caused numerous conditions from ADHD to heart diseases and brain cancer. Mercola has drawn sharp criticism for his anti-vaccinationism during the COVID-19 pandemic and was warned by the Food and Drug Administration to stop selling fake COVID-19 cures through his online alternative medicine business.

According to the *New York Times*, one origin of the 5G health controversy was an erroneous unpublished study that physicist Bill P. Curry did for the Broward County School Board in 2000 which indicated that the absorption of external microwaves by brain tissue increased with frequency. According to experts this was wrong, the millimeter waves used in 5G are safer than lower frequency microwaves because they cannot penetrate the skin and reach internal organs. Curry had confused *in vitro* and *in vivo* research. However Curry's study was widely distributed on the internet. Writing in *The New York Times* in 2019, William Broad reported that RT America began airing programming linking 5G to harmful health effects which "lack scientific support", such as "brain cancer, infertility, autism, heart tumors, and Alzheimer's disease". Broad asserted that the claims had increased. RT America had run seven programs on this theme by mid-April 2019 but only one in the whole of 2018. The network's coverage had spread to hundreds of blogs and websites.

In April 2019, the city of Brussels in Belgium blocked a 5G trial because of radiation rules. In Geneva, Switzerland, a planned upgrade to 5G was stopped for the same reason. The Swiss Telecommunications Association (ASUT) has said that studies have been unable to show that 5G frequencies have any health impact.

According to CNET, "Members of Parliament in the Netherlands are also calling on the government to take a closer look at 5G. Several leaders in the United States Congress have written to the Federal Communications Commission expressing concern about potential health risks. In Mill Valley, California, the city council blocked the deployment of new 5G wireless cells." Similar concerns were raised in Vermont and New Hampshire.

The US FDA is quoted saying that it "continues to believe that the current safety limits for cellphone radiofrequency energy exposure remain acceptable for protecting the public health." After campaigning by activist groups, a series of small localities in the UK, including Totnes, Brighton and Hove, Glastonbury, and Frome, passed resolutions against the implementation of further 5G infrastructure, though these resolutions have no impact on rollout plans.

Low-level EMF does have some effects on other organisms. Vian *et al.*, 2006 finds an effect of microwave on gene expression in plants. A meta-analysis of 95 *in vitro* and *in vivo* studies showed that an average of 80% of the *in vivo* research showed effects of such radiation, as did 58% of the *in vitro* research, but that the results were inconclusive as to whether any of these effects pose a health risk.

COVID-19 Conspiracy Theories and Arson Attacks

As the introduction of 5G technology coincided with the time of the COVID-19 pandemic, several conspiracy theories circulating online posited a link between COVID-19 and 5G.

This has led to dozens of arson attacks being made on telecom masts in the Netherlands (Amsterdam, Rotterdam, etc.), Ireland (Cork, etc.), Cyprus, the United Kingdom (Dagenham, Huddersfield, Birmingham, Belfast and Liverpool), Belgium (Pelt), Italy (Maddaloni), Croatia (Bibinje) and Sweden. It led to at least 61 suspected arson attacks against telephone masts in the United Kingdom alone and over twenty in The Netherlands.

In the early months of the pandemic, anti-lockdown protesters at protests over responses to the COVID-19 pandemic in Australia were seen with anti-5G signs, an early sign of what became a wider campaign by conspiracy theorists to link the pandemic with 5G technology. There are two versions of the 5G-COVID-19 conspiracy theory:

- The first version claims that radiation weakens the immune system, making the body more vulnerable to SARS-CoV-2 (the virus that causes COVID-19).
- The second version claims that 5G causes COVID-19. There are different variations on this. Some claim that the pandemic is coverup of illness caused by 5G radiation or that COVID-19 originated in Wuhan because that city was "the guinea-pig city for 5G".

Marketing of Non-5G Services

In various parts of the world, carriers have launched numerous differently branded technologies, such as "5G Evolution", which advertise improving existing networks with the use of "5G technology". However, these pre-5G networks are an improvement on specifications of existing LTE networks that are not exclusive to 5G. While the technology promises to deliver higher speeds, and is described by AT&T as a "foundation for our evolution to 5G while the 5G standards are being finalized", it cannot be considered to be true 5G. When AT&T announced 5G Evolution, 4x4 MIMO, the technology that AT&T is using to deliver the higher speeds, had already been put in place by T-Mobile without being branded with the 5G moniker. It is claimed that such branding is a marketing move that will cause confusion with consumers, as it is not made clear that such improvements are not true 5G.

Other Applications

- **Automobiles:** 5G Automotive Association have been promoting the C-V2X communication technology that will first be deployed in 4G. It provides for communication between vehicles and infrastructures.
- **Digital Twins:** A real time digital twin of the real object such as a turbine engine, aircraft, wind turbines, offshore platform and pipelines. 5G networks helps in building it due to the latency and throughput to capture near real-time IoT data and support digital twins.
- **Public Safety:** Mission-critical push-to-talk (MCPTT) and mission-critical video and data are expected to be furthered in 5G.
- **Fixed Wireless:** Fixed wireless connections will offer an alternative to fixed line broadband (ADSL, VDSL, Fiber optic, and DOCSIS connections) in some locations.
- **Wireless Video Transmission for Broadcast Applications:** Sony has tested the possibility of using local 5G networks to replace the SDI cables currently used in broadcast camcorders. The 5G Broadcast tests started around 2020 (Orkney, Bavaria, Austria, Central Bohemia) based

on FeMBMS (Further evolved multimedia broadcast multicast service). The aim is to serve unlimited number of mobile or fixed devices with video (TV) and audio (radio) streams without these consuming any data flow or even being authenticated in a network.

5.3.2 Role of Edge Computing in Enhancing 5G Capabilities

Edge computing complements 5G networks by decentralizing data processing and application management to the network edge, where data is generated and consumed. Edge computing infrastructure, comprising edge servers, gateways, and IoT devices, facilitates real-time analytics, content delivery, and application processing in close proximity to end-users. By integrating with 5G networks, edge computing enhances service agility, reduces latency, optimizes bandwidth usage, and supports innovative use cases requiring low-latency responses and localized data processing.

5.3.3 Benefits of 5G and Edge Computing Synergies

Ultra-Low Latency Applications

The combination of 5G and edge computing enables real-time applications, such as augmented reality (AR), virtual reality (VR), and autonomous systems, to operate seamlessly with minimal latency. Edge computing processes data locally, reducing round-trip times between devices and cloud servers, while 5G networks provide high-speed, low-latency connectivity for instantaneous data transmission.

High Bandwidth and Scalability

5G networks offer significantly higher bandwidth compared to previous generations, supporting bandwidth-intensive applications and massive data transfers. Edge computing optimizes bandwidth usage by processing data locally and prioritizing critical traffic, ensuring efficient resource allocation and scalability across distributed edge environments.

Enhanced Quality of Service (QoS)

Leveraging network slicing capabilities in 5G, service providers can create virtual network slices with customized QoS parameters, such as latency, reliability, and throughput, to meet specific application requirements. Edge computing enhances QoS by delivering consistent performance and responsiveness for latency-sensitive applications, such as real-time video streaming and autonomous operations.

Cost Efficiency and Network Optimization

Edge computing reduces data transmission costs and alleviates network congestion by offloading computational tasks and data processing to edge devices and local servers. 5G networks optimize network resources and spectrum allocation, supporting dynamic traffic management and efficient data routing across distributed edge environments.

5.3.4 Applications of 5G and Edge Computing Synergies

Autonomous Vehicles

5G networks provide ultra-low latency connectivity for real-time communication between autonomous vehicles, roadside infrastructure, and centralized control systems. Edge computing processes sensor data locally to enable autonomous decision-making, ensuring safe navigation, collision avoidance, and traffic management in dynamic environments.

Industrial Automation

In manufacturing and industrial sectors, 5G and edge computing support real-time monitoring of IoT-enabled devices, predictive maintenance, and process optimization.

Edge analytics analyze sensor data locally to detect anomalies, optimize equipment performance, and minimize downtime, while 5G networks facilitate reliable connectivity for mission-critical applications, such as robotic assembly lines and remote equipment monitoring.

Telemedicine and Healthcare

5G-enabled telemedicine solutions leverage edge computing for real-time analysis of medical data, enabling remote consultations, diagnostic imaging, and patient monitoring with minimal latency. Edge devices process sensitive health information locally, ensuring privacy compliance and delivering timely medical interventions and personalized treatment plans.

Smart Cities

5G networks and edge computing enhance smart city initiatives by supporting intelligent transportation systems, environmental monitoring, and public safety applications. Edge analytics process sensor data from IoT devices deployed across urban infrastructure, enabling adaptive traffic management, pollution control, and emergency response services in real time.

5.3.5 Challenges and Considerations

Despite their transformative potential, the integration of 5G and edge computing presents several challenges that require careful consideration and mitigation strategies.

Infrastructure Deployment

Deploying and maintaining edge computing infrastructure, including edge servers, gateways, and IoT devices, requires substantial investment in physical infrastructure, power management, and network connectivity.

Interoperability and Standards

Ensuring interoperability between diverse 5G networks, edge computing platforms, and legacy systems to facilitate seamless integration and data exchange across distributed edge environments.

Security and Privacy

Implementing robust security measures, such as encryption, authentication, and access controls, to protect sensitive data and prevent unauthorized access or cyber threats in edge computing deployments.

Regulatory Compliance

Addressing regulatory requirements and compliance standards, including data privacy laws and spectrum licensing regulations, to ensure lawful and ethical use of 5G and edge computing technologies in various applications and industries.

5.3.6 Future Directions

Looking ahead, ongoing advancements and emerging trends are expected to further accelerate the adoption and innovation of 5G and edge computing synergies.

Edge AI and Machine Learning

Integration of artificial intelligence (AI) and machine learning (ML) algorithms at the network edge to enable autonomous decision-making, predictive analytics, and adaptive learning for real-time applications.

5G Standalone (SA) Networks

Evolution towards standalone 5G networks, independent of legacy infrastructure, to support native edge computing capabilities and enable end-to-end network slicing for enhanced service customization and performance optimization.

Edge-to-Cloud Orchestration

Development of hybrid architectures that seamlessly orchestrate data processing tasks between edge devices, network slices, and centralized cloud servers to balance workload distribution, scalability, and cost-efficiency.

Edge-as-a-Service (EaaS)

Evolution of managed service offerings that simplify deployment, management, and scaling of 5G and edge computing solutions, enabling organizations to leverage on-demand services for innovative applications and business outcomes.

5.4 ENHANCING QUALITY OF SERVICE WITH EDGE COMPUTING

Quality of Service (QoS) refers to the performance characteristics of a network or service as perceived by users, encompassing parameters such as latency, reliability, throughput, and availability. Edge computing enhances QoS by decentralizing computational tasks and data processing closer to where data is generated and consumed, thereby optimizing service delivery, reducing latency, and improving user experiences across various applications and industries.

Edge computing enhances Quality of Service (QoS) by decentralizing data processing, optimizing resource allocation, and enabling real-time application delivery closer to end-users. By reducing latency, improving reliability, and enhancing scalability, edge computing empowers organizations to deliver responsive services, personalized experiences, and efficient operations across diverse industries. Addressing challenges related to infrastructure deployment, security, resource management, and regulatory compliance is essential to realizing the full potential of QoS enhancement with edge computing and driving forward the future of connected ecosystems. As technology continues to evolve, collaborative efforts among industry stakeholders, standardization bodies, and regulatory authorities will be crucial in fostering a secure, resilient, and scalable edge computing landscape that supports innovation and sustainable growth in the digital era.

5.4.1 Mechanisms of QoS Enhancement with Edge Computing

Reduced Latency

Edge computing reduces latency by minimizing the distance data travels between end-users and centralized cloud servers. By processing data locally at the network edge, edge devices and servers deliver faster response times for real-time applications, such as augmented reality (AR), virtual reality (VR), and autonomous systems requiring instantaneous data processing and decision-making.

Improved Reliability

Edge computing enhances reliability by ensuring continuous service availability and fault tolerance in distributed edge environments. Redundant edge nodes and failover mechanisms mitigate single points of failure, ensuring uninterrupted service delivery and resilience against network disruptions or hardware failures.

Bandwidth Optimization

Edge computing optimizes bandwidth usage by offloading computational tasks and data processing to edge devices and local servers. This minimizes data transmission over the network backbone, reduces congestion, and improves overall network efficiency for bandwidth-intensive applications, such as video streaming, large file transfers, and IoT data aggregation.

Customized Service Levels

Leveraging edge computing's proximity to end-users, service providers can create customized network slices with tailored QoS parameters, such as latency, throughput, and reliability, to meet specific application requirements. Dedicated network slices ensure consistent performance and optimized resource allocation for diverse use cases, ranging from industrial automation to mobile gaming and telemedicine.

5.4.2 Benefits of QoS Enhancement with Edge Computing

Real-Time Applications

Edge computing supports real-time applications, such as autonomous vehicles, remote surgery, and industrial automation, by reducing data processing delays and enabling instantaneous response times. Low-latency edge environments ensure seamless interaction and reliable operation of latency-sensitive systems, enhancing operational efficiency and user satisfaction.

Scalability and Flexibility

Edge computing enhances scalability by distributing computational tasks and data processing across distributed edge nodes and servers. Scalable edge architectures accommodate fluctuating workloads, dynamic user demands, and growing IoT deployments, ensuring responsive service delivery and resource optimization without compromising performance or reliability.

Cost Efficiency

Edge computing reduces operational costs by minimizing data transit times, optimizing bandwidth usage, and lowering dependency on centralized cloud resources. Localized data processing at the edge minimizes cloud service fees, data transmission costs, and network latency, contributing to overall cost savings and improved return on investment (ROI) for organizations deploying edge computing solutions.

Enhanced User Experience

Edge computing improves user experiences by delivering responsive applications, personalized content, and seamless connectivity across devices. Edge-driven optimizations, such as content caching, dynamic content delivery, and context-aware services, enhance interaction quality, reduce waiting times, and increase user engagement in digital environments.

5.4.3 Challenges and Considerations

Infrastructure Deployment

Deploying and managing edge computing infrastructure, including edge servers, gateways, and IoT devices, requires substantial investment in physical infrastructure, power management, and network connectivity. Addressing scalability and interoperability challenges ensures seamless integration and efficient resource utilization across distributed edge environments.

Security and Privacy

Implementing robust security measures, such as encryption, authentication, and access controls, is critical to protect sensitive data and prevent unauthorized access or cyber threats in edge computing deployments.

Ensuring compliance with data privacy regulations and industry standards safeguards user privacy and organizational data integrity in edge-driven applications.

Resource Management

Efficiently managing edge resources, including computing capacity, storage, and network bandwidth, requires dynamic resource allocation strategies and workload orchestration frameworks. Optimizing resource usage and mitigating performance bottlenecks ensure consistent QoS and operational resilience in dynamic edge environments.

Regulatory Compliance

Addressing regulatory requirements, such as data sovereignty, data localization, and industry-specific regulations, ensures lawful and ethical use of edge computing technologies in various applications and sectors. Compliance with regulatory standards supports trust, transparency, and accountability in data-driven decision-making and service delivery.

5.4.4 Applications of QoS Enhancement with Edge Computing

Telecommunications

Edge computing enhances QoS in telecommunications by supporting dynamic traffic management, content delivery, and network optimization. Edge-driven optimizations ensure reliable connectivity, low-latency communications, and high-quality multimedia streaming services for mobile users and IoT devices.

Healthcare

In healthcare applications, edge computing improves QoS by enabling real-time monitoring, diagnostic imaging, and telemedicine services with minimal latency. Edge-driven analytics facilitate remote patient monitoring, medical data analysis, and personalized treatment recommendations, enhancing healthcare delivery and patient outcomes.

Smart Cities

Edge computing enhances QoS in smart city initiatives by supporting intelligent transportation systems, environmental monitoring, and public safety applications. Edge-driven analytics optimize traffic flow, monitor air quality, and enable rapid emergency response services, ensuring efficient urban management and sustainable development.

Retail and E-commerce

Edge computing improves QoS in retail and e-commerce by enabling personalized customer experiences, real-time inventory management, and responsive online storefronts. Edge-driven insights enhance product recommendations, streamline order fulfillment, and optimize supply chain operations, enhancing customer satisfaction and loyalty.

5.4.5 Future Directions

Looking ahead, ongoing advancements and emerging trends are expected to further enhance QoS with edge computing.

AI-driven Edge Analytics

Integration of artificial intelligence (AI) and machine learning (ML) algorithms at the network edge to automate decision-making, predictive analytics, and adaptive QoS management for real-time applications.

5G and Edge Computing Integration

Evolution towards standalone 5G networks and native edge computing capabilities to support end-to-end QoS optimizations, network slicing, and service-level agreements (SLAs) tailored to specific application requirements.

Edge-to-Cloud Orchestration

Development of hybrid architectures that seamlessly orchestrate data processing tasks between edge devices, cloud servers, and centralized data centers to balance workload distribution, scalability, and cost-efficiency.

Edge-as-a-Service (EaaS)

Evolution of managed service offerings that simplify deployment, management, and scaling of edge computing solutions, enabling organizations to leverage on-demand services for innovative applications and business outcomes.

CHAPTER 6
EDGE SECURITY AND PRIVACY

6.1 SECURITY CHALLENGES IN EDGE COMPUTING

Edge computing introduces a distributed computing paradigm where data processing and storage occur closer to the data source, enabling real-time analytics, reduced latency, and improved service delivery. However, this decentralized architecture also introduces unique security challenges that organizations must address to safeguard sensitive data, protect against cyber threats, and ensure regulatory compliance.

Security challenges in edge computing necessitate proactive measures to protect sensitive data, mitigate cyber risks, and ensure operational resilience across distributed edge environments. By addressing vulnerabilities related to distributed architecture, data privacy, resource-constrained devices, network segmentation, physical security, data transmission, and edge management, organizations can strengthen their security posture and leverage the transformative potential of edge computing technologies securely. Embracing best practices, continuous monitoring, and collaborative efforts among stakeholders are essential to navigating the evolving threat landscape and safeguarding the integrity, availability, and confidentiality of data in edge-driven applications and ecosystems. As edge computing continues to evolve, prioritizing security as a foundational element ensures trust, resilience, and sustainable growth in the digital era.

6.1.1 Distributed Architecture and Attack Surface

Edge computing decentralizes data processing and storage across distributed edge nodes, including IoT devices, edge servers, and gateways, increasing the attack surface compared to centralized cloud environments. Each edge device and node represents a potential entry point for cyber attackers to exploit vulnerabilities and gain unauthorized access to sensitive data or disrupt critical operations. Securing a diverse and geographically dispersed edge infrastructure requires robust perimeter defenses, continuous monitoring, and proactive threat detection mechanisms to mitigate evolving cyber threats.

6.1.2 Data Privacy and Compliance

Edge computing involves processing sensitive data locally at the network edge, raising concerns about data privacy, regulatory compliance, and adherence to data protection laws such as GDPR, CCPA, and HIPAA. Ensuring data encryption, anonymization, and access controls at the edge helps mitigate privacy risks and safeguards personally identifiable information (PII) from unauthorized access or data breaches. Implementing privacy-enhancing technologies and conducting regular compliance audits are essential to maintaining regulatory compliance and earning user trust in edge-driven applications.

6.1.3 Resource-Constrained Devices and Security

Edge devices, including IoT sensors and consumer-grade devices, often operate with limited computational resources and firmware updates, making them susceptible to malware infections, denial-of-service (DoS) attacks, and exploitation by botnets. Securing resource-constrained devices requires lightweight security protocols, firmware integrity checks, and over-the-air (OTA) updates to patch vulnerabilities promptly and defend against emerging cyber threats. Implementing device authentication, secure boot mechanisms, and application sandboxing enhances resilience against unauthorized access and ensures the integrity of edge device ecosystems.

6.1.4 Network Segmentation and Isolation

Edge computing environments integrate diverse networked devices and systems, including operational technology (OT) and IT networks, which may lack adequate segmentation and isolation controls. Interconnected edge devices and applications share network resources, increasing the risk of lateral movement by attackers and cross-contamination of malware infections. Implementing network segmentation, micro-segmentation, and zero-trust architectures isolates critical assets and limits the impact of potential security incidents, ensuring data confidentiality, integrity, and availability in distributed edge environments.

6.1.5 Physical Security and Resilience

Edge computing deployments encompass a wide range of physical locations, including remote sites, mobile environments, and industrial settings, where physical security measures are crucial to protect edge infrastructure from theft, tampering, and unauthorized access. Securing edge facilities with access controls, surveillance cameras, and environmental monitoring systems mitigates physical threats and ensures the resilience of edge computing operations against natural disasters, physical intrusions, and physical damage to infrastructure.

6.1.6 Edge-to-Cloud Connectivity and Data Transmission

Edge computing relies on seamless connectivity between edge devices, edge servers, and centralized cloud services, exposing data to interception, eavesdropping, and man-in-the-middle (MitM) attacks during data transmission. Implementing secure communication protocols, such as Transport Layer Security (TLS) and Virtual Private Networks (VPNs), encrypts data in transit and authenticates endpoints to prevent unauthorized interception and tampering. Utilizing edge-to-cloud encryption, data masking techniques, and secure gateways ensures end-to-end data protection and maintains the confidentiality of sensitive information across hybrid edge-cloud architectures.

6.1.7 Management of Edge Security Policies and Updates

Managing security policies and updates across distributed edge environments presents operational challenges, including inconsistent security configurations, outdated firmware, and patch management inefficiencies. Establishing centralized management consoles, automation tools, and remote monitoring solutions facilitates the enforcement of uniform security policies, timely deployment of security patches, and proactive threat remediation across edge devices and nodes.

Continuous security posture assessments, vulnerability scanning, and incident response planning strengthen resilience against cyber threats and ensure the integrity of edge computing infrastructures.

6.1.8 Mitigating Edge Computing Security Risks: Best Practices and Strategies

Risk Assessment and Threat Modeling

Conducting comprehensive risk assessments and threat modeling exercises identifies potential vulnerabilities, prioritizes security controls, and aligns security measures with business objectives and regulatory requirements.

Security by Design

Integrating security considerations into the design phase of edge computing architectures ensures robust security controls, resilience against cyber threats, and adherence to industry best practices throughout the lifecycle of edge deployments.

Multi-Layered Defense Mechanisms

Implementing multi-layered security defenses, including network segmentation, endpoint protection, intrusion detection systems (IDS), and security information and event management (SIEM) solutions, enhances detection, prevention, and response capabilities against evolving cyber threats.

User Awareness and Training

Educating end-users, developers, and operational staff about cybersecurity best practices, data privacy policies, and incident response procedures promotes a culture of security awareness and proactive risk mitigation in edge computing environments.

Collaboration and Information Sharing

Engaging in industry collaborations, threat intelligence sharing, and cybersecurity partnerships fosters collective defense measures, enhances situational awareness, and strengthens resilience against global cyber threats affecting edge computing ecosystems.

6.2 DATA ENCRYPTION AND PRIVACY MEASURES

Data encryption and privacy measures play a critical role in safeguarding sensitive information, protecting user confidentiality, and ensuring regulatory compliance across various industries and applications. In the era of digital transformation and data-driven decision-making, organizations must adopt robust encryption techniques and privacy-enhancing technologies to mitigate data breaches, unauthorized access, and privacy violations.

Data encryption and privacy measures are essential components of cybersecurity strategies aimed at protecting sensitive information, mitigating cyber risks, and ensuring regulatory compliance in modern computing environments. By leveraging encryption algorithms, privacy-enhancing technologies, and best practices for key management, data classification, and security awareness, organizations can strengthen data protection, preserve user privacy, and foster trust among stakeholders.

Addressing challenges related to performance overhead, key management complexity, and interoperability facilitates seamless integration of encryption solutions and enhances the resilience of encrypted data against evolving cyber threats. As organizations continue to embrace digital transformation and data-driven innovation, prioritizing data encryption and privacy as core cybersecurity principles supports sustainable growth, resilience, and ethical data stewardship in the digital age.

6.2.1 Fundamentals of Data Encryption

Data encryption involves the transformation of plaintext data into ciphertext using cryptographic algorithms and keys, rendering it unreadable to unauthorized users or malicious attackers. Encryption ensures data confidentiality by securing sensitive information during storage, transmission, and processing across diverse computing platforms and communication channels. Key components of data encryption include:

- **Encryption Algorithms:** Symmetric (e.g., AES, DES) and asymmetric (e.g., RSA, ECC) encryption algorithms facilitate secure data transformation based on key management, cryptographic strength, and computational efficiency.

- **Encryption Keys:** Secret keys (symmetric encryption) and public-private key pairs (asymmetric encryption) manage data encryption and decryption processes, ensuring secure data access and confidentiality.
- **Data Integrity:** Hash functions and digital signatures verify data integrity and authenticity, preventing unauthorized modifications or tampering during data transmission and storage.

6.2.2 Types of Data Encryption

Data encryption encompasses various techniques and methods tailored to specific security requirements, operational environments, and regulatory compliance standards:

- **End-to-End Encryption (E2EE):** Protects data throughout its entire lifecycle, from origin to destination, ensuring confidentiality and preventing unauthorized access during transmission across networks or communication channels.
- **File and Disk Encryption:** Encrypts individual files, folders, or entire disk volumes to secure stored data on local devices, cloud storage platforms, or removable media from unauthorized access or physical theft.
- **Database Encryption:** Secures sensitive data stored in relational databases, NoSQL databases, or data warehouses using encryption at rest and in transit methods, safeguarding data integrity and confidentiality against insider threats and external attacks.

6.2.3 Benefits of Data Encryption

Implementing data encryption and privacy measures offers several strategic benefits for organizations, stakeholders, and end-users:

- **Confidentiality Protection:** Encryption safeguards sensitive data, intellectual property, and proprietary information from unauthorized access, ensuring confidentiality and minimizing the risk of data breaches or corporate espionage.
- **Compliance Assurance:** Facilitates regulatory compliance with data protection laws, industry standards (e.g., GDPR, HIPAA, PCI DSS), and contractual obligations by implementing encryption controls, data access controls, and audit trails to protect user privacy and mitigate legal liabilities.

- **Risk Mitigation:** Reduces cybersecurity risks, financial losses, and reputational damage associated with data breaches, ransomware attacks, and data leakage incidents by implementing encryption as a fundamental cybersecurity defense mechanism.
- **Trust and Reputation:** Enhances customer trust, brand reputation, and stakeholder confidence by demonstrating commitment to data security, privacy protection, and ethical data handling practices in business operations and customer interactions.

6.2.4 Challenges in Data Encryption

Despite its benefits, data encryption presents operational challenges and complexities that organizations must address to maximize effectiveness and mitigate potential risks:

- **Performance Overhead:** Encryption and decryption processes may introduce computational overhead and latency, impacting system performance, application responsiveness, and user experience in real-time data processing and transactional environments.
- **Key Management:** Secure key management practices, including key generation, storage, rotation, and distribution, are essential to maintaining data accessibility, encryption strength, and regulatory compliance across diverse IT infrastructures and encryption technologies.
- **Interoperability:** Ensuring interoperability and compatibility between encryption solutions, cryptographic protocols, and legacy systems to facilitate seamless data integration, data sharing, and secure collaboration across heterogeneous computing environments.

6.2.5 Privacy-Enhancing Technologies

In addition to data encryption, organizations leverage privacy-enhancing technologies to reinforce data protection, anonymize sensitive information, and uphold user privacy rights:

- **Anonymization and Pseudonymization:** Reduces the identifiability of personal data by replacing identifiable attributes with pseudonyms or anonymized identifiers, preserving data utility for analysis while protecting individual privacy.
- **Data Masking:** Masks or obfuscates sensitive data elements within datasets or databases to prevent unauthorized access, comply with data protection regulations, and mitigate privacy risks associated with data sharing and secondary usage.

- **Tokenization**: Replaces sensitive data elements (e.g., credit card numbers, social security numbers) with unique tokens or surrogate values, ensuring data security, PCI DSS compliance, and fraud prevention in payment processing and transactional systems.

6.2.6 Best Practices for Data Encryption and Privacy

Implementing effective data encryption and privacy measures requires adherence to industry best practices, standards, and guidelines to mitigate risks and strengthen security posture:

- **Data Classification**: Classify sensitive data based on confidentiality, integrity, and availability requirements to prioritize encryption controls, access permissions, and data protection strategies across organizational data assets.
- **Encryption Policies**: Develop and enforce encryption policies, procedures, and controls aligned with regulatory requirements, industry standards, and risk management frameworks to ensure consistent data protection and compliance.
- **Security Awareness and Training**: Educate employees, stakeholders, and third-party vendors about data privacy principles, encryption protocols, and cybersecurity hygiene practices to foster a culture of security awareness and proactive risk mitigation.
- **Continuous Monitoring and Auditing**: Implement real-time monitoring, intrusion detection systems (IDS), and security incident response capabilities to detect anomalous activities, unauthorized access attempts, and potential data breaches in encrypted data environments.

6.3 IDENTITY AND ACCESS MANAGEMENT AT THE EDGE

Identity and Access Management (IAM) at the edge encompasses strategies, technologies, and best practices for managing user identities, controlling access privileges, and securing resources in decentralized computing environments. As organizations embrace edge computing to enhance operational efficiency, reduce latency, and support real-time applications, effective IAM solutions play a crucial role in ensuring data security, regulatory compliance, and seamless user experiences.

IAM at the edge plays a pivotal role in securing user identities, controlling access to edge resources, and mitigating cybersecurity risks in decentralized computing environments. By implementing robust IAM strategies, leveraging advanced technologies, and adhering to best practices for identity federation, access controls, and secure device management, organizations can strengthen their security posture, achieve regulatory compliance, and optimize operational efficiency across distributed edge infrastructures. Addressing challenges related to distributed architecture, resource constraints, and regulatory compliance ensures scalable and resilient IAM solutions that support innovation, digital transformation, and secure collaboration in the era of edge computing. As organizations continue to embrace edge-driven initiatives and deploy mission-critical applications, prioritizing IAM as a foundational element fosters trust, resilience, and sustainable growth in the evolving landscape of connected ecosystems.

6.3.1 Fundamentals of IAM at the Edge

Identity management (IdM), also known as identity and access management (IAM or IdAM), is a framework of policies and technologies to ensure that the right users (that are part of the ecosystem connected to or within an enterprise) have the appropriate access to technology resources. IdM systems fall under the overarching umbrellas of IT security and data management. Identity and access management systems not only identify, authenticate, and control access for individuals who will be utilizing IT resources but also the hardware and applications employees need to access. IdM addresses the need to ensure appropriate access to resources across increasingly heterogeneous technology environments and to meet increasingly rigorous compliance requirements. The terms "identity management" (IdM) and "identity and access management" are used interchangeably in the area of identity access management.

Identity-management systems, products, applications and platforms manage identifying and ancillary data about entities that include individuals, computer-related hardware, and software applications. IdM covers issues such as how users gain an identity, the roles, and sometimes the permissions that identity grants, the protection of that identity, and the technologies supporting that protection (e.g., network protocols, digital certificates, passwords, etc.).

Definitions

Identity management (ID management) – or identity and access management (IAM) – is the organizational and technical processes for first registering and authorizing access rights in the configuration phase, and then in the operation phase for identifying, authenticating and controlling individuals or groups of people to have access to applications, systems or networks based on previously authorized access rights. Identity management (IdM) is the task of controlling information about users on computers. Such information includes information that authenticates the identity of a user, and information that describes data and actions they are authorized to access and/or perform. It also includes the management of descriptive information about the user and how and by whom that information can be accessed and modified. In addition to users, managed entities typically include hardware and network resources and even applications.

Function

In the real-world context of engineering online systems, identity management can involve five basic functions:

- **The Pure Identity Function:** Creation, management and deletion of identities without regard to access or entitlements;
- **The User Access (Log-on) Function:** For example: a smart card and its associated data used by a customer to log on to a service or services (a traditional view);
- **The Service Function:** A system that delivers personalized, role-based, online, on-demand, multimedia (content), presence-based services to users and their devices.
- **Identity Federation:** A system that relies on federated identity to authenticate a user without knowing their password.
- **Audit Function:** Monitor bottlenecks, malfunctions and suspect behavior.

Pure Identity

A general model of identity can be constructed from a small set of axioms, for example that all identities in a given namespace are unique, or that such identities bear a specific relationship to corresponding entities in the real world. Such an axiomatic model expresses "pure identity" in the sense that the model is not constrained by a specific application context. In general, an entity (real or virtual) can have multiple identities and each identity can encompass multiple attributes, some of which are unique within a given name space.

In most theoretical and all practical models of digital identity, a given identity object consists of a finite set of properties (attribute values). These properties record information about the object, either for purposes external to the model or to operate the model, for example in classification and retrieval. A "pure identity" model is strictly not concerned with the external semantics of these properties.

The most common departure from "pure identity" in practice occurs with properties intended to assure some aspect of identity, for example a digital signature or software token which the model may use internally to verify some aspect of the identity in satisfaction of an external purpose. To the extent that the model expresses such semantics internally, it is not a pure model.

Contrast this situation with properties that might be externally used for purposes of information security such as managing access or entitlement, but which are simply stored, maintained and retrieved, without special treatment by the model. The absence of external semantics within the model qualifies it as a "pure identity" model.

Identity management can thus be defined as a set of operations on a given identity model, or more generally, as a set of capabilities with reference to it. In practice, identity management often expands to express how model content is to be provisioned and reconciled among multiple identity models. The process of reconciling accounts may also be referred to as De-provisioning.

User Access

User access enables users to assume a specific digital identity across applications, which enables access controls to be assigned and evaluated against this identity. The use of a single identity for a given user across multiple systems eases tasks for administrators and users. It simplifies access monitoring and verification and allows the organizations to minimize excessive privileges granted to one user. Ensuring user access security is crucial in this process, as it involves protecting the integrity and confidentiality of user credentials and preventing unauthorized access. Implementing robust authentication mechanisms, such as multi-factor authentication (MFA), regular security audits, and strict access controls, helps safeguard user identities and sensitive data. User access can be tracked from initiation to termination of user access.

When organizations deploy an identity management process or system, their motivation is normally not primarily to manage a set of identities, but rather to grant appropriate access rights to those entities via their identities. In other words, access management is normally the motivation for identity management and the two sets of processes are consequently closely related.

Services

Organizations continue to add services for both internal users and by customers. Many such services require identity management to properly provide these services. Increasingly, identity management has been partitioned from application functions so that a single identity can serve many or even all of an organization's activities. For internal use identity management is evolving to control access to all digital assets, including devices, network equipment, servers, portals, content, applications and/or products. Services often require access to extensive information about a user, including address books, preferences, entitlements and contact information. Since much of this information is subject to privacy and/or confidentiality requirements, controlling access to it is vital.

Identity Federation

Identity federation comprises one or more systems that share user access and allow users to log in based on authenticating against one of the systems participating in the federation. This trust between several systems is often known as "Circle of Trust". In this setup, one system acts as the Identity Provider (IdP) and other system(s) acts as Service Provider (SP). When a user needs to access some service controlled by SP, they first authenticate against the IdP. Upon successful authentication, the IdP sends a secure "assertion" to the Service Provider. "SAML assertions, specified using a markup language intended for describing security assertions, can be used by a verifier to make a statement to a relying party about the identity of a claimant. SAML assertions may optionally be digitally signed."

- **Popular SAML Languages:** The most popular reference implementations of the SAML specifications are Shibboleth and Simple-SAML.php. Both of these languages also provide Single Sign on (SSO) capabilities.

System Capabilities

In addition to creation, deletion, modification of user identity data either assisted or self-service, identity management controls ancillary entity data for use by applications, such as contact information or location.

Authentication: Verification that an entity is who/what it claims to be using a password, biometrics such as a fingerprint, or distinctive behavior such as a gesture pattern on a touchscreen.

- **Authorization:** Managing authorization information that defines what operations an entity can perform in the context of a specific application. For example, one user might be authorized to enter a sales order, while a different user is authorized to approve the credit request for that order.
- **Roles:** Roles are groups of operations and/or other roles. Users are granted roles often related to a particular job or job function. Roles are granted authorizations, effectively authorizing all users which have been granted the role. For example, a user administrator role might be authorized to reset a user's password, while a system administrator role might have the ability to assign a user to a specific server.
- **Delegation:** Delegation allows local administrators or supervisors to perform system modifications without a global administrator or for one user to allow another to perform actions on their behalf. For example, a user could delegate the right to manage office-related information.

- **Interchange:** The SAML protocol is a prominent means used to exchange identity information between two identity domains. OpenID Connect is another such protocol.

Privacy

Putting personal information onto computer networks necessarily raises privacy concerns. Absent proper protections, the data may be used to implement a surveillance society. Social web and online social networking services make heavy use of identity management. Helping users decide how to manage access to their personal information has become an issue of broad concern.

Identity Theft

Identity theft happens when thieves gain access to identity information - such as the personal details needed to get access to a bank account.

Research

Research related to the management of identity covers disciplines such as technology, social sciences, humanities and the law. Decentralized identity management is identity management based on decentralized identifiers (DIDs).

European Research

Within the Seventh Research Framework Programme of the European Union from 2007 to 2013, several new projects related to Identity Management started. The PICOS Project investigates and develops a state-of-the-art platform for providing trust, privacy and identity management in mobile communities. PrimeLife develops concepts and technologies to help individuals to protect autonomy and retain control over personal information, irrespective of activities. SWIFT focuses on extending identity functions and federation to the network while addressing usability and privacy concerns and leverages identity technology as a key to integrate service and transport infrastructures for the benefit of users and the providers.

Organization Implications

In each organization there is normally a role or department that is responsible for managing the schema of digital identities of their staff and their own objects, which are represented by object identities or object identifiers (OID). The organizational policies and processes and procedures related to the oversight of identity management are sometimes referred to as *Identity Governance and Administration* (IGA). Commercial software tools exist to help automate and simplify such organizational-level identity management functions. How effectively and appropriately such tools are used falls within scope of broader governance, risk management, and compliance regimes. Since 2016 Identity and Access Management professionals have their own professional organization, IDPro. In 2018 the committee initiated the publication of An Annotated Bibliography, listing a number of important publications, books, presentations and videos.

Management Systems

An identity-management system refers to an information system, or to a set of technologies that can be used for enterprise or cross-network identity management. The following terms are used in relationship with "identity-management system":

- Access-governance system.
- Identity and access management system.
- Entitlement-management system.
- User provisioning system.

Identity management, otherwise known as identity and access management (IAM) is an identity security framework that works to authenticate and authorize user access to resources such as applications, data, systems, and cloud platforms. It seeks to ensure only the right people are being provisioned to the right tools, and for the right reasons. As our digital ecosystem continues to advance, so does the world of identity management.

"Identity management" and "access and identity management" (or AIM) are terms that are used interchangeably under the title of identity management while identity management itself falls under the umbrella of IT security and information privacy and privacy risk as well as usability and e-inclusion studies. There are three components of Identity and Access Management (IAM):

- Access management/Single sign-on to verify users' identities before they can access the network and applications.
- Identity governance to ensure that user access is being granted according to appropriate access policies for onboarding and role/ responsibility changes.
- Privileged access management to control and monitor access to highly privileged accounts, applications and system assets.

These technologies can be combined using identity governance, which provides the foundation for automated workflows and processes.

Modes of Identity Management

Identity is conceptualized in three different modes, according to an analysis:from the FIDIS Network of Excellence:

- **Idem-identity:** A third-person (i.e., objectified) attribution of sameness. Such an objectified perspective can not only be taken towards others but also towards oneself.
- **Ipse-identity:** The ipse-identity perspective is the first-person perspective on what constitutes oneself as a continuous being (idem) in the course of time, while experiencing multiplicity and difference in the here and now.
- **Me-identity:** The 'me' (G. H. Mead) is the organised set of attitudes of others which one assumes. It is coconstituted by the 'I', the first person perspective, which incorporates the variety of third person perspectives it encounters and develops. Thus, the 'me' is continuously reconstituted in the face of changing third person perspectives on the self.

In Bertino's and Takahashi's textbook, three categories of identity are defined that are to a degree overlapping with the FIDIS identity concepts:

- **"Me-Identity":** What I define as identity
- **"Our-Identity":** What others and I define as identity
- **"Their-Identity":** What others define as my identity

Purposes for Using Identity Management Systems

Identity management systems are concerned with the creation, the administration and the deployment of:

- **Identifiers:** Data used to identify a subject.
- **Credentials:** Data providing evidence for claims about identities or parts thereof.
- **Attributes:** Data describing characteristics of a subject.

The purposes of identity management systems are:

- **Identification:** Who is the user – used on logon or database lookup
- **Authentication:** Is this the real user? Systems needs to provide evidence!
- **Authorization and Non-Repudiation:** Authorization of documents or transaction with e-ID and most often with digital signature based on e-ID. Generates non-repudiation and receipts.

Commercial Solutions

Identity-management systems, products, applications, and platforms are commercial Identity-management solutions implemented for enterprises and organizations. Technologies, services, and terms related to identity management include Microsoft Windows active directory, service providers, identity providers, Web services, access control, digital identities, password managers, single sign-on, security tokens, security token services (STS), workflows, OpenID, WS-Security, WS-Trust, SAML 2.0, OAuth, and RBAC.

Electronic Identity Management

In general, electronic IdM can be said to cover the management of any form of digital identities. The focus on identity management goes back to the development of directories, such as X.500, where a namespace serves to hold named objects that represent real-life "identified" entities, such as countries, organizations, applications, subscribers or devices. The X.509 ITU-T standard defined certificates carried identity attributes as two directory names: the certificate subject and the certificate issuer. X.509 certificates and PKI systems operate to prove the online "identity" of a subject.

Therefore, in IT terms, one can consider identity management as the management of information (as held in a directory) that represents items identified in real life (e.g., users, organizations, devices, services, etc.). The design of such systems requires explicit information and identity engineering tasks.

The evolution of identity management follows the progression of Internet technology closely. In the environment of static web pages and static portals of the early 1990s, corporations investigated the delivery of informative web content such as the "white pages" of employees. Subsequently, as the information changed (due to employee turnover, provisioning and de-provisioning), the ability to perform self-service and help-desk updates more efficiently morphed into what became known as Identity Management today.

Solutions

Solutions which fall under the category of identity management may include:

Management of Identities:

- User account provisioning and de-provisioning.
- Workflow automation.
- Delegated administration.
- Password synchronization.
- Self-service password reset.

Access Control:

- Password manager.
- Single sign-on (SSO).

- Web single sign-on (Web SSO).
- Role-based access control (RBAC).
- Attribute based access control (ABAC).

Directory Services:

- x.500 and LDAP.
- Microsoft Active Directory.
- Microsoft Entra ID (Formally Microsoft Azure Active Directory).
- NetIQ eDirectory.
- Identity repository (directory services for the administration of user account attributes).
- Metadata replication and synchronization.
- Directory virtualization (Virtual directory).
- e-Business scale directory systems.
- Next-generation systems—Composite Adaptive Directory Services (CADS) and CADS SDP.

Other Categories:

- Federation of user access rights on web applications across otherwise untrusted networks.
- Directory-enabled networking and 802.1X EAP.

Standards:

- SAML 2.0.
- OAuth.
- OpenID.
- Liberty Alliance—A consortium promoting federated identity management.
- Shibboleth (Internet2) - Identity standards targeted towards educational environments.
- Global Trust Center.
- Central Authentication Service.
- NIST SP 800-63.

6.3.2 Challenges in IAM at the Edge

Deploying IAM solutions in edge computing environments presents unique challenges and complexities that organizations must address to mitigate security risks, ensure operational resilience, and maintain regulatory compliance:

- **Distributed Architecture**: Manages heterogeneous edge devices, platforms, and network segments with varying security capabilities, connectivity constraints, and operational dependencies, requiring scalable IAM architectures and interoperable identity protocols.
- **Resource-Constrained Devices**: Integrates IAM capabilities into resource-constrained edge devices, IoT sensors, or industrial controllers with limited processing power, memory, and firmware updates, necessitating lightweight authentication mechanisms and secure remote management solutions.
- **Data Privacy and Compliance**: Safeguards user privacy, sensitive data, and compliance with data protection regulations (e.g., GDPR, HIPAA) across distributed edge environments, implementing data encryption, anonymization, and audit trails for transparent access management and accountability.

6.3.3 Benefits of IAM at the Edge

Effective IAM strategies and technologies offer several strategic benefits for organizations deploying edge computing solutions:

- **Enhanced Security**: Strengthens data protection, mitigates insider threats, and prevents unauthorized access to edge resources through granular access controls, encryption, and continuous monitoring of user activities and device behaviors.
- **Operational Efficiency**: Streamlines user provisioning, authentication workflows, and policy enforcement across distributed edge nodes, reducing administrative overhead, improving service delivery, and ensuring consistent IAM policies and configurations.
- **Regulatory Compliance**: Facilitates compliance with industry regulations, data privacy laws, and contractual obligations by enforcing access controls, auditing IAM activities, and implementing security controls to protect sensitive information in edge-driven applications.

6.3.4 IAM Strategies and Best Practices

Implementing effective IAM strategies and best practices enhances security posture, operational efficiency, and user experiences in edge computing environments:

- **Identity Federation**: Integrates single sign-on (SSO) capabilities and federated identity management to authenticate users seamlessly across hybrid IT environments, cloud services, and edge computing platforms without compromising security or user convenience.

- **Role-Based Access Control (RBAC):** Assigns permissions based on predefined user roles, responsibilities, or organizational hierarchies to enforce least privilege principles, data segregation, and separation of duties in decentralized edge architectures.
- **Context-Aware Access Policies:** Adapts access policies based on user context, device attributes, location information, or environmental conditions to dynamically adjust access privileges and mitigate security risks in real-time edge computing scenarios.
- **Secure Device Onboarding:** Authenticates and provisions edge devices securely with unique identifiers, certificates, or cryptographic keys during initial setup, ensuring trusted device identities and secure communication channels in IoT and industrial IoT (IIoT) deployments.

6.3.5 Technologies and Tools for IAM at the Edge

Deploying IAM technologies and tools enhances visibility, control, and compliance across distributed edge infrastructures:

- **IAM Platforms:** Utilizes cloud-based IAM platforms, directory services, or identity as a service (IDaaS) solutions to centralize identity management, access controls, and policy enforcement across edge computing environments.
- **Edge Security Gateways:** Implements edge security gateways or secure access service edge (SASE) solutions to enforce IAM policies, inspect traffic, and protect edge resources from unauthorized access, malware threats, and data exfiltration attempts.
- **Blockchain and Distributed Ledger Technology:** Leverages blockchain-based identity management solutions, decentralized identifiers (DIDs), and verifiable credentials to establish trust, privacy, and tamper-resistant identity verification in edge computing ecosystems.

6.3.6 Future Trends and Considerations

Emerging trends and considerations in IAM at the edge are shaping the future of secure and scalable edge computing deployments:

- **AI-driven IAM:** Integrates artificial intelligence (AI) and machine learning (ML) algorithms to analyze user behavior, detect anomalies, and automate adaptive access controls in dynamic edge environments, enhancing threat detection and incident response capabilities.

- **Zero Trust Architecture:** Adopts zero trust principles to verify every request, device, or user attempting to access edge resources, enforcing least privilege access, continuous authentication, and micro-segmentation to mitigate lateral movement and insider threats.
- **Regulatory Alignment:** Aligns IAM strategies with evolving regulatory requirements, global privacy standards, and industry-specific compliance mandates to protect sensitive data, uphold user privacy rights, and maintain trust in edge computing ecosystems.

6.4 COMPLIANCE AND LEGAL CONSIDERATIONS

Edge computing introduces distributed computing architectures that process data closer to the source, enabling real-time analytics, low-latency applications, and enhanced user experiences. However, navigating compliance and legal considerations is crucial for organizations to mitigate risks, uphold regulatory requirements, and ensure ethical data handling practices in decentralized computing environments.

Compliance and legal considerations are critical to navigating regulatory complexities, protecting data privacy, and ensuring ethical data practices in edge computing environments. By adhering to regulatory frameworks, implementing best practices for data governance, risk management, and accountability, organizations can mitigate compliance risks, uphold legal obligations, and foster trust in decentralized computing ecosystems.

Addressing challenges related to data sovereignty, contractual agreements, liability frameworks, and industry standards promotes responsible innovation, regulatory alignment, and sustainable growth in the evolving landscape of edge computing. As organizations embrace edge-driven initiatives and deploy mission-critical applications, prioritizing compliance and legal considerations as integral components of edge computing strategies supports resilience, transparency, and ethical stewardship in the digital era.

6.4.1 Regulatory Frameworks and Data Protection Laws

Edge computing deployments must adhere to global, regional, and industry-specific regulatory frameworks governing data protection, privacy rights, and cybersecurity practices:

- **General Data Protection Regulation (GDPR):** Enforces data protection and privacy for individuals within the European Union (EU), regulating the collection, processing, and storage of personal data, including consent requirements, data subject rights, and cross-border data transfers.

- **California Consumer Privacy Act (CCPA):** Grants California residents rights to access, delete, and opt-out of the sale of personal information, imposing obligations on businesses to disclose data practices, secure sensitive data, and comply with consumer privacy preferences.
- **Health Insurance Portability and Accountability Act (HIPAA):** Safeguards protected health information (PHI) in healthcare settings, requiring covered entities and business associates to implement security safeguards, encryption, and access controls to protect patient privacy and prevent data breaches.
- **Payment Card Industry Data Security Standard (PCI DSS):** Ensures secure handling of credit card information by merchants and service providers, implementing encryption, access controls, and compliance assessments to protect cardholder data and mitigate payment fraud risks.

6.4.2 Key Legal Considerations in Edge Computing

Navigating legal considerations in edge computing involves addressing jurisdictional issues, contractual obligations, liability frameworks, and regulatory compliance across distributed edge environments:

- **Data Sovereignty and Jurisdiction:** Determines where data is stored, processed, or transmitted, addressing jurisdictional requirements, cross-border data transfers, and international data privacy laws governing data residency, localization, and lawful access by government authorities.
- **Contractual Agreements:** Establishes legal agreements, service-level agreements (SLAs), and data processing agreements (DPAs) between stakeholders, defining roles, responsibilities, liability provisions, data protection commitments, and dispute resolution mechanisms in edge computing contracts.
- **Liability and Risk Management:** Allocates liability for data breaches, cybersecurity incidents, and regulatory non-compliance among edge providers, customers, vendors, and third-party service providers, mitigating financial, reputational, and legal risks associated with edge computing operations.

6.4.3 Compliance Challenges and Best Practices

Addressing compliance challenges in edge computing requires adopting best practices, proactive risk management strategies, and regulatory alignment to protect data privacy, uphold legal obligations, and maintain trust in decentralized computing ecosystems:

- **Data Privacy by Design:** Integrates privacy principles, data minimization, and consent management into edge computing architectures, ensuring proactive data protection, transparency, and user-centric privacy controls in compliance with GDPR and CCPA requirements.
- **Security Controls and Risk Assessments:** Implements robust cybersecurity measures, encryption standards, access controls, and vulnerability assessments to mitigate data breaches, safeguard sensitive information, and comply with industry-specific security frameworks (e.g., HIPAA, PCI DSS).
- **Audits and Compliance Monitoring:** Conducts regular audits, compliance assessments, and privacy impact assessments (PIAs) to evaluate edge computing practices, identify regulatory gaps, and maintain adherence to data protection laws, industry standards, and internal policies.

6.4.4 Data Governance and Accountability

Establishes data governance frameworks, data stewardship responsibilities, and accountability mechanisms to oversee data lifecycle management, data quality, and ethical data use in edge computing environments:

- **Data Transparency and Accountability:** Provides transparency into data processing activities, data flows, and data sharing practices, enabling individuals to exercise data subject rights, request access to personal information, and monitor data usage consent preferences.
- **Ethical Considerations:** Adheres to ethical guidelines, responsible AI principles, and data ethics frameworks to promote fairness, non-discrimination, and ethical decision-making in edge-driven applications, minimizing biases and ensuring responsible use of data analytics.
- **Incident Response and Data Breach Notification:** Implements incident response plans, data breach notification procedures, and communication strategies to mitigate the impact of cybersecurity incidents, comply with legal reporting obligations, and restore trust in edge computing services.

6.4.5 Industry Standards and Best Practices

Adopts industry standards, certification programs, and cybersecurity frameworks to guide edge computing deployments, ensure interoperability, and demonstrate compliance with regulatory requirements:

- **National Institute of Standards and Technology (NIST):** Provides cybersecurity frameworks (e.g., NIST SP 800-53, NIST Cybersecurity Framework) and guidance on risk management, security controls, and continuous monitoring for edge computing environments.
- **International Organization for Standardization (ISO):** Offers ISO/IEC standards (e.g., ISO/IEC 27001, ISO/IEC 27018) for information security management, cloud computing, and privacy protection, supporting global conformity assessment, certification, and regulatory compliance in edge computing operations.
- **Edge Computing Consortiums:** Participates in industry consortia, collaborative initiatives, and regulatory working groups (e.g., Cloud Security Alliance, Edge Computing Consortium) to develop best practices, share threat intelligence, and promote cybersecurity resilience across distributed edge infrastructures.

6.4.6 Future Trends and Considerations

Emerging trends and considerations in compliance and legal frameworks are shaping the future of edge computing deployments:

- **Regulatory Evolution:** Monitors regulatory developments, emerging data privacy laws (e.g., Data Protection Act 2022), and regulatory guidance on edge computing, adapting compliance strategies to evolving legal requirements and regulatory expectations globally.
- **Cross-Sector Collaboration:** Collaborates with regulators, industry stakeholders, and academia to harmonize global standards, promote regulatory alignment, and address emerging challenges in data protection, cybersecurity, and ethical governance in edge computing ecosystems.
- **Technology Innovation:** Leverages advancements in encryption technologies, decentralized identity solutions (e.g., blockchain-based identity management), and AI-driven compliance automation to enhance data security, privacy protections, and regulatory compliance in edge computing deployments.

CHAPTER 7
EDGE COMPUTING USE CASES

7.1 EDGE COMPUTING IN HEALTHCARE

7.1.1 Introduction to Edge Computing in Healthcare

Edge computing is revolutionizing the healthcare industry by enabling real-time data processing, enhanced patient care delivery, and innovative medical applications at the network edge. This decentralized computing paradigm leverages edge devices, sensors, and local edge servers to process data closer to the point of care, improving operational efficiency, clinical decision-making, and patient outcomes. Edge computing is revolutionizing healthcare delivery by enabling real-time data processing, personalized patient care, and innovative medical applications at the network edge. By leveraging edge computing technologies, healthcare providers can enhance clinical decision-making, improve patient outcomes, and optimize healthcare operations while addressing challenges related to data interoperability, regulatory compliance, and cybersecurity risks. As organizations embrace edge-driven initiatives and deploy mission-critical healthcare applications, prioritizing patient privacy, regulatory compliance, and ethical considerations fosters trust, resilience, and sustainable innovation in the evolving landscape of decentralized healthcare ecosystems. Edge computing continues to shape the future of healthcare delivery by empowering healthcare providers, researchers, and patients with transformative capabilities for enhanced medical diagnostics, remote patient monitoring, and personalized treatment strategies in the digital era.

7.1.2 Applications of Edge Computing in Healthcare

Edge computing facilitates a wide range of applications and use cases across healthcare domains, transforming patient care delivery, medical diagnostics, and healthcare operations:

Remote Patient Monitoring

Remote patient monitoring (RPM) is a technology to enable monitoring of patients outside of conventional clinical settings, such as in the home or in a remote area, which may increase access to care and decrease healthcare delivery costs. RPM involves the constant remote care of patients by their physicians, often to track physical symptoms, chronic conditions, or post-hospitalization rehab.

Incorporating RPM in chronic-disease management may significantly improve an individual's quality of life, by allowing patients to maintain independence, prevent complications, and to minimize personal costs. RPM facilitates these goals by delivering care through telecommunications. This form of patient monitoring can be particularly important when patients are managing complex self-care processes such as home hemodialysis.

Key features of RPM, like remote monitoring and trend analysis of physiological parameters, enable early detection of deterioration; thereby reducing emergency department visits, hospitalizations, and the duration of hospital stays. While technologies are continually being developed to tackle this type of health care, physicians may utilize basic communication methods such as Zoom, Snapchat, or even landline phones.

Pilot programs for Remote Patient Monitoring began in 1970s when Kaiser Permanente created monitoring systems for rural communities in order to provide better healthcare to isolated regions. Literature related to Remote Patient Monitoring suggests that interventions based on health behavior models, care pathways, and personalized coaching lead to the best outcomes.

Research on the use of Remote Patient Monitoring technologies has helped determine that further development of telehealth ecosystems, in which physicians can give recommendations and means of care while also receiving transmitted health information, can lead to better patient outcomes and higher patient satisfaction. Researchers also note that Remote Patient Monitoring will become more important as healthcare changes from a volume focus to a value focus.

During the COVID-19 pandemic, Remote Patient Monitoring has been used extensively and allowed for more fields such as psychology or cardiology to use virtual care. By 2025, the Remote Patient Monitoring industry is expected to double, due to factors such as the COVID-19 pandemic and increased at-home care. Use of Remote Patient Monitoring has been proven to ultimately provide better patient compliance and improved physician management, while decreasing costs of care.

Key Features of RPM

- **Accessibly:** Both patients and care providers can access the RPM record anytime from anywhere. Instantaneous access is helpful in making accurate health decisions and improves clinical operations.
- **Cost-Effectiveness:** Not much evidence has been able to support whether or not telehealth is more cost effective or not. There is some research showing that it can be a less expensive way for doctors to provide care because they aren't using any of their physical resources on the patient. Sage journals published a case study researching if

telehealth is cost effective for the patient in the comfort of their home. Langabeer et al. (2017), stated that this study's method was to utilize telehealth resources when people called 911 and EMS responded. Once EMS was on scene, they would pull up a virtual system putting them in direct contact with an emergency department provider at the hospital. The provider was then able to triage the patient at the scene of the call and determine the best course of treatment potentially being no transport to the hospital. This in turn is more cost efficient for the patients and the medical providers both. This showed to be helpful in-patient outcomes because the provider was able to determine the critical level of the patient therefore allowing them to determine the best course of action at an earlier time.

- **Promptness:** RPM helps in faster decision-making. RPM collects, improves, and analyzes data promptly, which is time-saving. Report-making has become easy through RPM.

Technological Components

The diverse applications of RPM lead to numerous variations of RPM technology architecture. However, most RPM technologies follow a general architecture that consists of four components:

- Sensors on a device that is enabled by wireless communications to measure physiological parameters.
- Sensors can connect back to a central database by WiFi or cellular communication protocols depending on the manufacturer.
- Local data storage at patients' site that interfaces between sensors and other centralized data repository and/or healthcare providers.
- Centralized repository to store data sent from sensors, local data storage, diagnostic applications, and/or healthcare providers.
- Diagnostic application software that develops treatment recommendations and intervention alerts based on the analysis of collected data.

Depending on the disease and the parameters that are monitored, different combinations of sensors, storage, and applications may be deployed.

Applications

Physiological data such as blood pressure and subjective patient data are collected by sensors on peripheral devices. Examples of peripheral devices are: blood pressure cuff, pulse oximeter, and glucometer. The data are transmitted to healthcare providers or third parties via wireless telecommunication devices. The data are evaluated for potential problems by a healthcare professional or via a clinical decision support algorithm, and patient, caregivers, and health providers are immediately alerted if a problem is detected. As a result, timely intervention ensures positive patient outcomes. The newer applications also provide education, test and medication reminder alerts, and a means of communication between the patient and the provider. The following section illustrates examples of RPM applications, but RPM is not limited to those disease states

Cancer:

- Use of RPM among patients with cancer has been proven to improve outcomes overall, with studies showing improvements in re-hospitalization rates and decreased healthcare resource usage. These remote monitoring technologies help to lower severity of pain as well as improving depression. The RPM has improved the life expectancy of Cancer Patients up to 20%. Remote patient monitoring devices help in early interventions, prescriptions, chemotherapy modifications, etc. RPM has helped in reducing Cancer emergency room visits or prolonged chemotherapy treatments. It is estimated that the hospitalization rate of patients with RPM is 2.8% and without RPM is 13%

COVID-19:

- RPM can provide continuity of care for symptomatic COVID-19 patients post-discharge from hospital and those with mild to moderate oxygen desaturation levels that do not require hospitalization, and patients with long-COVID symptoms. Due to the nature of the pandemic, RPM is a necessary means of providing care to at-risk patients such as elderly or immunocompromised people. Studies show that the use of RPM during the pandemic has helped to reduce hospitalizations and decrease the use of acute care resources. The FDA has given emergency authorized use of RPM technologies for the purpose of decreasing the spread of COVID-19 and to prevent overload for healthcare resources and personnel.

Chronic Obstructive Pulmonary Disease (COPD):

- For patients with chronic obstructive pulmonary disease, RPM may contribute to increased patient knowledge, earlier interventions, and shared decision making. However, the evidence is varying and issues of cost, and the shift of responsibilities to patients have also been raised.

Dementia and Falls:

- For patients with dementia that are at risk for falls, RPM technology promotes safety and prevents harm through continuous surveillance.

RPM sensors can be affixed to the individual or their assistive mobility devices such as canes and walkers. The sensors monitor an individual's location, gait, linear acceleration and angular velocity, and utilize a mathematical algorithm to predict the likelihood for falls, detect movement changes, and alert caregivers if the individual has fallen. Furthermore, tracking capabilities via Wi-Fi, global positioning system (GPS) or radio frequency enables caregivers to locate wandering elders.

Diabetes:

- Diabetes management requires control of multiple parameters: blood pressure, weight, and blood glucose. The real-time delivery of blood glucose and blood pressure readings enables immediate alerts for patient and healthcare providers to intervene when needed. There is evidence to show that daily diabetes management involving RPM is just as effective as usual clinic visit every 3 months.

Congestive Heart Failure:

- A systematic review of the literature on home monitoring for heart failure patients indicates that RPM improves quality of life, improves patient-provider relationships, shortens duration of stay in hospitals, decreases mortality rate, and reduces costs to the healthcare system.

Infertility:

- A recent study of a remote patient monitoring solution for infertility demonstrated that for appropriately screened patients who had been seeking In-Vitro Fertilization (IVF) treatment, a six-month remote monitoring program had the same pregnancy rate as a cycle of IVF. The remote patient monitoring product and service used had a cost-per-patient of $800, compared to the average cost of a cycle of IVF of $15,000, suggesting a 95% reduction in the cost of care for the same outcome.

Surgery:

- When compared to standard of care with no devices, a 2021 study showed that post-surgical remote patient monitoring detected 30% more medication errors, 10-14% reduction in patient paint, and a 5% reduction in hospital re-admissions. The randomized study, conducted by PJ Devereaux and Micheal McGillion, split 905 patients between a standard of care group and a RPM group, which used at-home clinical grade vital sign devices to transfer their vital signs to a Clinician Portal where they were monitored remotely and could communicate through text, chat, or video calls. The scientists (Devereaux and McGillion) are now conducting two follow-up studies (PVC-RAM 2 and PVC-RAM 3) to investigate secondary findings of PVC RAM1.

Telemedicine in Prison Systems:

- A forerunner to RPM, Florida first experimented with "primitive" telemedicine use in its prisons during the latter 1980s. Working with Doctors Oscar W. Boultinghouse and Michael J. Davis, from the early 1990s to 2007, Glenn G. Hammack led the University of Texas Medical Branch's development of a pioneering telehealth program in Texas state prisons. Many of the studies conducted on telehealth have focused on the effectiveness in rural or remote communities so an article published by plos one looked at a study done focusing on the effectiveness of telehealth in the prison system. This review looked at 29 different studies that all utilized telehealth in the prison slightly different. The parameters and interventions delivered varied causing the outcomes to vary. The overall systemic review provided mixed evidence on the impact and outcomes of telehealth usage in prisons. Considering the fact, the world population is growing this means so is the prison population which also means the spectrum of health issues is also broadening. This being the main reason for these studies to have been conducted. This leads to the conclusion that more testing and studies must be completed too fully determine the effectiveness in patient outcomes. There was definitely evidence in the studies showing a positive effect from telehealth in the prison system and it did in some cases prove to be effective with positive impacts. It also showed in some cases to be just as effective as normal conventional care. The study stated that the idea to consider is what is being treated and what the context of the situation being addressed is. If the situation is critical, then other measures or responses may be necessary.

Veterans Health Administration:

- The Veterans Health Administration (VHA), United States' largest integrated healthcare system, is an early adopter which became highly involved in the implementation and evaluation of RPM technologies. It has expanded use of RPM beyond common chronic disease applications, to post-traumatic stress disorder, cancer and palliative care. VHA's findings indicate improvements in a wide range of metrics, including decrease in emergency department visits, hospitalizations, and nursing home admissions. Findings from the VHA Care Coordination/Home Telehealth program show that RPM deployment resulted in significant savings to the organization.

Limitations

RPM is highly dependent on the individual's motivation to manage their health. Without the patient's willingness to be an active participant in their care, RPM implementation will likely fail. The shift of accountability associated with RPM brings up liability issues. There are no clear guidelines in respect to whether clinicians have to intervene every time they receive an alert regardless of the urgency. The continuous flow of patient data requires a dedicated team of health care providers to handle the information, which may, in fact, increase the workload. Although technology is introduced with the intent to increase efficiency, it can become a barrier to some healthcare providers that are not technological. There are common obstacles that health informatics technologies encounter that applies to RPM. Depending on the comorbidities monitored, RPM involves a diverse selection of devices in its implementation. Standardization is required for data exchange and interoperability among multiple components. Furthermore, RPM deployment is highly dependent on an extensive wireless telecommunications infrastructure, which may not be available or feasible in rural areas. Since RPM involves transmission of sensitive patient data across telecommunication networks, information security is a concern. Debate surrounds the potential cybersecurity issues of RPM, including the likelihood of hacks which could pull personal medical data. Additionally, most remote monitoring devices are limited to single-user applications, and could be expanded in the future for better inclusion of multi-user technologies.

Reimbursement

United States:

- Since 2020, Medicare fully covers doctors and other medical staff receiving payment for RPM patient setup and training. This is then followed by a fixed monthly amount for operating health monitoring devices and logging patient readings. Medicaid also covers these procedures in 34 states. Cigna, Humana and UnitedHealth Care are among the large private U.S. private health insurance companies that offer members to track certain health data, such as blood pressure, glucose values and other metrics, and send them to their virtual primary care providers who can review the data during patient visits. Some of these plans include coverage of the use of medical devices for remote patient monitoring.

Germany:

- Digital health applications (known as DiGA in German: "Digitale Gesundheitsanwendungen") have been eligible for nationwide insurance coverage since the end of 2019 through a fast-track application process.

Medical devices that are used for remote patient monitoring through apps, have to be considered Category I (low risk) or IIa (low-medium risk) to be eligible. Telehealth and coaching, even when combined with remote patient monitoring through wearables, is not directly covered by the DiGA directive, but needs to be reimbursed separately under different provisions.

Telemedicine

Telehealth is the distribution of health-related services and information via electronic information and telecommunication technologies. It allows long-distance patient and clinician contact, care, advice, reminders, education, intervention, monitoring, and remote admissions. Telemedicine is sometimes used as a synonym, or is used in a more limited sense to describe remote clinical services, such as diagnosis and monitoring. When rural settings, lack of transport, a lack of mobility, conditions due to outbreaks, epidemics or pandemics, decreased funding, or a lack of staff restrict access to care, telehealth may bridge the gap as well as provide distance-learning; meetings, supervision, and presentations between practitioners; online information and health data management and healthcare system integration. Telehealth could include two clinicians discussing a case over video conference; a robotic surgery occurring through remote access; physical therapy done via digital monitoring instruments, live feed and application combinations; tests being forwarded between facilities for interpretation by a higher specialist; home monitoring through continuous sending of patient health data; client to practitioner online conference; or even videophone interpretation during a consult.

History

The development and history of telehealth or telemedicine (terms used interchangeably in literature) is deeply rooted in the history and development in not only technology but also society itself. Humans have long sought to relay important messages through torches, optical telegraphy, electroscopes, and wireless transmission. Early forms of telemedicine achieved with telephone and radio have been supplemented with videotelephony, advanced diagnostic methods supported by distributed client/server applications, and additionally with telemedical devices to support in-home care.

In the 21st century, with the advent of the internet, portable devices and other such digital devices are taking a transformative role in healthcare and its delivery.

Although, traditional medicine relies on in-person care, the need and want for remote care has existed from the Roman and pre-Hippocratic periods in antiquity. The elderly and infirm who could not visit temples for medical care sent representatives to convey information on symptoms and bring home a diagnosis as well as treatment. In Africa, villagers would use smoke signals to warn neighboring villages of disease outbreak. The beginnings of telehealth have existed through primitive forms of communication and technology. The exact date of origin for Telehealth is unknown, but it was known to have been used during the Bubonic Plague. That version of telehealth was far different from how we know it today. During that time, they were communicating by heliograph and bonfire. Those were used to notify other groups of people about famine and war. Those are not using any form of technology yet but are starting to spread the idea of connectivity among groups of people who geographically could not be together.

As technology developed and wired communication became increasingly commonplace, the ideas surrounding telehealth began emerging. The earliest telehealth encounter can be traced to Alexander Graham Bell in 1876, when he used his early telephone as a means of getting help from his assistant Mr. Watson after he spilt acid on his trousers. Another instance of early telehealth, specifically telemedicine was reported in *The Lancet* in 1879. An anonymous writer described a case where a doctor successfully diagnosed a child over the telephone in the middle of the night. This Lancet issue, also further discussed the potential of Remote Patient Care in order to avoid unnecessary house visits, which were part of routine health care during the 1800s. Other instances of telehealth during this period came from the American Civil War, during which telegraphs were used to deliver mortality lists and medical care to soldiers. As the 1900s started, physicians quickly found a use for the telephone making it a prime communication channel to contact patients and other physicians. Over the next fifty-plus years, the telephone was a staple for medical communication. As the 1930s came around, radio communication played a key role, especially during World War I. It was specifically used to communicate with remote areas such as Alaska and Australia. They used the radio to communicate medical information. During the Vietnam War, radio communication had become more advanced and was now used to send medical teams in helicopters to help. This then brought together the Aerial Medical Service (AMS) who used telegraphs, radios, and planes to help care for people who lived in remote areas.

From the late 1800s to the early 1900s the early foundations of wireless communication were laid down. Radios provided an easier and near instantaneous form of communication. The use of radio to deliver healthcare became accepted for remote areas. The Royal Flying Doctor Service of Australia is an example of the early adoption of radios in telehealth.

In 1925 the inventor Hugo Gernsback wrote an article for the magazine *Science and Invention* which included a prediction of a future where patients could be treated remotely by doctors through a device he called a “teledactyl”. His descriptions of the device are similar to what would later become possible with new technology.

When the American National Aeronautics and Space Administration (NASA) began plans to send astronauts into space, the need for telemedicine became clear. In order to monitor their astronauts in space, telemedicine capabilities were built into the spacecraft as well as the first spacesuits. Additionally, during this period, telehealth and telemedicine were promoted in different countries especially the United States and Canada. Carrier Sekani Family Services helped pioneer telehealth in British Columbia and Canada, according to its CEO Warner Adam. After the telegraph and telephone started to successfully help physicians treat patients from remote areas, telehealth became more recognized. Technological advancements occurred when NASA sent men to space. Engineers for NASA created biomedical telemetry and telecommunications systems. NASA technology monitored vitals such as blood pressure, heart rate, respiration rate, and temperature. After the technology was created, it then became the base of telehealth medicine for the public.

Massachusetts General Hospital and Boston’s Logan International Airport had a role in the early use of telemedicine, which more or less coincided with NASA’s foray into telemedicine through the use of physiologic monitors for astronauts. On October 26, 1960, a plane struck a flock of birds upon takeoff, killing many passengers and leaving a number wounded. Due to the extreme complexity of trying to get all the medical personnel out from the hospital, the practical solution became telehealth. This was expanded upon in 1967, when Kenneth Bird at Massachusetts General founded one of the first telemedicine clinics. The clinic addressed the fundamental problem of delivering occupational and emergency health services to employees and travellers at the airport, located three congested miles from the hospital. Clinicians at the hospital would provide consultation services to patients who were at the airport. Consultations were achieved through microwave audio as well as video links. The airport began seeing over a hundred patients a day at its nurse-run clinic that cared for victims of plane crashes and other accidents, taking vital signs, electrocardiograms, and video images that were sent to Massachusetts General. Over 1,000 patients are documented as having received remote treatment from doctors at MGH using the clinic’s two-way audiovisual microwave circuit. One notable story featured a woman who got off a flight in Boston and was experiencing chest pain. They performed a workup at the airport, took her to the telehealth suite where Raymond Murphy appeared on the television, and had a conversation with her. While this was happening, another doctor took notes and the nurses took vitals and any test that Murphy ordered. At this point, telehealth was becoming more mainstream and was starting to become more technologically advanced, which created a viable option for patients.

In 1964, the Nebraska Psychiatric Institute began using television links to form two-way communication with the Norfolk State Hospital which was 112 miles away for the education and consultation purposes between clinicians in the two locations.

In 1972 the Department of Health, Education and Welfare in the United States approved funding for seven telemedicine projects across different states. This funding was renewed and two further projects were funded the following year.

In March 1972, the San Bernardino County Medical Society officially implemented its Tel-Med program, a system of prerecorded health-related messages, with a log of 50 tapes. The nonprofit initiative began in 1971 as a local medical project to ease the doctor shortage in the expanding San Bernardino Valley and improve the public's access to sound medical information. It covered subjects ranging from cannabis to vaginitis. In January 1973, in response to the developing "London flu" epidemic hitting California and the country, a tape providing information on the disease was on air within a week after news broke of the flu spreading in the state. That spring, programs were implemented in San Diego and Indianapolis, Indiana, signaling a national acceptance of the concept. By 1979, its system offered messages on over 300 different subjects, 200 of which were available in Spanish as well as English, and serviced over 65 million people in 180 cities around the country.

Telehealth projects underway before and during the 1980s would take off but fail to enter mainstream healthcare. As a result, this period of telehealth history is called the "maturation" stage and made way for sustainable growth. Although state funding in North America was beginning to run low, different hospitals began to launch their own telehealth initiatives. NASA provided an ATS-3 satellite to enable medical care communications of American Red Cross and Pan American Health Organization response teams, following the 1985 Mexico City earthquake. The agency then launched its SateLife/HealthNet programme to increase health service connectivity in developing countries. In 1997, NASA sponsored Yale's Medical Informatics and Technology Applications Consortium project.

Florida first experimented with "primitive" telehealth in its prisons during the latter 1980s. Working with Doctors Oscar W. Boultinghouse and Michael J. Davis, from the early 1990s to 2007; Glenn G. Hammack led the University of Texas Medical Branch (UTMB) development of a pioneering telehealth program in Texas state prisons. The three UTMB alumni would, in 2007, co-found telehealth provider NuPhysician.

The first interactive telemedicine system, operating over standard telephone lines, designed to remotely diagnose and treat patients requiring cardiac resuscitation (defibrillation) was developed and launched by an American company, MedPhone Corporation, in 1989. A year later under the leadership of its President/CEO S Eric

Wachtel, MedPhone introduced a mobile cellular version, the MDPhone. Twelve hospitals in the U.S. served as receiving and treatment centers.

As the expansion of telehealth continued in 1990 Maritime Health Services (MHS) was a big part of the initiation for occupational health services. They sent a medical officer aboard the Pacific trawler that allowed for round-the-clock communication with a physician. The system that allows for this is called the Medical Consultation Network (MedNet). MedNet is a video chatting system that has live audio and visual so the physician on the other end of the call can see and hear what is happening. MetNet can be used from anywhere, not just aboard ships. Being able to provide onsite visual information allows remote patients expert emergency help and medical attention that saves money as well as lives. This has created a demand for at-home monitoring. At-home care has also become a large part of telehealth. Doctors or nurses will now give pre-op and post-op phone calls to check-in. There are also companies such as Lifeline, which give the elderly a button to press in case of an emergency. That button will automatically call for emergency help. If someone has surgery and then is sent home, telehealth allows physicians to see how the patient is progressing without them having to stay in the hospital. TeleDiagnostic Systems of San Francisco is a company that has created a device that monitors sleep patterns, so people with sleep disorders do not have to stay the night at the hospital. Another at-home device that was created was the Wanderer, which was attached to Alzheimer's patients or people who had dementia. It was attached to them so when they wandered off it notified the staff to allow them to go after them. All these devices allowed healthcare beyond hospitals to improve, which means that more people are being helped efficiently.

The advent of high-speed Internet, and the increasing adoption of ICT in traditional methods of care, spurred advances in telehealth delivery. Increased access to portable devices, like laptops and mobile phones, made telehealth more plausible; the industry then expanded into health promotion, prevention and education.

In 2002, G. Byron Brooks, a former NASA surgeon and engineer who had also helped manage the UTMB Telemedicine program, co-founded Teladoc in Dallas, Texas, which was then launched in 2005 as the first national telehealth provider.

In the 2010s, integration of smart home telehealth technologies, such as health and wellness devices, software, and integrated IoT, has accelerated the industry. Healthcare organizations are increasingly adopting the use of self-tracking and cloud-based technologies, and innovative data analytic approaches to accelerate telehealth delivery.

In 2015, Mercy Health system opened Mercy Virtual, in Chesterfield, Missouri, the world's first medical facility dedicated solely to telemedicine.

Telehealth expanded significantly during the COVID-19 pandemic, becoming a vital means of medical communication. It allows doctors to return to humanizing the patient. It forces them to listen to what people have to say and from there make a diagnosis. Studies have demonstrated high trust in telehealth expressed by patients during the COVID-19 pandemic. Some researchers claim this creates an environment that encourages greater vulnerability among patients in self disclosure in the practice of narrative medicine. Telehealth allows for Zoom calls and video chats from across the world checking in on patients and speaking to physicians. Universities are now ensuring that medical students graduate with proficient telehealth communication skills. Experts suggest that telehealth has become a vital part of medical care; with more virtual options becoming available. The pandemic era also identified the "potential to significantly improve global health equity" through telehealth and other virtual care technologies.

Telehealth versus Telemedicine

Telehealth is sometimes discussed interchangeably with telemedicine, the latter being more common than the former. The Health Resources and Services Administration distinguishes telehealth from telemedicine in its scope, defining telemedicine only as describing remote clinical services, such as diagnosis and monitoring, while telehealth includes preventative, promotive, and curative care delivery. This includes the above-mentioned non-clinical applications, like administration and provider education.

The United States Department of Health and Human Services states that the term telehealth includes "non-clinical services, such as provider training, administrative meetings, and continuing medical education", and that the term telemedicine means "remote clinical services". The World Health Organization uses telemedicine to describe all aspects of health care including preventive care. The American Telemedicine Association uses the terms telemedicine and telehealth interchangeably, although it acknowledges that telehealth is sometimes used more broadly for remote health not involving active clinical treatments.

eHealth is another related term, used particularly in the U.K. and Europe, as an umbrella term that includes telehealth, electronic medical records, and other components of health information technology.

Methods and Modalities

Telehealth requires good Internet access by participants, usually in the form of a strong, reliable broadband connection, and broadband mobile communication technology of at least the fourth generation (4G) or long-term evolution (LTE) standard to overcome issues with video stability and bandwidth restrictions. As broadband infrastructure has improved, telehealth usage has become more widely feasible. Healthcare providers often begin telehealth with a needs assessment which assesses hardships which can be improved by telehealth such as travel time, costs or time off work. Collaborators, such as technology companies can ease the transition. Delivery can come within four distinct domains: live video (synchronous), store-and-forward (asynchronous), remote patient monitoring, and mobile health.

- **Store and Forward:** Store-and-forward telemedicine involves acquiring medical data (like medical images, biosignals etc.) and then transmitting this data to a doctor or medical specialist at a convenient time for assessment offline. It does not require the presence of both parties at the same time. Dermatology (cf: teledermatology), radiology, and pathology are common specialties that are conducive to asynchronous telemedicine. A properly structured medical record preferably in electronic form should be a component of this transfer. The 'store-and-forward' process requires the clinician to rely on a history report and audio/video information in lieu of a physical examination.
- **Remote Monitoring:** Remote monitoring, also known as self-monitoring or testing, enables medical professionals to monitor a patient remotely using various technological devices. This method is primarily used for managing chronic diseases or specific conditions, such as heart disease, diabetes mellitus, or asthma. These services can provide comparable health outcomes to traditional in-person patient encounters, supply greater satisfaction to patients, and may be cost-effective. Examples include home-based nocturnal dialysis and improved joint management.
- **Real-Time Interactive:** Electronic consultations are possible through interactive telemedicine services which provide real-time interactions between patient and provider. Videoconferencing has been used in a wide range of clinical disciplines and settings for various purposes including management, diagnosis, counseling and monitoring of patients.
- **Videotelephony:** Videotelephony comprises the technologies for the reception and transmission of audio-video signals by users at different locations, for communication between people in real-time. At the dawn of the technology, videotelephony also included *image phones* which would exchange still images between units every few seconds over conventional POTS-type telephone lines, essentially the same as slow scan TV systems. Currently, videotelephony is particularly useful to the deaf and speech-impaired who can use them with sign language and also with a video relay service, and well as to those with mobility issues

or those who are located in distant places and are in need of telemedical or tele-educational services.

Emergency Care

Common daily emergency telemedicine is performed by SAMU Regulator Physicians in France, Spain, Chile and Brazil. Aircraft and maritime emergencies are also handled by SAMU centres in Paris, Lisbon and Toulouse.

A recent study identified three major barriers to adoption of telemedicine in emergency and critical care units. They include:

- **Regulatory Challenges:** Related to the difficulty and cost of obtaining licensure across multiple states, malpractice protection and privileges at multiple facilities
- **Financial Barrier:** Lack of acceptance and reimbursement by government payers and some commercial insurance carriers, which places the investment burden squarely upon the hospital or healthcare system.
- **Cultural Barriers:** Occurring from the lack of desire, or unwillingness, of some physicians to adapt clinical paradigms for telemedicine applications.

Emergency Telehealth is also gaining acceptance in the United States. There are several modalities currently being practiced that include but are not limited to TeleTriage, TeleMSE and ePPE.

An example of telehealth in the field is when EMS arrives on scene of an incident and is able to take an EKG that is then sent directly to a physician at the hospital to be read. Therefore, allowing instant care and management.

Telenursing

Telenursing refers to the use of telecommunications and information technology in order to provide nursing services in health care whenever a large physical distance exists between patient and nurse, or between any number of nurses. As a field it is part of telehealth, and has many points of contacts with other medical and non-medical applications, such as telediagnosis, teleconsultation, telemonitoring, etc.

Telenursing is achieving significant growth rates in many countries due to several factors: the preoccupation in reducing the costs of health care, an increase in the number of aging and chronically ill population, and the increase in coverage of health care to distant, rural, small or sparsely populated regions. Among its benefits, telenursing may help solve increasing shortages of nurses; to reduce distances and save travel time, and to keep patients out of hospital. A greater degree of job satisfaction has been registered among telenurses.

In Australia, during January 2014, Melbourne tech startup Small World Social collaborated with the Australian Breastfeeding Association to create the first hands-free breastfeeding Google Glass application for new mothers. The application, named Google Glass Breastfeeding app trial, allows mothers to nurse their baby while viewing instructions about common breastfeeding issues (latching on, posture etc.) or call a lactation consultant via a secure Google Hangout, who can view the issue through the mother's Google Glass camera. The trial was successfully concluded in Melbourne in April 2014, and 100% of participants were breastfeeding confidently.

Telepalliative Care

Palliative care is an interdisciplinary medical caregiving approach aimed at optimizing quality of life and mitigating suffering among people with serious, complex, and often terminal illnesses. In the past, palliative care was a disease specific approach, but today the World Health Organization (WHO) takes a broader approach suggesting that palliative care should be applied as early as possible to any chronic and fatal illness. As in many aspects of healthcare, telehealth is increasingly being used in palliative care and is often referred to as telepalliative care. The types of technology applied in telepalliative care are typically telecommunication technologies, such as video conferencing or messaging for follow-up, or digital symptom assessments through digital questionnaires generating alerts to health care professionals. Telepalliative care has been shown to be a feasible approach to deliver palliative care among patients, caregivers and health care professionals. Telepalliative care can provide an added support system that enable patients to remain at home through self-reporting of symptoms and tailoring care to specific patients. Studies have shown that the use of telehealth in palliative care is mostly well received by patients, and that telepalliative care may improve access to health care professionals at home and enhance feelings of security and safety among patients receiving palliative care. Further, telepalliative care may enable more efficient utilization of healthcare resources, promotes collaboration between different levels of healthcare and makes healthcare professionals more responsive to changes in patients' condition.

Challenging aspects of the use of telehealth in palliative care have also been described. Generally, palliative care is a diverse medical specialty, involving interdisciplinary professionals from different professional traditions and cultures, delivering care to a heterogenous cohort of patients with diverse diseases, conditions and symptoms. This makes it a challenge to develop telehealth that is suitable for all patients and in all contexts of palliative care. Some of the barriers to telepalliative care relate to inflexible reporting of complex and fluctuating symptoms and circumstances using electronic questionnaires. Further, palliative care emphasizes a holistic approach that should address existential, spiritual and mental distress related to serious illness. However, few studies have included the self-reporting of existential or spiritual concerns, emotions, and well-being. Healthcare professionals may also be uncomfortable providing emotional or psychological care remotely. Palliative care has been characterized as high-touch rather than high-tech, limiting the interest in applying technological advancements when developing interventions. To optimize the advantages and minimize the challenges with the use of telehealth in home-based palliative care, future research should include users in the design and development process. Understanding the potential of telehealth to support therapeutic relationships between patients and health care professionals and being aware of the possible difficulties and tensions it may create are critical to its successful and acceptable use.

Telepharmacy

Telepharmacy is the delivery of pharmaceutical care via telecommunications to patients in locations where they may not have direct contact with a pharmacist. It is an instance of the wider phenomenon of telemedicine, as implemented in the field of pharmacy. Telepharmacy services include drug therapy monitoring, patient counseling, prior authorization and refill authorization for prescription drugs, and monitoring of formulary compliance with the aid of teleconferencing or videoconferencing. Remote dispensing of medications by automated packaging and labeling systems can also be thought of as an instance of telepharmacy. Telepharmacy services can be delivered at retail pharmacy sites or through hospitals, nursing homes, or other medical care facilities. This approach allows patients in remote or underserved areas to receive pharmacy services that would otherwise be unavailable to them, enhancing access to care and ensuring continuity in medication management. Health outcomes appear similar when pharmacy services are delivered by telepharmacy compared to traditional service delivery. The term can also refer to the use of videoconferencing in pharmacy for other purposes, such as providing education, training, and management services to pharmacists and pharmacy staff remotely.

Telepsychiatry

Telepsychiatry or telemental health refers to the use of telecommunications technology (mostly videoconferencing and phone calls) to deliver psychiatric care remotely for people with mental health conditions. It is a branch of telemedicine. Telepsychiatry can be effective in treating people with mental health conditions. In the short-term it can be as acceptable and effective as face-to-face care. It can improve access to mental health services for some but might also represent a barrier for those lacking access to a suitable device, the internet or the necessary digital skills. Factors such as poverty that are associated with lack of internet access are also associated with greater risk of mental health problems, making digital exclusion an important problem of telemental health services. During the COVID-19 pandemic mental health services were adapted to telemental health in high-income countries. It proved effective and acceptable for use in an emergency situation but there were concerns regarding its long-term implementation.

Teledentistry

Teledentistry is the use of information technology and telecommunications for dental care, consultation, education, and public awareness in the same manner as telehealth and telemedicine.

Teleaudiology

Tele-audiology is the utilization of telehealth to provide audiological services and may include the full scope of audiological practice. This term was first used by Gregg Givens in 1999 in reference to a system being developed at East Carolina University in North Carolina, US.

Teleneurology

Teleneurology describes the use of mobile technology to provide neurological care remotely, including care for stroke, movement disorders like Parkinson's disease, seizure disorders (e.g., epilepsy), etc. The use of teleneurology gives us the opportunity to improve health care access for billions around the globe, from those living in urban locations to those in remote, rural locations. Evidence shows that individuals with Parkinson's disease prefer personal connection with a remote specialist to their local clinician. Such home care is convenient but requires access to and familiarity with internet. A 2017 randomized controlled trial of "virtual house calls" or video visits with individuals diagnosed with Parkinson disease evidences patient preference for the remote specialist vs their local clinician after one year. Teleneurology for patients with Parkison's disease is found to be cheaper than in person visits by reducing transportation and travel time A recent systematic review by Ray Dorsey et al. describes both the limitations and potential benefits of teleneurology to improve care for patients with chronic neurological conditions, especially in low-income countries. White, well educated and technologically savvy people are the biggest consumers of telehealth services for Parkinson's disease. as compared to ethnic minorities in the US.

Teleneurosurgery

Telemedicine in neurosurgery was historically primarily used for follow-up visits by patients that had to travel far to undergo surgery. In the last decade, telemedicine was also used for remote ICU rounding as well as prompt evaluation for acute ischemic stroke and administration of IV alteplase in conjunction with

Neurology. From the onset of the COVID-19 pandemic, there was a rapid surge in the use of telemedicine across all divisions of neurosurgery: vascular, oncology, spine, and functional neurosurgery. Not only for follow-up visits, but it has gained popularity for seeing new patients or following established patients regardless of whether they underwent surgery. Telemedicine is not limited to direct patient care only; there are a number of new research groups and companies focused on using telemedicine for clinical trials involving patients with neurosurgical diagnoses.

Teleneuropsychology

Teleneuropsychology is the use of telehealth/videoconference technology for the remote administration of neuropsychological tests. Neuropsychological tests are used to evaluate the cognitive status of individuals with known or suspected brain disorders and provide a profile of cognitive strengths and weaknesses. Through a series of studies, there is growing support in the literature showing that remote videoconference-based administration of many standard neuropsychological tests results in test findings that are similar to traditional in-person evaluations, thereby establishing the basis for the reliability and validity of teleneuropsychological assessment.

Telenutrition

Telenutrition refers to the use of video conferencing/ telephony to provide online consultation by a nutritionist or dietician. Patient or clients upload their vital statistics, diet logs, food pictures etc. on a telenutrition portal which are then used by nutritionist or dietician to analyze their current health condition. Nutritionist or dietician can then set goals for their respective client/ patients and monitor their progress regularly by follow-up consultations. Telenutrition portals can help people seek remote consultation for themselves and/or their family. This can be extremely helpful for elderly or bed ridden patients who can consult their dietician from comfort of their homes. Telenutrition showed to be feasible and the majority of patients trusted the nutritional televisits, in place of the scheduled but not provided follow-up visits during the lockdown of the COVID-19 pandemic.

Telerehabilitation

Telerehabilitation (or *e-rehabilitation*) is the delivery of rehabilitation services over telecommunication networks and the Internet. Most types of services fall into two categories: clinical assessment (the patient's functional abilities in his or her environment), and clinical therapy. Some fields of rehabilitation practice that have explored telerehabilitation are: neuropsychology, speech–language pathology, audiology, occupational therapy, and physical therapy. Telerehabilitation can deliver therapy to people who cannot travel to a clinic because the patient has a disability or because of travel time. Telerehabilitation also allows experts in rehabilitation to engage in a clinical consultation at a distance.

Most telerehabilitation is highly visual. As of 2014, the most commonly used mediums are webcams, videoconferencing, phone lines, videophones and webpages containing rich web applications. The visual nature of telerehabilitation technology limits the types of rehabilitation services that can be provided. It is most widely used for neuropsychological rehabilitation; fitting of rehabilitation equipment such as wheelchairs, braces or artificial limbs; and in speech-language pathology. Rich web applications for neuropsychological rehabilitation (aka cognitive rehabilitation) of cognitive impairment (from many etiologies) were first introduced in 2001. This endeavor has expanded as a teletherapy application for cognitive skills enhancement programs for school children. Tele-audiology (hearing assessments) is a growing application. Physical therapy and psychology interventions delivered via telehealth may result in similar outcomes as those delivered in-person for a range of health conditions.

Two important areas of telerehabilitation research are (1) demonstrating equivalence of assessment and therapy to in-person assessment and therapy, and (2) building new data collection systems to digitize information that a therapist can use in practice. Ground-breaking research in telehaptics (the sense of touch) and virtual reality may broaden the scope of telerehabilitation practice, in the future.

In the United States, the National Institute on Disability and Rehabilitation Research's (NIDRR) supports research and the development of telerehabilitation. NIDRR's grantees include the "Rehabilitation Engineering and Research Center" (RERC) at the University of Pittsburgh, the Rehabilitation Institute of Chicago, the State University of New York at Buffalo, and the National Rehabilitation Hospital in Washington DC. Other federal funders of research are the Veterans Health Administration, the Health Services Research Administration in the US Department of Health and Human Services, and the Department of Defense. Outside the United States, excellent research is conducted in Australia and Europe.

Only a few health insurers in the United States, and about half of Medicaid programs, reimburse for telerehabilitation services. If the research shows that teleassessments and teletherapy are equivalent to clinical encounters, it is more likely that insurers and Medicare will cover telerehabilitation services.

In India, the Indian Association of Chartered Physiotherapists (IACP) provides telerehabilitation facilities. With the support and collaboration of local clinics and private practitioners and the Members IACP, IACP runs the facility, named Telemedicine. IACP has maintained an internet-based list of their members on their website, through which patients can make online appointments.

Teletrauma Care

Telemedicine can be utilized to improve the efficiency and effectiveness of the delivery of care in a trauma environment. Examples include:

- **Telemedicine for Trauma Triage:** Using telemedicine, trauma specialists can interact with personnel on the scene of a mass casualty or disaster situation, via the internet using mobile devices, to determine the severity of injuries. They can provide clinical assessments and determine whether those injured must be evacuated for necessary care. Remote trauma specialists can provide the same quality of clinical assessment and plan of care as a trauma specialist located physically with the patient.

Telemedicine for intensive care unit (ICU) rounds: Telemedicine is also being used in some trauma ICUs to reduce the spread of infections. Rounds are usually conducted at hospitals across the country by a team of approximately ten or more people to include attending physicians, fellows, residents and other clinicians. This group usually moves from bed to bed in a unit discussing each patient. This aids in the transition of care for patients from the night shift to the morning shift, but also serves as an educational experience for new residents to the team. A new approach features the team conducting rounds from a conference room using a video-conferencing system.

The trauma attending, residents, fellows, nurses, nurse practitioners, and pharmacists are able to watch a live video stream from the patient's bedside. They can see the vital signs on the monitor, view the settings on the respiratory ventilator, and/or view the patient's wounds. Video-conferencing allows the remote viewers two-way communication with clinicians at the bedside.

Telemedicine for trauma education: some trauma centers are delivering trauma education lectures to hospitals and health care providers worldwide using video conferencing technology. Each lecture provides fundamental principles, firsthand knowledge and evidenced-based methods for critical analysis of established clinical practice standards, and comparisons to newer advanced alternatives. The various sites collaborate and share their perspective based on location, available staff, and available resources.

Telemedicine in the trauma operating room: trauma surgeons are able to observe and consult on cases from a remote location using video conferencing. This capability allows the attending to view the residents in real time. The remote surgeon has the capability to control the camera (pan, tilt and zoom) to get the best angle of the procedure while at the same time providing expertise in order to provide the best possible care to the patient.

Telecardiology

ECGs, or electrocardiographs, can be transmitted using telephone and wireless. Willem Einthoven, the inventor of the ECG, actually did tests with transmission of ECG via telephone lines. This was because the hospital did not allow him to move patients outside the hospital to his laboratory for testing of his new device. In 1906 Einthoven came up with a way to transmit the data from the hospital directly to his lab.

One of the oldest known telecardiology systems for teletransmissions of ECGs was established in Gwalior, India in 1975 at GR Medical college by Ajai Shanker, S. Makhija, P.K. Mantri using an indigenous technique for the first time in India.

This system enabled wireless transmission of ECG from the moving ICU van or the patients home to the central station in ICU of the department of Medicine. Transmission using wireless was done using frequency modulation which eliminated noise. Transmission was also done through telephone lines. The ECG output was connected to the telephone input using a modulator which converted ECG into high frequency sound. At the other end a demodulator reconverted the sound into ECG with a good gain accuracy. The ECG was converted to sound waves with a frequency varying from 500 Hz to 2500 Hz with 1500 Hz at baseline.

This system was also used to monitor patients with pacemakers in remote areas. The central control unit at the ICU was able to correctly interpret arrhythmia. This technique helped medical aid reach in remote areas.

In addition, electronic stethoscopes can be used as recording devices, which is helpful for purposes of telecardiology. There are many examples of successful telecardiology services worldwide.

In Pakistan three pilot projects in telemedicine were initiated by the Ministry of IT & Telecom, Government of Pakistan (MoIT) through the Electronic Government Directorate in collaboration with Oratier Technologies (a pioneer company within Pakistan dealing with healthcare and HMIS) and PakDataCom (a bandwidth provider). Three hub stations through were linked via the Pak Sat-I communications satellite, and four districts were linked with another hub. A 312 Kb link was also established with remote sites and 1 Mbit/s bandwidth was provided at each hub. Three hubs were established: the Mayo Hospital (the largest hospital in Asia), JPMC Karachi and Holy Family Rawalpindi. These 12 remote sites were connected and on average of 1,500 patients were treated per month per hub. The project was still running smoothly after two years. Wireless ambulatory ECG technology, moving beyond previous ambulatory ECG technology such as the Holter monitor, now includes smartphones and Apple Watches which can perform at-home cardiac monitoring and send the data to a physician via the internet.

Teleradiology

Teleradiology is the ability to send radiographic images (x-rays, CT, MR, PET/CT, SPECT/CT, MG, US...) from one location to another. For this process to be implemented, three essential components are required, an image sending station, a transmission network, and a receiving-image review station. The most typical implementation are two computers connected via the Internet. The computer at the receiving end will need to have a high-quality display screen that has been tested and cleared for clinical purposes. Sometimes the receiving computer will have a printer so that images can be printed for convenience.

The teleradiology process begins at the image sending station. The radiographic image and a modem or other connection are required for this first step. The image is scanned and then sent via the network connection to the receiving computer.

Today's high-speed broadband based Internet enables the use of new technologies for teleradiology: the image reviewer can now have access to distant servers in order to view an exam. Therefore, they do not need particular workstations to view the images; a standard personal computer (PC) and digital subscriber line (DSL) connection is enough to reach Keosys' central server. No particular software is necessary on the PC and the images can be reached from anywhere in the world. Teleradiology is the most popular use for telemedicine and accounts for at least 50% of all telemedicine usage.

Telepathology

Telepathology is the practice of pathology at a distance. It uses telecommunications technology to facilitate the transfer of image-rich pathology data between distant locations for the purposes of diagnosis, education, and research. Performance of telepathology requires that a pathologist selects the video images for analysis and the rendering diagnoses. The use of "television microscopy", the forerunner of telepathology, did not require that a pathologist have physical or virtual "hands-on" involvement is the selection of microscopic fields-of-view for analysis and diagnosis.

A pathologist, Ronald S. Weinstein, M.D., coined the term "telepathology" in 1986. In an editorial in a medical journal, Weinstein outlined the actions that would be needed to create remote pathology diagnostic services. He, and his collaborators, published the first scientific paper on robotic telepathology. Weinstein was also granted the first U.S. patents for robotic telepathology systems and telepathology diagnostic networks. Weinstein is known to many as the "father of telepathology". In Norway, Eide and Nordrum implemented the first sustainable clinical telepathology service in 1989. This is still in operation, decades later. A number of clinical telepathology services have benefited many thousands of patients in North America, Europe, and Asia.

Telepathology has been successfully used for many applications including the rendering histopathology tissue diagnoses, at a distance, for education, and for research. Although digital pathology imaging, including virtual microscopy, is the mode of choice for telepathology services in developed countries, analog telepathology imaging is still used for patient services in some developing countries.

Teledermatology

Teledermatology allows dermatology consultations over a distance using audio, visual and data communication, and has been found to improve efficiency, access to specialty care, and patient satisfaction. Applications comprise health care management such as diagnoses, consultation and treatment as well as (continuing medical) education. The dermatologists Perednia and Brown were the first to coin the term *teledermatology* in 1995, where they described the value of a teledermatologic service in a rural area underserved by dermatologists.

Teleophthalmology

Teleophthalmology is a branch of telemedicine that delivers eye care through digital medical equipment and telecommunications technology. Today, applications of teleophthalmology encompass access to eye specialists for patients in remote areas, ophthalmic disease screening, diagnosis and monitoring; as well as distant learning. Teleophthalmology may help reduce disparities by providing remote, low-cost screening tests such as diabetic retinopathy screening to low-income and uninsured patients. In Mizoram, India, a hilly area with poor roads, between 2011 and 2015, teleophthalmology provided care to over 10,000 patients. These patients were examined by ophthalmic assistants locally but surgery was done on appointment after the patient images were viewed online by eye surgeons in the hospital 6–12 hours away. Instead of an average five trips for say, a cataract procedure, only one was required for surgery alone as even post-op care like removal of stitches and appointments for glasses was done locally. There were large cost savings in travel as well.

In the United States, some companies allow patients to complete an online visual exam and within 24 hours receive a prescription from an optometrist valid for eyeglasses, contact lenses, or both. Some US states such as Indiana have attempted to ban these companies from doing business.

Telesurgery

Remote surgery (also known as telesurgery) is the ability for a doctor to perform surgery on a patient even though they are not physically in the same location. It is a form of telepresence. Remote surgery combines elements of robotics, cutting-edge telecommunications such as high-speed data connections, telehaptics and elements of management information systems. While the field of robotic surgery is fairly well established, most of these robots are controlled by surgeons at the location of the surgery.

Remote surgery is remote work for surgeons, where the physical distance between the surgeon and the patient is immaterial. It promises to allow the expertise of specialized surgeons to be available to patients worldwide, without the need for patients to travel beyond their local hospital.

Remote surgery or telesurgery is performance of surgical procedures where the surgeon is not physically in the same location as the patient, using a robotic teleoperator system controlled by the surgeon. The remote operator may give tactile feedback to the user. Remote surgery combines elements of robotics and high-speed data connections. A critical limiting factor is the speed, latency and reliability of the communication system between the surgeon and the patient, though trans-Atlantic surgeries have been demonstrated.

Teleabortion

Telemedicine has been used globally to increase access to abortion care, specifically medical abortion, in environments where few abortion care providers exist or abortion is legally restricted. Clinicians are able to virtually provide counseling, review screening tests, observe the administration of an abortion medication, and directly mail abortion pills to people. In 2004, Women on Web (WoW), Amsterdam, started offering online consultations, mostly to people living in areas where abortion was legally restricted, informing them how to safely use medical abortion drugs to end a pregnancy. People contact the Women on Web service online; physicians review any necessary lab results or ultrasounds, mail mifepristone and misoprostol pills to people, then follow up through online communication. In the United States, medical abortion was introduced as a telehealth service in Iowa by Planned Parenthood of the Heartland in 2008 to allow a patient at one health facility to communicate via secure video with a health provider at another facility. In this model a person seeking abortion care must come to a health facility. An abortion care provider communicates with the person located at another site using clinic-to-clinic videoconferencing to provide medical abortion after screening tests and consultation with clinic staff. In 2018, the website Aid Access was launched by the founder of Women on Web, Rebecca Gomperts. It offers a similar service as Women on Web in the United States, but the medications are prescribed to an Indian pharmacy, then mailed to the United States.

The TelAbortion study conducted by Gynuity Health Projects, with special approval from the U.S. Food and Drug Administration (FDA), aims to increase access to medical abortion care without requiring an in-person visit to a clinic. This models was expanded during the COVID-19 pandemic and as of March 2020 exists in 13 U.S.

states and has enrolled over 730 people in the study. The person receives counseling and instruction from an abortion care provider via videoconference from a location of their choice. The medications necessary for the abortion, mifepristone and misoprostol, are mailed directly to the person and they have a follow-up video consultation in 7–14 days. A systematic review of telemedicine abortion has found the practice to be safe, effective, efficient, and satisfactory.

In the United States, eighteen states require the clinician to be physically present during the administration of medications for abortion which effectively bans telehealth of medication abortion: five states explicitly ban telemedicine for medication abortion, while thirteen states require the prescriber (usually required to be a physician) to be physically present with the patient. In the UK, the Royal College of Obstetricians and Gynecologists approved a no-test protocol for medication abortion, with mifepristone available through a minimal-contact pick-up or by mail.

Other Specialist Care Delivery

Telemedicine can facilitate specialty care delivered by primary care physicians according to a controlled study of the treatment of hepatitis C. Various specialties are contributing to telemedicine, in varying degrees.Other specialist conditions for which telemedicine has been used include perinatal mental health.

In light of the COVID-19 pandemic, primary care physicians have relied on telehealth to continue to provide care in outpatient settings. The transition to virtual health has been beneficial in providing patients access to care (especially care that does not require a physical exam e.g., medication changes, minor health updates) and avoid putting patients at risk of COVID-19. This included providing services to pediatric patients during the pandemic, where issues of last minute cancelation and rescheduling were frequently related to a lack of technicality and engagement, two factors often understudied in the literature.

Telemedicine has also been beneficial in facilitating medical education to students while still allowing for adequate social distancing during the COVID-19 pandemic. Many medical schools have shifted to alternate forms of virtual curriculum and are still able to engage in meaningful telehealth encounters with patients.

Medication assisted treatment (MAT) is the treatment of opioid use disorder (OUD) with medications, often in combination with behavioral therapy As a response to the COVID-19 pandemic the use of telemedicine has been granted by the Drug Enforcement Administration to start or maintain people OUD on buprenorphine (trade name Suboxone) via telemedicine without the need for an initial in-person examination. On March 31, 2020, QuickMD became the first national TeleMAT service in the United States to provide Medication-assisted Treatment with

Suboxone online – without the need of an in-person visit; with others announcing to follow soon.

Health Promotion

Telehealth can also increase health promotion efforts. These efforts can now be more personalised to the target population and professionals can extend their help into homes or private and safe environments in which patients of individuals can practice, ask and gain health information. Health promotion using telehealth has become increasingly popular in underdeveloped countries where there are very poor physical resources available. There has been a particular push toward mHealth applications as many areas, even underdeveloped ones have mobile phone and smartphone coverage.

In a 2015 article reviewing research on the use of a mobile health application in the United Kingdom, authors describe how a home-based application helped patients manage and monitor their health and symptoms independently. The mobile health application allows people to rapidly self-report their symptoms – 95% of patients were able to report their daily symptoms in less than 100 seconds, which is less than the 5 minutes (plus commuting) taken to measure vital signs by nurses in hospitals. Online applications allow patients to remain at home to keep track of the progression of their chronic illnesses. The downside of using mHealth applications is that not everyone, especially in developing countries, has daily access to internet or electronic devices.

In developed countries, health promotion efforts using telehealth have been met with some success. The Australian hands-free breastfeeding Google Glass application reported promising results in 2014. This application made in collaboration with the Australian Breastfeeding Association and a tech startup called Small World Social, helped new mothers learn how to breastfeed. Breastfeeding is beneficial to infant health and maternal health and is recommended by the World Health Organisation and health organisations all over the world. Widespread breastfeeding can prevent 820,000 infant deaths globally but the practice is often stopped prematurely or intents to do are disrupted due to lack of social support, know-how or other factors. This application gave mother's hands-free information on breastfeeding, instructions on how to breastfeed and also had an option to call a lactation consultant over Google Hangout. When the trial ended, all participants were reported to be confident in breastfeeding.

Health Care Quality and Barriers to Adoption

A scientific review indicates that, in general, outcomes of telemedicine are or can be as good as in-person care with health care use staying similar. Advantages of the nonexclusive adoption of already existing telemedicine technologies such as smartphone videotelephony may include reduced infection risks, increased control of disease during epidemic conditions, improved access to care, reduced stress and exposure to other pathogens during illness for better recovery, reduced time and labor costs, efficient more accessible matching of patients with particular symptoms and clinicians who are experts for such, and reduced travel while disadvantages may include privacy breaches (e.g., due to software backdoors and vulnerabilities or sale of data), dependability on Internet access and, depending on various factors, increased health care use.

Theoretically, the whole health system could benefit from telehealth. There are indications telehealth consumes fewer resources and requires fewer people to operate it with shorter training periods to implement initiatives. Commenters suggested that lawmakers may fear that making telehealth widely accessible, without any other measures, would lead to patients using unnecessary health care services. Telemedicine could also be used for connected networks between health care professionals.

Telemedicine also can eliminate the possible transmission of infectious diseases or parasites between patients and medical staff. This is particularly an issue where MRSA is a concern. Additionally, some patients who feel uncomfortable in a doctors office may do better remotely. For example, white coat syndrome may be avoided. Patients who are home-bound and would otherwise require an ambulance to move them to a clinic are also a consideration.

However, whether or not the standard of health care quality is increasing is debatable, with some literature refuting such claims. Research has reported that clinicians find the process difficult and complex to deal with. Furthermore, there are concerns around informed consent, legality issues as well as legislative issues. A recent study also highlighted that the swift and large-scale implementation of telehealth across the United Kingdom NHS Allied Health Professional (AHP) services might increase disparities in health care access for vulnerable populations with limited digital literacy. Although health care may become affordable with the help of technology, whether or not this care will be "good" is the issue. Many studies indicate high satisfaction with telemedicine among patients. Among the factors associated with a good trust in telemedicine, the use of known and user-friendly video services and confidence in the data protection policies were the two variables contributing most to trust in telemedicine.

Major problems with increasing adoption include technically challenged staff, resistance to change or habits and age of patient. Focused policy could eliminate several barriers.

A review lists a number of potentially good practices and pitfalls, recommending the use of "virtual handshakes" for confirming identity, taking consent for conducting remote consultation over a conventional meeting, and professional standardized norms for protecting patient privacy and confidentiality. It also found that the COVID-19 pandemic substantially increased, voluntarily, the adoption of telephone or video consultation and suggests that telemedicine technology "is a key factor in delivery of health care in the future".

Economic Evaluations

Due to its digital nature it is often assumed that telehealth saves the health system money. However, the evidence to support this is varied. When conducting economic evaluations of telehealth services, the individuals evaluating them need to be aware of potential outcomes and extraclinical benefits of the telehealth service. Economic viability relies on the funding model within the country being examined (public vs private), the consumers willingness-to-pay, and the expected remuneration by the clinicians or commercial entities providing the services (examples of research on these topics from teledermoscopy in Australia)

In a UK telehealth trial done in 2011, it was reported that the cost of health could be dramatically reduced with the use of telehealth monitoring. The usual cost of in vitro fertilisation (IVF) per cycle would be around $15,000; with telehealth it was reduced to $800 per patient. In Alaska the Federal Health Care Access Network, which connects 3,000 healthcare providers to communities, engaged in 160,000 telehealth consultations from 2001 and saved the state $8.5 million in travel costs for just Medicaid patients.

Digital interventions for mental health conditions seem to be cost-effective compared to no intervention or non-therapeutic responses such as monitoring. However, when compared to in-person therapy or medication their added value is currently uncertain.

Virtual Consultations

Online consultations or e-consultations refer to an exchange between government and citizens using the Internet. They are one form of online deliberation. Further, online consultation consists in using the Internet to ask a group of people their opinion on one or more specific topics, allowing for trade-offs between participants. Generally, an agency consults a group of people to get their thoughts on an issue when a project or a policy is being developed or implemented, e.g., to identify or access options, or to evaluate ongoing activities. This enables governments to draft more citizen-centered policy.

As the Internet gains popularity with the public for voicing opinion, citizen participation in policy development through cyberspace is changing the face of democracy. The rise of the Internet has given way to buzzwords such as e-democracy, referring to citizen participation in politics, government issues and policy development through electronic technologies and the Internet, and eGovernment, pertaining to providing citizens with government information and services online. Online consultation is an extension of these concepts. Through online engagement, government is enabled to hold interactive dialogues with the public as they have a more direct route to citizen opinion via the Internet.

The California Report Card (CRC) facilitates online consultation, working to support collaboration between citizens and the government though the Internet. Gavin Newsom, Lt. Governor of California, and the Center for Information Technology Research in the Interest of Society at University of California, Berkeley jointly launched the CRC in January 2014. The CRC allows for Californians to vote online on six timely issues. The site then redirects users to an electronic "cafe" using Principal Component Analysis. In the "cafe", participants can textually submit their own suggestions and assess the ideas of other users. The CRC offers a means of connecting the public to the California government.

While this definition is framed in the Canadian context, other countries like the UK, Denmark, Scotland, and Australia can also be considered leaders in the field. These and many other countries are integrating online consultations and engagement using various methods and for a range of purposes. The European Union also utilises online consultations. These complement face-to-face consultations and help to create greater transparency of the democratic process. Online consultations are also increasingly being used by the United Nations and its Specialized Agencies. The Food and Agriculture Organization of the UN hosts online consultations to allow for more inclusive drafting processes of policy guidelines, reports and strategy papers. The Global Forum on Food Security and Nutrition (FSN Forum) is tasked with carrying out many of these consultations.

Channels

Online consultations and engagement activities can utilize:

- Websites, discussion boards, and electronic mailing lists, which have the ability to aid in policy development by providing the public with pertinent information and engaging them in order to extract feedback on issues.
- Weblogs and real time online chat that can often put the public in direct contact with government officials, such as their MP, deputy or other political figure with whom they can share opinion and concerns

Medical Imaging

Medical imaging is the technique and process of imaging the interior of a body for clinical analysis and medical intervention, as well as visual representation of the function of some organs or tissues (physiology). Medical imaging seeks to reveal internal structures hidden by the skin and bones, as well as to diagnose and treat disease. Medical imaging also establishes a database of normal anatomy and physiology to make it possible to identify abnormalities. Although imaging of removed organs and tissues can be performed for medical reasons, such procedures are usually considered part of pathology instead of medical imaging.

Measurement and recording techniques that are not primarily designed to produce images, such as electroencephalography (EEG), magnetoencephalography (MEG), electrocardiography (ECG), and others, represent other technologies that produce data susceptible to representation as a parameter graph versus time or maps that contain data about the measurement locations. In a limited comparison, these technologies can be considered forms of medical imaging in another discipline of medical instrumentation.

As of 2010, 5 billion medical imaging studies had been conducted worldwide. Radiation exposure from medical imaging in 2006 made up about 50% of total ionizing radiation exposure in the United States. Medical imaging equipment is manufactured using technology from the semiconductor industry, including CMOS integrated circuit chips, power semiconductor devices, sensors such as image sensors (particularly CMOS sensors) and biosensors, and processors such as microcontrollers, microprocessors, digital signal processors, media processors and system-on-chip devices. As of 2015, annual shipments of medical imaging chips amount to 46 million units and $1.1 billion. The term "noninvasive" is used to denote a procedure where no instrument is introduced into a patient's body, which is the case for most imaging techniques used.

Types

In the clinical context, "invisible light" medical imaging is generally equated to radiology or "clinical imaging". "Visible light" medical imaging involves digital video or still pictures that can be seen without special equipment. Dermatology and wound care are two modalities that use visible light imagery. Interpretation of medical images is generally undertaken by a physician specialising in radiology known as a *radiologist*; however, this may be undertaken by any healthcare professional who is trained and certified in radiological clinical evaluation. Increasingly interpretation is being undertaken by non-physicians, for example radiographers frequently train in interpretation as part of expanded practice. Diagnostic radiography designates the technical aspects of medical imaging and in particular the acquisition of medical images. The radiographer (also known as a radiologic technologist) is usually responsible for acquiring medical images of diagnostic quality; although other professionals may train in this area, notably some radiological interventions performed by radiologists are done so without a radiographer.

As a field of scientific investigation, medical imaging constitutes a sub-discipline of biomedical engineering, medical physics or medicine depending on the context: Research and development in the area of instrumentation, image acquisition (e.g., radiography), modeling and quantification are usually the preserve of biomedical engineering, medical physics, and computer science; Research into the application and interpretation of medical images is usually the preserve of radiology and the medical sub-discipline relevant to medical condition or area of medical science (neuroscience, cardiology, psychiatry, psychology, etc.) under investigation. Many of the techniques developed for medical imaging also have scientific and industrial applications.

Radiography

Two forms of radiographic images are in use in medical imaging. Projection radiography and fluoroscopy, with the latter being useful for catheter guidance. These 2D techniques are still in wide use despite the advance of 3D tomography due to the low cost, high resolution, and depending on the application, lower radiation dosages with 2D technique. This imaging modality uses a wide beam of X-rays for image acquisition and is the first imaging technique available in modern medicine.

- **Fluoroscopy:** Produces real-time images of internal structures of the body in a similar fashion to radiography, but employs a constant input of X-rays, at a lower dose rate. Contrast media, such as barium, iodine, and air are used to visualize internal organs as they work. Fluoroscopy is also used in image-guided procedures when constant feedback during a procedure is required. An image receptor is required to convert the radiation into an image after it has passed through the area of interest. Early on, this was a fluorescing screen, which gave way to an Image Amplifier (IA) which was a large vacuum tube that had the receiving end coated with cesium iodide, and a mirror at the opposite end. Eventually the mirror was replaced with a TV camera.
- **Projectional Radiographs:** More commonly known as X-rays, are often used to determine the type and extent of a fracture as well as for detecting pathological changes in the lungs. With the use of radio-opaque contrast media, such as barium, they can also be used to visualize the structure of the stomach and intestines – this can help diagnose ulcers or certain types of colon cancer.

Magnetic Resonance Imaging

A magnetic resonance imaging instrument (MRI scanner), or "nuclear magnetic resonance (NMR) imaging" scanner as it was originally known, uses powerful magnets to polarize and excite hydrogen nuclei (i.e., single protons) of water molecules in human tissue, producing a detectable signal which is spatially encoded, resulting in images of the body. The MRI machine emits a radio frequency (RF) pulse at the resonant frequency of the hydrogen atoms on water molecules. Radio frequency antennas ("RF coils") send the pulse to the area of the body to be examined. The RF pulse is absorbed by protons, causing their direction with respect to the primary magnetic field to change. When the RF pulse is turned off, the protons "relax" back to alignment with the primary magnet and emit radio-waves in the process. This radio-frequency emission from the hydrogen-atoms on water is what is detected and reconstructed into an image. The resonant frequency of a spinning magnetic dipole (of which protons are one example) is called the Larmor frequency and is determined by the strength of the main magnetic field and the chemical environment of the nuclei of interest. MRI uses three electromagnetic fields: a very strong (typically 1.5 to 3 teslas) static magnetic field to polarize the hydrogen nuclei, called the primary field; gradient fields that can be modified to vary in space and time (on the order of 1 kHz) for spatial encoding, often simply called gradients; and a spatially homogeneous radio-frequency (RF) field for manipulation of the hydrogen nuclei to produce measurable signals, collected through an RF antenna.

Like CT, MRI traditionally creates a two-dimensional image of a thin "slice" of the body and is therefore considered a tomographic imaging technique. Modern MRI instruments are capable of producing images in the form of 3D blocks, which may be considered a generalization of the single-slice, tomographic, concept. Unlike CT, MRI does not involve the use of ionizing radiation and is therefore not associated with the same health hazards. For example, because MRI has only been in use since the early 1980s, there are no known long-term effects of exposure to strong static fields and therefore there is no limit to the number of scans to which an individual can be subjected, in contrast with X-ray and CT. However, there are well-identified health risks associated with tissue heating from exposure to the RF field and the presence of implanted devices in the body, such as pacemakers. These risks are strictly controlled as part of the design of the instrument and the scanning protocols used.

Because CT and MRI are sensitive to different tissue properties, the appearances of the images obtained with the two techniques differ markedly. In CT, X-rays must be blocked by some form of dense tissue to create an image, so the image quality when looking at soft tissues will be poor. In MRI, while any nucleus with a net nuclear spin can be used, the proton of the hydrogen atom remains the most widely used, especially in the clinical setting, because it is so ubiquitous and returns a large signal. This nucleus, present in water molecules, allows the excellent soft-tissue contrast achievable with MRI.

A number of different pulse sequences can be used for specific MRI diagnostic imaging (multiparametric MRI or mpMRI). It is possible to differentiate tissue characteristics by combining two or more of the following imaging sequences, depending on the information being sought: T1-weighted (T1-MRI), T2-weighted (T2-MRI), diffusion weighted imaging (DWI-MRI), dynamic contrast enhancement (DCE-MRI), and spectroscopy (MRI-S). For example, imaging of prostate tumors is better accomplished using T2-MRI and DWI-MRI than T2-weighted imaging alone. The number of applications of mpMRI for detecting disease in various organs continues to expand, including liver studies, breast tumors, pancreatic tumors, and assessing the effects of vascular disruption agents on cancer tumors.

Nuclear Medicine

Nuclear medicine encompasses both diagnostic imaging and treatment of disease, and may also be referred to as molecular medicine or molecular imaging and therapeutics. Nuclear medicine uses certain properties of isotopes and the energetic particles emitted from radioactive material to diagnose or treat various pathology. Different from the typical concept of anatomic radiology, nuclear medicine enables assessment of physiology. This function-based approach to medical evaluation has useful applications in most subspecialties, notably oncology, neurology, and cardiology. *Gamma cameras* and *PET scanners* are used in e.g., scintigraphy, SPECT and PET to detect regions of biologic activity that may be associated with a disease. Relatively short-lived isotope, such as Tc is administered to the patient. Isotopes are often preferentially absorbed by biologically active tissue in the body, and can be used to identify tumors or fracture points in bone. Images are acquired after collimated photons are detected by a crystal that gives off a light signal, which is in turn amplified and converted into count data.

- **Scintigraphy:** Scintigraphy (“scint”) is a form of diagnostic test wherein radioisotopes are taken internally, for example, intravenously or orally. Then, gamma cameras capture and form two-dimensional images from the radiation emitted by the radiopharmaceuticals.
- **SPECT:** SPECT is a 3D tomographic technique that uses gamma camera data from many projections and can be reconstructed in different planes. A dual detector head gamma camera combined with a CT scanner, which provides localization of functional SPECT data, is termed a SPECT-CT camera, and has shown utility in advancing the field of molecular imaging. In most other medical imaging modalities, energy is passed through the body and the reaction or result is read by detectors. In SPECT imaging, the patient is injected with a radioisotope, most commonly Thallium 201TI, Technetium 99mTC, Iodine 123I, and Gallium 67Ga. The radioactive gamma rays are emitted through the

body as the natural decaying process of these isotopes takes place. The emissions of the gamma rays are captured by detectors that surround the body. This essentially means that the human is now the source of the radioactivity, rather than the medical imaging devices such as X-ray or CT.

- **Positron Emission Tomography (PET):** Uses coincidence detection to image functional processes. Short-lived positron emitting isotope, such as F, is incorporated with an organic substance such as glucose, creating F18-fluorodeoxyglucose, which can be used as a marker of metabolic utilization. Images of activity distribution throughout the body can show rapidly growing tissue, like tumor, metastasis, or infection. PET images can be viewed in comparison to computed tomography scans to determine an anatomic correlate. Modern scanners may integrate PET, allowing PET-CT, or PET-MRI to optimize the image reconstruction involved with positron imaging. This is performed on the same equipment without physically moving the patient off of the gantry. The resultant hybrid of functional and anatomic imaging information is a useful tool in non-invasive diagnosis and patient management.

Fiduciary markers are used in a wide range of medical imaging applications. Images of the same subject produced with two different imaging systems may be correlated (called image registration) by placing a fiduciary marker in the area imaged by both systems. In this case, a marker which is visible in the images produced by both imaging modalities must be used. By this method, functional information from SPECT or positron emission tomography can be related to anatomical information provided by magnetic resonance imaging (MRI). Similarly, fiducial points established during MRI can be correlated with brain images generated by magnetoencephalography to localize the source of brain activity.

Ultrasound

Medical ultrasound uses high frequency broadband sound waves in the megahertz range that are reflected by tissue to varying degrees to produce (up to 3D) images. This is commonly associated with imaging the fetus in pregnant women. Uses of ultrasound are much broader, however. Other important uses include imaging the abdominal organs, heart, breast, muscles, tendons, arteries and veins. While it may provide less anatomical detail than techniques such as CT or MRI, it has several advantages which make it ideal in numerous situations, in particular that it studies the function of moving structures in real-time, emits no ionizing radiation, and contains speckle that can be used in elastography. Ultrasound is also used as a popular research tool for capturing raw data, that can be made available through an ultrasound research interface, for the purpose of tissue characterization and implementation of new image processing techniques. The concepts of ultrasound differ from other medical imaging modalities in the fact that it is operated by the transmission and receipt of sound waves. The high frequency sound waves are sent into the tissue and depending on the composition of the different tissues; the signal will be attenuated and returned at separate intervals. A path of reflected sound waves in a multilayered structure can be defined by an input acoustic impedance (ultrasound sound wave) and the Reflection and transmission coefficients of the relative structures. It is very safe to use and does not appear to cause any adverse effects. It is also relatively inexpensive and quick to perform. Ultrasound scanners can be taken to critically ill patients in intensive care units, avoiding the danger caused while moving the patient to the radiology department. The real-time moving image obtained can be used to guide drainage and biopsy procedures. Doppler capabilities on modern scanners allow the blood flow in arteries and veins to be assessed.

Elastography

Elastography is a relatively new imaging modality that maps the elastic properties of soft tissue. This modality emerged in the last two decades. Elastography is useful in medical diagnoses, as elasticity can discern healthy from unhealthy tissue for specific organs/growths. For example, cancerous tumours will often be harder than the surrounding tissue, and diseased livers are stiffer than healthy ones. There are several elastographic techniques based on the use of ultrasound, magnetic resonance imaging and tactile imaging. The wide clinical use of ultrasound elastography is a result of the implementation of technology in clinical ultrasound machines. Main branches of ultrasound elastography include Quasistatic Elastography/Strain Imaging, Shear Wave Elasticity Imaging (SWEI), Acoustic Radiation Force Impulse imaging (ARFI), Supersonic Shear Imaging (SSI), and Transient Elastography. In the last decade, a steady increase of activities in the field of elastography is observed demonstrating successful application of the technology in various areas of medical diagnostics and treatment monitoring.

Photoacoustic Imaging

Photoacoustic imaging is a recently developed hybrid biomedical imaging modality based on the photoacoustic effect. It combines the advantages of optical absorption contrast with an ultrasonic spatial resolution for deep imaging in (optical) diffusive or quasi-diffusive regime. Recent studies have shown that photoacoustic imaging can be used in vivo for tumor angiogenesis monitoring, blood oxygenation mapping, functional brain imaging, and skin melanoma detection, etc.

Tomography

Tomography is the imaging by sections or sectioning. The main such methods in medical imaging are:

- X-ray computed tomography (CT), or Computed Axial Tomography (CAT) scan, is a helical tomography technique (latest generation), which traditionally produces a 2D image of the structures in a thin section of the body. In CT, a beam of X-rays spins around an object being examined and is picked up by sensitive radiation detectors after having penetrated the object from multiple angles. A computer then analyses the information received from the scanner's detectors and constructs a detailed image of the object and its contents using the mathematical principles laid out in the Radon transform. It has a greater ionizing radiation dose burden than projection radiography; repeated scans must be limited to avoid health effects. CT is based on the same principles as X-ray projections but in this case, the patient is enclosed in a surrounding ring of detectors assigned with 500–1000 scintillation detectors (fourth-generation X-ray CT scanner geometry). Previously in older generation scanners, the X-ray beam was paired by a translating source and detector. Computed tomography has almost completely replaced focal plane tomography in X-ray tomography imaging.
- Positron emission tomography (PET) also used in conjunction with computed tomography, PET-CT, and magnetic resonance imaging PET-MRI.
- Magnetic resonance imaging (MRI) commonly produces tomographic images of cross-sections of the body.

Echocardiography

When ultrasound is used to image the heart it is referred to as an echocardiogram. Echocardiography allows detailed structures of the heart, including chamber size, heart function, the valves of the heart, as well as the pericardium (the sac around the heart) to be seen. Echocardiography uses 2D, 3D, and Doppler imaging to create pictures of the heart and visualize the blood flowing through each of the four heart valves.

Echocardiography is widely used in an array of patients ranging from those experiencing symptoms, such as shortness of breath or chest pain, to those undergoing cancer treatments. Transthoracic ultrasound has been proven to be safe for patients of all ages, from infants to the elderly, without risk of harmful side effects or radiation, differentiating it from other imaging modalities. Echocardiography is one of the most commonly used imaging modalities in the world due to its portability and use in a variety of applications. In emergency situations, echocardiography is quick, easily accessible, and able to be performed at the bedside, making it the modality of choice for many physicians.

Functional Near-Infrared Spectroscopy

FNIR Is a relatively new non-invasive imaging technique. NIRS (near infrared spectroscopy) is used for the purpose of functional neuroimaging and has been widely accepted as a brain imaging technique.

Magnetic Particle Imaging

Using superparamagnetic iron oxide nanoparticles, magnetic particle imaging (MPI) is a developing diagnostic imaging technique used for tracking superparamagnetic iron oxide nanoparticles. The primary advantage is the high sensitivity and specificity, along with the lack of signal decrease with tissue depth. MPI has been used in medical research to image cardiovascular performance, neuroperfusion, and cell tracking.

In Pregnancy

Medical imaging may be indicated in pregnancy because of pregnancy complications, a pre-existing disease or an acquired disease in pregnancy, or routine prenatal care. Magnetic resonance imaging (MRI) without MRI contrast agents as well as obstetric ultrasonography are not associated with any risk for the mother or the fetus, and are the imaging techniques of choice for pregnant women. Projectional radiography, CT scan and nuclear medicine imaging result some degree of ionizing radiation exposure, but have with a few exceptions much lower absorbed doses than what are associated with fetal harm. At higher dosages, effects can include miscarriage, birth defects and intellectual disability.

Maximizing Imaging Procedure Use

The amount of data obtained in a single MR or CT scan is very extensive. Some of the data that radiologists discard could save patients time and money, while reducing their exposure to radiation and risk of complications from invasive procedures. Another approach for making the procedures more efficient is based on utilizing additional constraints, e.g., in some medical imaging modalities one can improve the efficiency of the data acquisition by taking into account the fact the reconstructed density is positive.

Creation of Three-Dimensional Images

Volume rendering techniques have been developed to enable CT, MRI and ultrasound scanning software to produce 3D images for the physician. Traditionally CT and MRI scans produced 2D static output on film. To produce 3D images, many scans are made and then combined by computers to produce a 3D model, which can then be manipulated by the physician. 3D ultrasounds are produced using a somewhat similar technique. In diagnosing disease of the viscera of the abdomen, ultrasound is particularly sensitive on imaging of biliary tract, urinary tract and female reproductive organs (ovary, fallopian tubes). As for example, diagnosis of gallstone by dilatation of common bile duct and stone in the common bile duct. With the ability to visualize important structures in great detail, 3D visualization methods are a valuable resource for the diagnosis and surgical treatment of many pathologies. It was a key resource for the famous, but ultimately unsuccessful attempt by Singaporean surgeons to separate Iranian twins Ladan and Laleh Bijani in 2003. The 3D equipment was used previously for similar operations with great success.

Other proposed or developed techniques include:

- Diffuse optical tomography.
- Elastography.
- Electrical impedance tomography.
- Optoacoustic imaging.
- Ophthalmology:
  - A-scan.
  - B-scan.
  - Corneal topography.
  - Optical coherence tomography.
  - Scanning laser ophthalmoscopy.
  - Some of these techniques are still at a research stage and not yet used in clinical routines.

Non-Diagnostic Imaging

Neuroimaging has also been used in experimental circumstances to allow people (especially disabled persons) to control outside devices, acting as a brain computer interface. Many medical imaging software applications are used for non-diagnostic imaging, specifically because they do not have an FDA approval and not allowed to use in clinical research for patient diagnosis. Note that many clinical research studies are not designed for patient diagnosis anyway.

Archiving and Recording

Used primarily in ultrasound imaging, capturing the image produced by a medical imaging device is required for archiving and telemedicine applications. In most scenarios, a frame grabber is used in order to capture the video signal from the medical device and relay it to a computer for further processing and operations.

- **DICOM:** The Digital Imaging and Communication in Medicine (DICOM) Standard is used globally to store, exchange, and transmit medical images. The DICOM Standard incorporates protocols for imaging techniques such as radiography, computed tomography (CT), magnetic resonance imaging (MRI), ultrasound, and radiation therapy.

- **Compression of Medical Images:** Medical imaging techniques produce very large amounts of data, especially from CT, MRI and PET modalities. As a result, storage and communications of electronic image data are prohibitive without the use of compression. JPEG 2000 image compression is used by the DICOM standard for storage and transmission of medical images. The cost and feasibility of accessing large image data sets over low or various bandwidths are further addressed by use of another DICOM standard, called JPIP, to enable efficient streaming of the JPEG 2000 compressed image data.
- **Medical Imaging in the Cloud:** There has been growing trend to migrate from on-premise PACS to a cloud-based PACS. A recent article by Applied Radiology said, "As the digital-imaging realm is embraced across the healthcare enterprise, the swift transition from terabytes to petabytes of data has put radiology on the brink of information overload. Cloud computing offers the imaging department of the future the tools to manage data much more intelligently."

Use in Pharmaceutical Clinical Trials

Medical imaging has become a major tool in clinical trials since it enables rapid diagnosis with visualization and quantitative assessment. A typical clinical trial goes through multiple phases and can take up to eight years. Clinical endpoints or outcomes are used to determine whether the therapy is safe and effective. Once a patient reaches the endpoint, he or she is generally excluded from further experimental interaction. Trials that rely solely on clinical endpoints are very costly as they have long durations and tend to need large numbers of patients.

In contrast to clinical endpoints, surrogate endpoints have been shown to cut down the time required to confirm whether a drug has clinical benefits. Imaging biomarkers (a characteristic that is objectively measured by an imaging technique, which is used as an indicator of pharmacological response to a therapy) and surrogate endpoints have shown to facilitate the use of small group sizes, obtaining quick results with good statistical power.

Imaging is able to reveal subtle change that is indicative of the progression of therapy that may be missed out by more subjective, traditional approaches. Statistical bias is reduced as the findings are evaluated without any direct patient contact.

Imaging techniques such as positron emission tomography (PET) and magnetic resonance imaging (MRI) are routinely used in oncology and neuroscience areas. For example, measurement of tumour shrinkage is a commonly used surrogate endpoint in solid tumour response evaluation. This allows for faster and more objective assessment of the effects of anticancer drugs. In Alzheimer's disease, MRI scans of the entire brain can accurately assess the rate of hippocampal atrophy, while PET scans can measure the brain's metabolic activity by measuring regional glucose metabolism, and beta-amyloid plaques using tracers such as Pittsburgh compound B (PiB).

Historically less use has been made of quantitative medical imaging in other areas of drug development although interest is growing.

An imaging-based trial will usually be made up of three components:

- **A Realistic Imaging Protocol:** The protocol is an outline that standardizes (as far as practically possible) the way in which the images are acquired using the various modalities (PET, SPECT, CT, MRI). It covers the specifics in which images are to be stored, processed and evaluated.
- An imaging centre that is responsible for collecting the images, perform quality control and provide tools for data storage, distribution and analysis. It is important for images acquired at different time points are displayed in a standardised format to maintain the reliability of the evaluation. Certain specialised imaging contract research organizations provide end to end medical imaging services, from protocol design and site management through to data quality assurance and image analysis.
- Clinical sites that recruit patients to generate the images to send back to the imaging centre.

Risks and Safety Issues

Medical imaging can lead to patient and healthcare provider harm through exposure to ionizing radiation, iodinated contrast, magnetic fields Safety of magnetic resonance imaging, and other hazards. Lead is the main material used for radiographic shielding against scattered X-rays. In magnetic resonance imaging, there is MRI RF shielding as well as magnetic shielding to prevent external disturbance of image quality.

Privacy Protection

Medical imaging are generally covered by laws of medical privacy. For example, in the United States the Health Insurance Portability and Accountability Act (HIPAA) sets restrictions for health care providers on utilizing protected health information, which is any individually identifiable information relating to the past, present, or future physical or mental health of any individual. While there has not been any definitive legal decision in the matter, at least one study has indicated that medical imaging may contain biometric information that can uniquely identify a person, and so may qualify as PHI. The UK General Medical Council's ethical guidelines indicate that the Council does not require consent prior to secondary uses of X-ray images.

Industry

Organizations in the medical imaging industry include manufacturers of imaging equipment, freestanding radiology facilities, and hospitals. The global market for manufactured devices was estimated at $5 billion in 2018. Notable manufacturers as of 2012 included Fujifilm, GE, Siemens Healthineers, Philips, Shimadzu, Toshiba, Carestream Health, Hitachi, Hologic, and Esaote. In 2016, the manufacturing industry was characterized as oligopolistic and mature; new entrants included in Samsung and Neusoft Medical. In the United States, as estimate as of 2015 places the US market for imaging scans at about $100b, with 60% occurring in hospitals and 40% occurring in freestanding clinics, such as the RadNet chain.

Real-Time Analytics

Real-time data (RTD) is information that is delivered immediately after collection. There is no delay in the timeliness of the information provided. Real-time data is often used for navigation or tracking. Such data is usually processed using real-time computing although it can also be stored for later or off-line data analysis.

Real-time data is not the same as dynamic data. Real-time data can be dynamic (e.g., a variable indicating current location) or static (e.g., a fresh log entry indicating location at a specific time).

Real-time economic data, and other official statistics, are often based on preliminary estimates, and therefore are frequently adjusted as better estimates become available. These later adjusted data are called "revised data". The terms real-time economic data and real-time economic analysis were coined by Francis X. Diebold and Glenn D. Rudebusch. Macroeconomist Glenn D. Rudebusch defined real-time analysis as 'the use of sequential information sets that were actually available as history unfolded.'

Macroeconomist Athanasios Orphanides has argued that economic policy rules may have very different effects when based on error-prone real-time data (as they inevitably are in reality) than they would if policy makers followed the same rules but had more accurate data available.

In order to better understand the accuracy of economic data and its effects on economic decisions, some economic organizations, such as the Federal Reserve Bank of St. Louis, Federal Reserve Bank of Philadelphia and the Euro-Area Business Cycle Network (EABCN), have made databases available that contain both real-time data and subsequent revised estimates of the same data.

Real-timebiddingisprogrammaticreal-timeauctionsthatselldigital-adimpressions. Entities on both the buying and selling sides require almost instantaneous access to data in order to make decisions, forcing real-time data to the forefront of their needs. To support these needs, new strategies and technologies, such Druid have arisen and are quickly evolving.

7.1.3 Benefits of Edge Computing in Healthcare

Edge computing offers several strategic benefits for healthcare providers, patients, and stakeholders.

Reduced Latency and Improved Responsiveness

Minimizes data transmission delays and latency issues by processing critical healthcare data locally at the edge, ensuring real-time responsiveness for telemedicine consultations, remote monitoring, and emergency medical interventions.

Enhanced Data Privacy and Security

Protects patient confidentiality, medical records, and sensitive healthcare information by encrypting data, implementing access controls, and maintaining compliance with healthcare data protection regulations (e.g., HIPAA) in edge computing environments.

Scalability and Cost Efficiency

Optimizes healthcare IT infrastructure costs, bandwidth usage, and operational expenses by distributing computing resources, storage capabilities, and network bandwidth across distributed edge nodes, minimizing data storage requirements and network congestion.

7.1.4 Challenges and Considerations

Despite its benefits, deploying edge computing in healthcare presents challenges and considerations that organizations must address to maximize effectiveness and mitigate risks.

Data Interoperability and Integration

Integrates heterogeneous healthcare IT systems, electronic health records (EHRs), and medical devices with edge computing platforms, ensuring seamless data interoperability, standardized data formats, and secure data exchange protocols.

Regulatory Compliance

Adheres to healthcare regulatory requirements, patient privacy laws (e.g., GDPR, CCPA), and industry standards for data security, confidentiality, and consent management in edge-driven healthcare applications and medical IoT deployments.

Cybersecurity Risks

Mitigates cybersecurity threats, data breaches, and ransomware attacks by implementing robust security controls, encryption standards, and intrusion detection systems (IDS) to protect patient data integrity and healthcare information systems.

7.1.5 Future Trends and Innovations

Emerging trends and innovations in edge computing are shaping the future of healthcare delivery, patient engagement, and medical research.

Edge AI and Machine Learning

Advances in edge AI algorithms, deep learning models, and federated learning techniques enable personalized medicine, disease prediction, and treatment optimization using patient-specific data insights at the point of care.

Blockchain Technology

Integrates blockchain-based solutions for secure medical data sharing, interoperable EHRs, and patient identity management, enhancing transparency, data provenance, and trust in edge computing ecosystems for healthcare providers and patients.

5G Network Integration

Leverages high-speed 5G networks and edge computing capabilities to support bandwidth-intensive healthcare applications, telemedicine services, and remote surgical procedures with ultra-low latency, high reliability, and real-time connectivity.

7.1.6 Ethical and Social Implications

Addressing ethical considerations and societal impacts of edge computing in healthcare involves preserving patient autonomy, informed consent, and equitable access to healthcare services, while safeguarding against biases, discrimination, and algorithmic transparency issues in AI-driven healthcare decision-making.

7.2 EDGE COMPUTING IN SMART CITIES

Edge computing is revolutionizing urban infrastructure and governance by enabling real-time data processing, intelligent decision-making, and enhanced services delivery within smart city environments. This decentralized computing paradigm leverages edge devices, IoT sensors, and localized computing resources to optimize resource management, improve public safety, and enhance urban sustainability.

Edge computing is transforming smart city development and governance by enabling real-time data processing, intelligent decision-making, and enhanced service delivery across urban infrastructures. By leveraging edge computing technologies, municipal authorities can optimize resource management, improve public safety, and promote environmental sustainability while addressing challenges related to infrastructure interoperability, data governance, and regulatory compliance. As cities embrace edge-driven initiatives and deploy innovative applications, prioritizing citizen privacy, community engagement, and ethical considerations fosters trust, resilience, and inclusive growth in the evolving landscape of smart city ecosystems. Edge computing continues to play a pivotal role in shaping the future of urban living by empowering cities, residents, and stakeholders with transformative capabilities for sustainable development, innovation, and quality of life improvements in the digital era.

7.2.1 Applications of Edge Computing in Smart Cities

Traffic Management

Traffic management is a key branch within logistics. It concerns the planning, control and purchasing of transport services needed to physically move vehicles (for example aircraft, road vehicles, rolling stock and watercraft) and freight. Traffic management is implemented by people working with different job titles in different branches:

- **Within Freight and Cargo Logistics:** Traffic manager, assessment of hazardous and awkward materials, carrier choice and fees, demurrage, documentation, expediting, freight consolidation, insurance, reconsignment and tracking.
- **Within Air Traffic Management:** Air traffic controller.
- **Within Rail Traffic Management:** Rail traffic controller, train dispatcher or signalman.
- **Within Road Traffic Management:** Traffic controller.

Traffic Optimization

Traffic optimization is the methods by which time stopped in road traffic (particularly, at traffic signals) is reduced.

Need for Traffic Optimization

Texas Transportation Institute estimates travel delays of between 17–55 hours of delay per person per year relating to congestion on the streets. Traffic device optimization hence becomes a significant aspect of operations.

Techniques

Several techniques exist to reduce the delay of traffic. Generally the algorithms attempt to reduce delays (user time), stops, exhaust gas emissions, or some other measure of effectiveness. Many optimization software are geared towards pre-timed coordinated systems.

Normally optimization of signals along a road is a challenging and expensive task, because the sources for traffic monitoring have been limited to inductive loops, cameras or manually counting. However, due to recent advances in information technology, portable devices with Bluetooth and Wi-Fi communication are becoming more common, enabling real-time continuous traffic monitoring and adjustments to traffic signal timing.

By placing sensors along roads, tracking Bluetooth and Wi-Fi devices in passing vehicles, the solution can accurately detect and record how long it takes a car to drive along a corridor, segment by segment and in total. This provides historical data for traditional timing methods but also enables real-time feedback to changes in signal programs along with the ability to continuously detect traffic levels and travel time to trigger transitions among programs.

Excessive city traffic can be the most frustrating part about living in urban areas. The solution to metro traffic is a well-balanced mixture of expanded public transit options, remote work, differentiated hubs within the metro area, and electronic tolls. Public transit will help commuters arrive safely at their place of work while eliminating the stress of bumper to bumper traffic. Toll roads, especially those with fluctuating tolls dependent upon the time of day and/or level of traffic, also help to improve the level of traffic by deterring some from driving the roadways. Some may choose to work remotely, or run their errands at a different time of day. Finally, differentiated business hubs within a metro area can help alleviate traffic by directing it to several different areas, rather than one centralized location. Cities that spend time and resources on making travel efficient within their borders will attract a healthier, wealthier, and happier population.

Real Time Traffic Control

Several systems are capable of monitoring the traffic arrivals and adjusting timings based on the detected inputs. Traffic Detectors may range from Metal Detectors to Detectors that use Image Detection. Metal detectors are the most popular in use. Image detection devices exhibit numerous problems including degradation during bad weather and lighting.

Traffic actuated signal systems use detectors to adjust timing for:

- **Only the Main Street:** Semi-actuated system
- **Both Main and Cross Streets:** Fully actuated system.

The above method is primitive real-time signal optimization at best. This method will optimize one traffic signal at a time. However, in the real world, a motorist's commute involves driving through multiple signals. Thus, multiple traffic signals need to be collectively synchronized in order to be effective. One such system that has gained significant popularity in the United States is InSync.

Criticism

It has been suggested that the benefits of traffic optimization have never been scientifically justified. It inherently favors motorized traffic over alternate modes such as pedestrians, bicyclists, and transit users and may promote more auto use. It is suggested that an alternate approach could involve traffic calming, and a conceptual focus on the movement of people and goods rather than vehicles. It can be argued that Traffic optimization inherently calms traffic due to discouraging speeding and limits acceleration and deceleration thus reducing the noise pollution produced by vehicles.

Road Traffic Safety

Road traffic safety refers to the methods and measures used to prevent road users from being killed or seriously injured. Typical road users include pedestrians, cyclists, motorists, vehicle passengers, and passengers of on-road public transport (mainly buses and trams).

Best practices in modern road safety strategy:

- The basic strategy of a Safe System approach is to ensure that in the event of a crash, the impact energies remain below the threshold likely to produce either death or serious injury. This threshold will vary from crash scenario to crash scenario, depending upon the level of protection offered to the road users involved. For example, the chances of survival for an unprotected pedestrian hit by a vehicle diminish rapidly at speeds greater than 30 km/h, whereas for a properly restrained motor vehicle occupant the critical impact speed is 50 km/h (for side impact crashes) and 70 km/h (for head-on crashes).—*International Transport Forum, Towards Zero, Ambitious Road Safety Targets and the Safe System Approach, Executive Summary page 19*

As sustainable solutions for classes of road safety have not been identified, particularly low-traffic rural and remote roads, a hierarchy of control should be applied, similar to classifications used to improve occupational safety and health. At the highest level is sustainable prevention of serious injury and death crashes, with sustainable requiring all key result areas to be considered. At the second level is real-time risk reduction, which involves providing users at severe risk with a specific warning to enable them to take mitigating action. The third level is about reducing the crash risk which involves applying the road-design standards and guidelines (such as from AASHTO), improving driver behavior and enforcement.

It is important to note that drivers' traffic behaviors are significantly influenced by their perceptions and attitudes. Traffic safety has been studied as a science for more than 75 years.

Background

Road traffic crashes have become one of the world's largest public-health and injury-prevention problems. The issue is all the more acute because the victims are overwhelmingly healthy before their crashes. According to the World Health Organization (WHO), more than 1 million people are killed on the world's roads each year. A report published by the WHO in 2004 estimated that some 1.2 million people were killed and 50 million injured in traffic collisions on the roads around the world each year and that traffic accidents were the leading cause of death among children 10–19 years of age. The report also noted that the problem was most severe in developing countries and that simple prevention-measures could halve the number of deaths.

The standard measures used in assessing road safety interventions are fatalities and killed-or-seriously-injured (KSI) rates, usually expressed per billion (10) passenger kilometres. Countries using older road-safety paradigms replace KSI rates with crash rates – for example, crashes per million vehicle-miles.

Vehicle speed within the human tolerances for avoiding serious injury and death is a key goal of modern road-design, because impact speed affects the severity of injury both to vehicle occupants and to pedestrians. For occupants, Joksch (1993) found the probability of death for drivers in multi-vehicle collisions increased as the fourth power of impact speed (often referred to by the mathematical term δv ("delta V"), meaning change in velocity). Injuries are caused by sudden, severe acceleration (or deceleration); this is difficult to measure. However, crash reconstruction techniques can estimate vehicle speeds before a crash. Therefore, the change in speed is used as a surrogate for acceleration. This enabled the Swedish Road Administration to identify the KSI risk curves using actual crash-reconstruction data which led to the human tolerances for serious injury and death referenced above.

Interventions are generally much easier to identify in the modern road-safety paradigm, which focusses on the human tolerances for serious injury and death. For example, the elimination of head-on KSI crashes simply required the installation of an appropriate median crash-barrier. Also, roundabouts, often with speed-reducing approaches, feature very few KSI crashes.

The old road-safety paradigm of purely crash risk is a far more complex matter. Contributing factors to highway crashes may be related to the driver (such as driver error, illness, or fatigue), the vehicle (brake, steering, or throttle failures), or the road itself (lack of sight distance, poor roadside clear- zones, etc.). Interventions may seek to reduce or compensate for these factors, or to reduce the severity of crashes. A comprehensive outline of interventions areas can be seen in management systems for road safety. Study conducted in Finland revealed that the fatality risk is increased most when a collision type is either pedestrian or meeting of the vehicles.

In addition to management systems, which apply predominantly to networks in built-up areas, another class of interventions relates to the design of roadway networks for new districts. Such interventions explore the configurations of a network that will inherently reduce the probability of collisions.

Interventions for the prevention of road traffic injuries are often evaluated; the Cochrane Library has published a wide variety of reviews of interventions for the prevention of road-traffic injuries.

For the purposes of road-traffic safety it can be helpful to classify roads into three usages:

- built-up urban streets with slower speeds, greater densities, and more diversity among road users,
- non built-up rural roads with higher speeds, and
- major highways (motorways/ Interstates/ freeways/ Autobahns, autostrade, etc.) reserved for motor-vehicles, and which are often designed to minimize and attenuate crashes.

Built-up Areas

On neighborhood roads where many vulnerable road users, such as pedestrians and bicyclists can be found, traffic calming can be a tool for road safety. Though not strictly a traffic calming measure, mini-traffic circles implanted in normal intersections of neighbourhood streets have been shown to reduce collisions at intersections dramatically. Shared space schemes, which rely on human instincts and interactions, such as eye contact, for their effectiveness, and are characterised by the removal of traditional traffic signals and signs, and even by the removal of the distinction between carriageway (roadway) and footway (sidewalk), are also becoming increasingly popular. Both approaches can be shown to be effective.

For planned neighbourhoods, studies recommend new network configurations, such as the Fused Grid or 3-Way Offset. These layout models organize a neighbourhood area as a zone of no cut-through traffic by means of loops or dead-end streets. They also ensure that pedestrians and bicycles have a distinct advantage by introducing exclusive shortcuts by path connections through blocks and parks. Such a principle of organization is referred to as "Filtered Permeability" implying a preferential treatment of active modes of transport. These new patterns, which are recommended for laying out neighbourhoods, are based on analyses of collision data of large regional districts and over extended periods. They show that four-way intersections combined with cut-through traffic are the most significant contributors to increased collisions.

Modern safety barriers are designed to absorb impact energy and minimize the risk to the occupants of cars and bystanders. For example, most side rails are now anchored to the ground, so that they cannot skewer a passenger compartment. Most light poles are designed to break at the base rather than violently stop a car that hits them. Some road fixtures such as signs and fire hydrants are designed to collapse on impact. authorities have removed trees in the vicinity of roads; while the idea of "dangerous trees" has attracted a certain amount of skepticism, unforgiving objects such as trees can cause severe damage and injury to errant road users. Safety barriers can provide some combination of physical protection and visual protection depending on their environment. Physical protection is important for protecting sensitive building and pedestrian areas. Visual protection is necessary to alert drivers to changes in road patterns.

Most roads are cambered (crowned), that is, made so that they have rounded surfaces, to reduce standing water and ice, primarily to prevent frost damage but also increasing traction in poor weather. Some sections of road are now surfaced with porous bitumen to enhance drainage; this is particularly done on bends. These are just a few elements of highway engineering. As well as that, there are often grooves cut into the surface of cement highways to channel water away, and rumble strips at the edges of highways to rouse inattentive drivers with the loud noise they make when driven over. In some cases, there are raised markers between lanes to reinforce the lane boundaries; these are often reflective. In pedestrian areas, speed bumps are often placed to slow cars, preventing them from going too fast near pedestrians.

Poor road surfaces can lead to safety problems. If too much asphalt or bituminous binder is used in asphalt concrete, the binder can 'bleed' or flush' to the surface, leaving a very smooth surface that provides little traction when wet. Certain kinds of stone aggregate become very smooth or polished under the constant wearing action of vehicle tyres, again leading to poor wet-weather traction. Either of these problems can increase wet-weather crashes by increasing braking distances or contributing to loss of control. If the pavement is insufficiently sloped or poorly drained, standing water on the surface can also lead to wet-weather crashes due to hydroplaning.

Lane markers in some countries and states are marked with cat's eyes, Botts' dots or reflective raised pavement markers that do not fade like paint. Botts dots are not used where it is icy in the winter, because frost and snowplows can break the glue that holds them to the road, although they can be embedded in short, shallow trenches carved in the roadway, as is done in the mountainous regions of California.

Road hazards and intersections in some areas are now usually marked several times, roughly five, twenty, and sixty seconds in advance so that drivers are less likely to attempt violent manoeuvres.

Most road signs and pavement marking materials are retro-reflective, incorporating small glass spheres or prisms to more efficiently reflect light from vehicle headlights back to the driver's eyes.

Turning Across Traffic

Turning across traffic (i.e., turning left in right-hand drive countries, turning right in left-hand drive countries) poses several risks. The more serious risk is a collision with oncoming traffic. Since this is nearly a head-on collision, injuries are common. It is the most common cause of fatalities in a built-up area. Another major risk is involvement in a rear-end collision while waiting for a gap in oncoming traffic.

Countermeasures for this type of collision include:

- Addition of left turn lanes.
- Providing protected turn phasing at signalized intersections.
- Using indirect turn treatments such as the Michigan left.
- Converting conventional intersections to roundabouts.

In the absence of these facilities as a driver about to turn:

- Keep your wheels straight, so that in the event of a rear end shunt, you are not pushed into on-coming traffic.
- When you think it is clear, look away, to the road that you are entering. There is an optical illusion that, after a time, presents an oncoming vehicle as further away and travelling slower. Looking away breaks this illusion.

There is no presumption of negligence which arises from the bare fact of a collision at an intersection, and circumstances may dictate that a left turn is safer than to turn right.

The American Association of State Highway Transportation Officials (AASHTO) recommends in their publication Geometric Design of Highways and Streets that left or right turns are to be provided the *same* time gap. Some states have recognized this in statute, and a presumption of negligence is only raised *because* of the *turn* if and only if the turn was prohibited by an erected sign. Turns across traffic have been shown to be problematic for older drivers.

Designing for Pedestrians and Cyclists

Pedestrians and cyclists are among the most vulnerable road users and in some countries constitute over half of all road deaths. Interventions aimed at improving safety of non-motorised users:

- Sidewalks (or pavements in British English) of suitable width for pedestrian traffic.
- Pedestrian crossings close to the desire line which allow pedestrians to cross roads safely.
- Segregated pedestrian routes and cycle lanes away from the main highway.
- Overbridges (tend to be unpopular with pedestrians and cyclists due to additional distance and effort).
- Underpasses (these can pose heightened risk from crime if not designed well, can work for cyclists in some cases).
- Traffic calming and speed humps.
- Low speed limits that are rigorously enforced, possibly by speed cameras.
- Shared space schemes giving ownership of the road space and equal priority to all road users, regardless of mode of use.
- Pedestrian barriers to prevent pedestrians crossing dangerous locations
- Cycling infrastructure.
- Protected intersection.

American passive traffic safety measures which were adopted in the mid-20th century created roadways which were forgiving to motorists traveling at high speeds but which de-prioritized cycling and pedestrian facilities. Passive traffic safety policies led to excessively wide streets, clear zones adjacent to roadways, wide turn radii and a focus on protecting drivers from the consequences of high speeds. Passive traffic safety measures sought to avoid influencing the behavior of drivers while giving automobiles maximum convenience. Recent complete street policies seek to create design-oriented traffic safety improvements which actively slow drivers down by narrowing roadways while better accommodating pedestrians and cyclists.

Pedestrians' advocates question the equitability of schemes if they impose extra time and effort on the pedestrian to remain safe from vehicles, for example overbridges with long slopes or steps up and down, underpasses with steps and addition possible risk of crime and at-grade crossings off the desired crossing line.

Make Roads Safe was criticised in 2007 for proposing such features. Successful pedestrian schemes tend to avoid over-bridges and underpasses and instead use at-grade crossings (such as pedestrian crossings) close to the intended route. Successful cycling schemes by contrast avoid frequent stops even if some additional distance is involved, because cyclists expend more energy when starting off.

In Costa Rica 57% of road deaths are pedestrians. However, a partnership between AACR, Cosevi, MOPT and iRAP has proposed the construction of 190 km of pedestrian footpaths and 170 pedestrian crossings which could save over 9000 fatal or serious injuries over 20 years.

Shared Space

By 1947 the Pedestrians' Association was suggesting that many of the safety features being introduced (speed limits, traffic calming, road signs and road markings, traffic lights, Belisha beacons, pedestrian crossings, cycle lanes, etc.) were potentially self-defeating because "every nonrestrictive safety measure, however admirable in itself, is treated by the drivers as an opportunity for more speeding, so that the net amount of danger is increased and the latter state is worse than the first."

During the 1990s a new approach, known as 'shared space' was developed which removed many of these features in some places has attracted the attention of authorities around the world. The approach was developed by Hans Monderman who believed that "if you treat drivers like idiots, they act as idiots" and proposed that trusting drivers to behave was more successful than forcing them to behave. Professor John Adams, an expert on risk compensation suggested that traditional traffic engineering measures assumed that motorists were "selfish, stupid, obedient automatons who had to be protected from their own stupidity" and non-motorists were treated as "vulnerable, stupid, obedient automatons who had to be protected from cars – and their own stupidity".

Reported results indicate that the 'shared space' approach leads to significantly reduced traffic speeds, the virtual elimination of road casualties, and a reduction in congestion. Living streets share some similarities with shared spaces. The woonerven also sought to reduce traffic speeds in community and housing zones by the use of lower speed limits enforced by the use of special signage and road markings, the introduction of traffic calming measures, and by giving pedestrians priority over motorists.

Major Highways

Major highways including motorways, freeways, Autobahnen, autostrade and interstates are designed for safer high-speed operation and generally have lower levels of injury per vehicle km than other roads; for example, in 2013, the German autobahn fatality rate of 1.9 deaths per billion-travel-kilometers compared favorably with the 4.7 rate on urban streets and 6.6 rate on rural roads.

Safety features include:

- Limited access from the properties and local roads.
- Grade separated junctions.
- Median dividers between opposite-direction traffic to reduce likelihood of head-on collisions.
- Removing roadside obstacles.
- Prohibition of more vulnerable road users and slower vehicles.
- Placements of energy attenuation devices (e.g., guard rails, wide grassy areas, sand barrels).
- Eliminating road toll booths.

The ends of some guard in rails on high-speed highways in the United States are protected with impact attenuators, designed to gradually absorb the kinetic energy of a vehicle and slow it more gently before it can strike the end of the guard rail head on, which would be devastating at high speed. Several mechanisms are used to dissipate kinetic energy. Fitch Barriers, a system of sand-filled barrels, uses momentum transfer from the vehicle to the sand. Many other systems are tear or deform steel members to absorb energy and gradually stop the vehicle.

In some countries major roads have "tone bands" impressed or cut into the edges of the legal roadway, so that drowsing drivers are awakened by a loud hum as they release the steering and drift off the edge of the road. Tone bands are also referred to as "rumble strips", owing to the sound they create. An alternative method is the use of "Raised Rib" markings, which consists of a continuous line marking with ribs across the line at regular intervals.

They were first specially authorised for use on motorways as an edge line marking to separate the edge of the hard shoulder from the main carriageway. The objective of the marking is to achieve improved visual delineation of the carriageway edge in wet conditions at night.

It also provides an audible/vibratory warning to vehicle drivers, should they stray from the carriageway, and run onto the marking.

Better motorways are banked on curves to reduce the need for tire-traction and increase stability for vehicles with high centers of gravity.

The US has developed a prototype automated roadway, to reduce driver fatigue and increase the carrying capacity of the roadway. Roadside units participating in future wireless vehicle safety communications networks have been studied.

Motorways are far more expensive and space-consumptive to build than ordinary roads, so are only used as principal arterial routes. In developed nations, motorways bear a significant portion of motorized travel; for example, the United Kingdom's 3533 km of motorways represented less than 1.5% of the United Kingdom's roadways in 2003, but carry 23% of road traffic.

The proportion of traffic borne by motorways is a significant safety factor. For example, even though the United Kingdom had a higher fatality rates on both motorways and non-motorways than Finland, both nations shared the same overall fatality rate in 2003. This result was due to the United Kingdom's higher proportion of motorway travel.

Similarly, the reduction of conflicts with other vehicles on motorways results in smoother traffic flow, reduced collision rates, and reduced fuel consumption compared with stop-and-go traffic on other roadways.

The improved safety and fuel economy of motorways are common justifications for building more motorways. However, the planned capacity of motorways is often exceeded in a shorter timeframe than initially planned, due to the under estimation of the extent of the suppressed demand for road travel. In developing nations, there is significant public debate on the desirability of continued investment in motorways.

With effect from January 2005 and based primarily on safety grounds, the UK's Highways Agency's policy is that all new motorway schemes are to use high containment concrete step barriers in the central reserve. All existing motorways will introduce concrete barriers into the central reserve as part of ongoing upgrades and through replacement as and when these systems have reached the end of their useful life. This change of policy applies only to barriers in the central reserve of high speed roads and not to verge side barriers. Other routes will continue to use steel barriers.

More people die on the hard shoulder than on the highway itself. Without other vehicles passing a parked car, following drivers are unaware that the vehicle is parked, despite hazard lights. Truck drivers indicate that they are parked by putting their cab seat behind their truck. In the UK, the AA and police park their vehicles on the hard shoulder at a slight angle so that following drivers can see down the side of their vehicle and are therefore aware that they are stopped. 30% of highway crashes occur in the vicinity of toll collection booths in the countries that have them, these can be reduced by switching to electronic toll systems.

Traffic Camera

A traffic camera is a video camera which observes vehicular traffic on a road. Typically, traffic cameras are put along major roads such as highways, freeways, expressways and arterial roads, and are connected by optical fibers buried alongside or under the road, with electricity provided either by mains power in urban areas, by solar panels or other alternative power sources which provide consistent imagery without the threat of power outages.

A monitoring center receives the live video in real-time, and serves as a dispatcher if there is a traffic collision, some other disruptive incident or safety issue.

Traffic cameras form a part of most intelligent transportation systems. They are especially valuable in tunnels, where safety equipment can be activated remotely based on information provided by the cameras and other sensors. On surface roads, they are typically mounted on high poles or masts, sometimes with street lights. On arterial roads, they are often mounted on traffic light poles at intersections, where problems are most likely. In remote areas beyond the electrical grid, they are usually powered by a renewable source such as solar power, which also provides a backup source to urban camera infrastructure.

Traffic cameras are distinct from road safety cameras, which are put in specific places to enforce rules of the road by taking still photos in a much higher image resolution upon a trigger. Traffic cameras are only for observation and continuously take lower-resolution video, often in full motion, though they may be remotely controlled to focus on an incident in the distance or at an orientation normally outside its field of view, such as a frontage road. Many transmit in analog television formats, though many are being converted to high definition or 4K resolution video as equipment is replaced. Some have a compass built in which displays the cardinal direction at which the camera is aimed, though many installers also provide a reference image with the cardinal direction. These cameras are required to be able to resist weather conditions permanently.

A non-public use for traffic cameras is video tolling, where motorists drive through open road tolling gantries, have an image of their license plate taken, and then are billed after automatic number-plate recognition has read the license plate and cross-referenced it with motor vehicle databases.

Many transportation departments have linked their camera networks to the internet so that travelers can view traffic conditions. They may show either streaming video or still imagery which refreshes at a set interval, helping travelers determine whether an alternate route should be taken.

In the United States and Canada, these often are displayed on state or municipally-run 5-1-1 websites (511 being a telephone service relaying traffic information). These images may be combined with in-road sensors that measure traffic timing and mapping providers such as Google Maps/Waze that allow user-generated traffic information.

Many states and provinces consider this information public domain, thus many television stations air live traffic camera imagery during traffic reports on their local news broadcasts, or simply as a moving background during newscasts. Some cable TV systems provide these pictures full-time on a governmental access channel, and some broadcast stations set aside a full digital subchannel solely for traffic information and camera imagery, such as WMVT-DT3 in Milwaukee and WFMZ-DT2 in Allentown, Pennsylvania. However, in some cases for toll roads and other private road authorities, such as the Illinois State Toll Highway Authority, these images are the property of the toll agency (or private company which runs a toll road), and are released exclusively to one station (e.g., ISTHA feeds only to WMAQ-TV).

Sustainability and Environmental Management

At the global scale sustainability and environmental management involves managing the oceans, freshwater systems, land and atmosphere, according to sustainability principles. Land use change is fundamental to the operations of the biosphere because alterations in the relative proportions of land dedicated to urbanisation, agriculture, forest, woodland, grassland and pasture have a marked effect on the global water, carbon and nitrogen biogeochemical cycles. Management of the Earth's atmosphere involves assessment of all aspects of the carbon cycle to identify opportunities to address human-induced climate change and this has become a major focus of scientific research because of the potential catastrophic effects on biodiversity and human communities. Ocean circulation patterns have a strong influence on climate and weather and, in turn, the food supply of both humans and other organisms.

Atmosphere

In March 2009, at a meeting of the Copenhagen Climate Council, 2,500 climate experts from 80 countries issued a keynote statement that there is now "no excuse" for failing to act on global warming and without strong carbon reduction targets "abrupt or irreversible" shifts in climate may occur that "will be very difficult for contemporary societies to cope with". Management of the global atmosphere now involves assessment of all aspects of the carbon cycle to identify opportunities to address human-induced climate change and this has become a major focus of scientific research because of the potential catastrophic effects on biodiversity and human communities.

Other human impacts on the atmosphere include the air pollution in cities, the pollutants including toxic chemicals like nitrogen oxides, sulphur oxides, volatile organic compounds and airborne particulate matter that produce photochemical smog and acid rain, and the chlorofluorocarbons that degrade the ozone layer.

Anthropogenic particulates such as sulfate aerosols in the atmosphere reduce the direct irradiance and reflectance (albedo) of the Earth's surface. Known as global dimming the decrease is estimated to have been about 4% between 1960 and 1990 although the trend has subsequently reversed. Global dimming may have disturbed the global water cycle by reducing evaporation and rainfall in some areas. It also creates a cooling effect and this may have partially masked the effect of greenhouse gases on global warming.

Oceans

Ocean circulation patterns have a strong influence on climate and weather and, in turn, the food supply of both humans and other organisms. Scientists have warned of the possibility, under the influence of climate change, of a sudden alteration in circulation patterns of ocean currents that could drastically alter the climate in some regions of the globe. Major human environmental impacts occur in the more habitable regions of the ocean fringes – the estuaries, coastline and bays. Eight point five of the world's population – about 600 million people – live in low-lying areas vulnerable to sea level rise. Trends of concern that require management include: over-fishing (beyond sustainable levels); coral bleaching due to ocean warming, and ocean acidification due to increasing levels of dissolved carbon dioxide; and sea level rise due to climate change. Because of their vastness oceans also act as a convenient dumping ground for human waste. Remedial strategies include: more careful waste management, statutory control of overfishing by adoption of sustainable fishing practices and the use of environmentally sensitive and sustainable aquaculture and fish farming, reduction of fossil fuel emissions and restoration of coastal and other marine habitats.

Freshwater

Water covers 71% of the Earth's surface. Of this, 97.5% is the salty water of the oceans and only 2.5% freshwater, most of which is locked up in the Antarctic ice sheet. The remaining freshwater is found in lakes, rivers, wetlands, the soil, aquifers and atmosphere. All life depends on the solar-powered global water cycle, the evaporation from oceans and land to form water vapour that later condenses from clouds as rain, which then becomes the renewable part of the freshwater supply. Awareness of the global importance of preserving water for ecosystem services has only recently emerged as: during the 20th century, more than half the world's wetlands have been lost along with their valuable environmental services. Biodiversity-rich freshwater ecosystems are currently declining faster than marine or land ecosystems making them the world's most vulnerable habitats. Increasing urbanization pollutes clean water supplies and much of the world still does not have access to clean, safe water. In the industrial world demand management has slowed absolute usage rates but increasingly water is being transported over vast distances from water-rich natural areas to population-dense urban areas and energy-hungry desalination is becoming more widely used. Greater emphasis is now being placed on the improved management of blue (harvestable) and green (soil water available for plant use) water, and this applies at all scales of water management.

Land

Loss of biodiversity originates largely from the habitat loss and fragmentation produced by artificial land development, forestry and agriculture as natural capital is progressively converted to man-made capital. Land-use change is fundamental to the operations of the biosphere because alterations in the relative proportions of land dedicated to urbanisation, agriculture, forest, woodland, grassland and pasture have a marked effect on the global water, carbon and nitrogen biogeochemical cycles and this can negatively impact both natural and human systems. At the local human scale major sustainability benefits accrue from the pursuit of green cities and sustainable parks and gardens.

Forests

Since the Neolithic Revolution, human consumption has reduced the world's forest cover by about 47%. Present-day forests occupy about a quarter of the world's ice-free land with about half of these occurring in the tropics. In temperate and boreal regions forest area is gradually increasing (with the exception of Siberia), but deforestation in the tropics is of major concern.

Forests moderate the local climate and the global water cycle through their light reflectance (albedo) and evapotranspiration. They also conserve biodiversity, protect water quality, preserve soil and soil quality, provide fuel and pharmaceuticals, and purify the air. These free ecosystem services are not given a market value under most current economic systems, and so forest conservation has little appeal when compared with the economic benefits of logging and clearance which, through soil degradation and organic decomposition returns carbon dioxide to the atmosphere. The United Nations Food and Agriculture Organization (FAO) estimates that about 90% of the carbon stored in land vegetation is locked up in trees and that they sequester about 50% more carbon than is present in the atmosphere. Changes in land use currently contribute about 20% of total global carbon emissions (heavily logged Indonesia and Brazil are a major source of emissions). Climate change can be mitigated by sequestering carbon in reafforestation schemes, plantations and timber products. Also wood biomass can be utilized as a renewable carbon-neutral fuel. The FAO has suggested that, over the period 2005–2050, effective use of tree planting could absorb about 10–20% of man-made emissions – so monitoring the condition of the world's forests must be part of a global strategy to mitigate emissions and protect ecosystem services. However, climate change may preempt this FAO scenario as a study by the International Union of Forest Research Organizations in 2009 concluded that the stress of a 2.5 °C (36.5 °F) temperature rise above pre-industrial levels could result in the release of vast amounts of carbon so the potential of forests to act as carbon "sinks" is "at risk of being lost entirely".

Cultivated Land

Feeding more than seven billion human bodies takes a heavy toll on the Earth's resources. This begins with the appropriation of about 38% of the Earth's land surface and about 20% of its net primary productivity. Added to this are the resource-hungry activities of industrial agribusiness – everything from the crop need for irrigation water, synthetic fertilizers and pesticides to the resource costs of food packaging, transport (now a major part of global trade) and retail. Food is essential to life. But the list of environmental costs of food production is a long one: topsoil depletion, erosion and conversion to desert from constant tillage of annual crops; overgrazing; salinization; sodification; waterlogging; high levels of fossil fuel use; reliance on inorganic fertilisers and synthetic organic pesticides; reductions in genetic diversity by the mass use of monocultures; water resource depletion; pollution of waterbodies by run-off and groundwater contamination; social problems including the decline of family farms and weakening of rural communities.

All of these environmental problems associated with industrial agriculture and agribusiness are now being addressed through such movements as sustainable agriculture, organic farming and more sustainable business practices.

Extinctions

Although biodiversity loss can be monitored simply as loss of species, effective conservation demands the protection of species within their natural habitats and ecosystems. Following human migration and population growth, species extinctions have progressively increased to a rate unprecedented since the Cretaceous–Paleogene extinction event. Known as the Holocene extinction event this current human-induced extinction of species ranks as one of the world's six mass extinction events. Some scientific estimates indicate that up to half of presently existing species may become extinct by 2100. Current extinction rates are 100 to 1000 times their prehuman levels with more than 10% birds and mammals threatened, about 8% of plants, 5% of fish and more than 20% of freshwater species.

The 2008 IUCN Red List warns that long-term droughts and extreme weather put additional stress on key habitats and, for example, lists 1,226 bird species as threatened with extinction, which is one eighth of all bird species. The Red List Index also identifies 44 tree species in Central Asia as under threat of extinction due to over-exploitation and human development and threatening the region's forests which are home to more than 300 wild ancestors of modern domesticated fruit and nut cultivars.

Biological Invasions

In many parts of the industrial world land clearing for agriculture has diminished and here the greatest threat to biodiversity, after climate change, has become the destructive effect of invasive species. Increasingly efficient global transport has facilitated the spread of organisms across the planet. The potential danger of this aspect of globalization is starkly illustrated through the spread of human diseases like HIV AIDS, mad cow disease, bird flu and swine flu, but invasive plants and animals are also having a devastating impact on native biodiversity. Non-indigenous organisms can quickly occupy disturbed land and natural areas where, in the absence of their natural predators, they are able to thrive. At the global scale this issue is being addressed through the Global Invasive Species Information Network but there is improved international biosecurity legislation to minimise the transmission of pathogens and invasive organisms. Also, through CITES legislation there is control the trade in rare and threatened species. Increasingly at the local level public awareness programs are alerting communities, gardeners, the nursery industry, collectors, and the pet and aquarium industries, to the harmful effects of potentially invasive species.

Resistance to Change

The environmental sustainability problem has proven difficult to solve. The modern environmental movement has attempted to solve the problem in a large variety of ways. But little progress has been made, as shown by severe ecological footprint overshoot and lack of sufficient progress on the climate change problem. Something within the human system in preventing change to a sustainable mode of behavior. That system trait is systemic change resistance. Change resistance is also known as organizational resistance, barriers to change, or policy resistance.

Environmental Monitoring

Environmental monitoring describes the processes and activities that need to take place to characterize and monitor the quality of the environment. Environmental monitoring is used in the preparation of environmental impact assessments, as well as in many circumstances in which human activities carry a risk of harmful effects on the natural environment. All monitoring strategies and programs have reasons and justifications which are often designed to establish the current status of an environment or to establish trends in environmental parameters. In all cases, the results of monitoring will be reviewed, analyzed statistically, and published. The design of a monitoring program must therefore have regard to the final use of the data before monitoring starts. Environmental monitoring includes monitoring of air quality, soils and water quality.

Air Quality Monitoring

Air pollutants are atmospheric substances—both naturally occurring and anthropogenic—which may potentially have a negative impact on the environment and organism health. With the evolution of new chemicals and industrial processes has come the introduction or elevation of pollutants in the atmosphere, as well as environmental research and regulations, increasing the demand for air quality monitoring.

Air quality monitoring is challenging to enact as it requires the effective integration of multiple environmental data sources, which often originate from different environmental networks and institutions. These challenges require specialized observation equipment and tools to establish air pollutant concentrations, including sensor networks, geographic information system (GIS) models, and the Sensor Observation Service (SOS), a web service for querying real-time sensor data. Air dispersion models that combine topographic, emissions, and meteorological data to predict air pollutant concentrations are often helpful in interpreting air monitoring data. Additionally, consideration of anemometer data in the area between sources and the monitor often provides insights on the source of the air contaminants recorded by an air pollution monitor.

Air quality monitors are operated by citizens, regulatory agencies, non-governmental organisations and researchers to investigate air quality and the effects of air pollution. Interpretation of ambient air monitoring data often involves a consideration of the spatial and temporal representativeness of the data gathered, and the health effects associated with exposure to the monitored levels. If the interpretation reveals concentrations of multiple chemical compounds, a unique "chemical fingerprint" of a particular air pollution source may emerge from analysis of the data.

Air Sampling

Passive or "diffusive" air sampling depends on meteorological conditions such as wind to diffuse air pollutants to a sorbent medium. Passive samplers, such as diffusion tubes, have the advantage of typically being small, quiet, and easy to deploy, and they are particularly useful in air quality studies that determine key areas for future continuous monitoring.

Air pollution can also be assessed by biomonitoring with organisms that bioaccumulate air pollutants, such as lichens, mosses, fungi, and other biomass. One of the benefits of this type of sampling is how quantitative information can be obtained via measurements of accumulated compounds, representative of the environment from which they came. However, careful considerations must be made in choosing the particular organism, how it's dispersed, and relevance to the pollutant. Other sampling methods include the use of a denuder, needle trap devices, and microextraction techniques.

Soil Monitoring

Soil monitoring involves the collection and/or analysis of soil and its associated quality, constituents, and physical status to determine or guarantee its fitness for use. Soil faces many threats, including compaction, contamination, organic material loss, biodiversity loss, slope stability issues, erosion, salinization, and acidification. Soil monitoring helps characterize these threats and other potential risks to the soil, surrounding environments, animal health, and human health.

Assessing these threats and other risks to soil can be challenging due to a variety of factors, including soil's heterogeneity and complexity, scarcity of toxicity data, lack of understanding of a contaminant's fate, and variability in levels of soil screening.

This requires a risk assessment approach and analysis techniques that prioritize environmental protection, risk reduction, and, if necessary, remediation methods. Soil monitoring plays a significant role in that risk assessment, not only aiding in the identification of at-risk and affected areas but also in the establishment of base background values of soil.

Soil monitoring has historically focused on more classical conditions and contaminants, including toxic elements (e.g., mercury, lead, and arsenic) and persistent organic pollutants (POPs). Historically, testing for these and other aspects of soil, however, has had its own set of challenges, as sampling in most cases is of a destructive in nature, requiring multiple samples over time. Additionally, procedural and analytical errors may be introduced due to variability among references and methods, particularly over time.

However, as analytical techniques evolve and new knowledge about ecological processes and contaminant effects disseminate, the focus of monitoring will likely broaden over time and the quality of monitoring will continue to improve.

Soil Sampling

The two primary types of soil sampling are grab sampling and composite sampling. Grab sampling involves the collection of an individual sample at a specific time and place, while composite sampling involves the collection of a homogenized mixture of multiple individual samples at either a specific place over different times or multiple locations at a specific time.

Soil sampling may occur both at shallow ground levels or deep in the ground, with collection methods varying by level collected from. Scoops, augers, core barrel, and solid-tube samplers, and other tools are used at shallow ground levels, whereas split-tube, solid-tube, or hydraulic methods may be used in deep ground.

Soil Contamination Monitoring

Soil contamination monitoring helps researchers identify patterns and trends in contaminant deposition, movement, and effect. Human-based pressures such as tourism, industrial activity, urban sprawl, construction work, and inadequate agriculture/forestry practices can contribute to and make worse soil contamination and lead to the soil becoming unfit for its intended use. Both inorganic and organic pollutants may make their way to the soil, having a wide variety of detrimental effects. Soil contamination monitoring is therefore important to identify risk areas, set baselines, and identify contaminated zones for remediation. Monitoring efforts may range from local farms to nationwide efforts, such as those made by China in the late 2000s, providing details such as the nature of contaminants, their quantity, effects, concentration patterns, and remediation feasibility. Monitoring and analytical equipment will ideally will have high response times, high levels of resolution and automation, and a certain degree of self-sufficiency. Chemical techniques may be used to measure toxic elements and POPs using chromatography and spectrometry, geophysical techniques may assess physical properties of large terrains, and biological techniques may use specific organisms to gauge not only contaminant level but also byproducts of contaminant biodegradation. These techniques and others are increasingly becoming more efficient, and laboratory instrumentation is becoming more precise, resulting in more meaningful monitoring outcomes.

Soil Erosion Monitoring

Soil erosion monitoring helps researchers identify patterns and trends in soil and sediment movement. Monitoring programs have varied over the years, from long-term academic research on university plots to reconnaissance-based surveys of biogeoclimatic areas. In most methods, however, the general focus is on identifying and measuring all the dominant erosion processes in a given area. Additionally, soil erosion monitoring may attempt to quantify the effects of erosion on crop productivity, though challenging "because of the many complexities in the relationship between soils and plants and their management under a variable climate."

Soil Salinity Monitoring

Soil salinity monitoring helps researchers identify patterns and trends in soil salt content. Both the natural process of seawater intrusion and the human-induced processes of inappropriate soil and water management can lead to salinity problems in soil, with up to one billion hectares of land affected globally (as of

2013). Salinity monitoring at the local level may look closely at the root zone to gauge salinity impact and develop management options, whereas at the regional and national level salinity monitoring may help with identifying areas at-risk and aiding policymakers in tackling the issue before it spreads. The monitoring process itself may be performed using technologies such as remote sensing and geographic information systems (GIS) to identify salinity via greenness, brightness, and whiteness at the surface level. Direct analysis of soil up close, including the use of electromagnetic induction techniques, may also be used to monitor soil salinity.

Design of Environmental Monitoring Programmes

Water quality monitoring is of little use without a clear and unambiguous definition of the reasons for the monitoring and the objectives that it will satisfy. Almost all monitoring (except perhaps remote sensing) is in some part invasive of the environment under study and extensive and poorly planned monitoring carries a risk of damage to the environment.

This may be a critical consideration in wilderness areas or when monitoring very rare organisms or those that are averse to human presence. Some monitoring techniques, such as gill netting fish to estimate populations, can be very damaging, at least to the local population and can also degrade public trust in scientists carrying out the monitoring.

Almost all mainstream environmentalism monitoring projects form part of an overall monitoring strategy or research field, and these field and strategies are themselves derived from the high levels objectives or aspirations of an organisation. Unless individual monitoring projects fit into a wider strategic framework, the results are unlikely to be published and the environmental understanding produced by the monitoring will be lost.

Monitoring Programmes

All scientifically reliable environmental monitoring is performed in line with a published programme. The programme may include the overall objectives of the organisation, references to the specific strategies that helps deliver the objective and details of specific projects or tasks within those strategies the key feature of any programme is the listing of what is being monitored and how that monitoring is to take place and the time-scale over which it should all happen. Typically, and often as an appendix, a monitoring programme will provide a table of locations, dates and sampling methods that are proposed and which, if undertaken in full, will deliver the published monitoring programme. There are a number of commercial software packages which can assist with the implementation of the programme, monitor its progress and flag up inconsistencies or omissions but none of these can provide the key building block which is the programme itself.

Environmental Monitoring Data Management Systems

Given the multiple types and increasing volumes and importance of monitoring data, commercial software Environmental Data Management Systems (EDMS) or E-MDMS are increasingly in common use by regulated industries. They provide a means of managing all monitoring data in a single central place. Quality validation, compliance checking, verifying all data has been received, and sending alerts are generally automated. Typical interrogation functionality enables comparison of data sets both temporarily and spatially. They will also generate regulatory and other reports.

One formal certification scheme exists specifically for environmental data management software. This is provided by the Environment Agency in the U.K. under its Monitoring Certification Scheme (MCERTS).

Sampling Methods

There are a wide range of sampling methods which depend on the type of environment, the material being sampled and the subsequent analysis of the sample. At its simplest a sample can be filling a clean bottle with river water and submitting it for conventional chemical analysis. At the more complex end, sample data may be produced by complex electronic sensing devices taking sub-samples over fixed or variable time periods.

Sampling methods include judgmental sampling, simple random sampling, stratified sampling, systematic and grid sampling, adaptive cluster sampling, grab samples, semi-continuous monitoring and continuous, passive sampling, remote surveillance, remote sensing, biomonitoring and other sampling methods.

Smart Grid

The smart grid is an enhancement of the 20th century electrical grid, using two-way communications and distributed so-called intelligent devices. Two-way flows of electricity and information could improve the delivery network. Research is mainly focused on three systems of a smart grid – the infrastructure system, the management system, and the protection system. Electronic power conditioning and control of the production and distribution of electricity are important aspects of the smart grid.

The smart grid represents the full suite of current and proposed responses to the challenges of electricity supply. Numerous contributions to the overall improvement of the efficiency of energy infrastructure are anticipated from the deployment of smart grid technology, in particular including demand-side management. The improved flexibility of the smart grid permits greater penetration of highly variable renewable energy sources such as solar power and wind power, even without the addition of energy storage. Smart grids could also monitor/control residential devices that are noncritical during periods of peak power consumption, and return their function during nonpeak hours.

A smart grid includes a variety of operation and energy measures:

- Advanced metering infrastructure (of which smart meters are a generic name for any utility side device even if it is more capable e.g., a fiber optic router).
- Smart distribution boards and circuit breakers integrated with home control and demand response (*behind the meter* from a utility perspective) :
  - Load control switches and smart appliances, often financed by efficiency gains on municipal programs (e.g. PACE financing).
- Renewable energy resources, including the capacity to charge parked (electric vehicle) batteries or larger arrays of batteries recycled from these, or other energy storage.
- Energy efficient resources.
- Electric surplus distribution by power lines and auto-smart switch.
- Sufficient utility grade fiber broadband to connect and monitor the above, with wireless as a backup. Sufficient spare if "dark" capacity to ensure failover, often leased for revenue.

Concerns with smart grid technology mostly focus on smart meters, items enabled by them, and general security issues. Roll-out of smart grid technology also implies a fundamental re-engineering of the electricity services industry, although typical usage of the term is focused on the technical infrastructure.

Smart grid policy is organized in Europe as Smart Grid European Technology Platform. Policy in the United States is described in 42 U.S.C. ch. 152, subch. IX § 17381.

Energy Management

Energy management includes planning and operation of energy production and energy consumption units as well as energy distribution and storage. Objectives are resource conservation, climate protection and cost savings, while the users have permanent access to the energy they need. It is connected closely to environmental management, production management, logistics and other established business functions. The VDI-Guideline 4602 released a definition which includes the economic dimension: "Energy management is the proactive, organized and systematic coordination of procurement, conversion, distribution and use of energy to meet the requirements, taking into account environmental and economic objectives". It is a systematic endeavor to optimize energy efficiency for specific political, economic, and environmental objectives through Engineering and Management techniques.

One of the initial steps for an effective energy cost control program is the base line energy assessment, which examines the pattern of existing energy usage by the government or any sub-entity of the government or private organization. This program will set the reference point for improvements in energy efficiency. Energy efficiency can improve the existing energy usage and benchmarking of every individual section such as area, sub-area, and the industry.

It is important to integrate the energy management in the organizational structure, so that the energy management can be implemented. Responsibilities and the interaction of the decision makers should be regularized. The delegation of functions and competencies extend from the top management to the executive worker. Furthermore, a comprehensive coordination can ensure the fulfillment of the tasks.

It is advisable to establish a separate organizational unit "energy management" in large or energy-intensive companies. This unit supports the senior management and keeps track. It depends on the basic form of the organizational structure, where this unit is connected. In case of a functional organization the unit is located directly between the first (CEO) and the second hierarchical level (corporate functions such as production, procurement, marketing). In a divisional organization, there should be a central and several sector-specific energy management units. So the diverse needs of the individual sectors and the coordination between the branches and the head office can be fulfilled. In a matrix organization the energy management can be included as a matrix function and thus approach most functions directly.

Facility management is an important part of energy management, because a huge proportion (average 25 per cent) of complete operating costs are energy costs. According to the International Facility Management Association (IFMA), facility management is "a profession that encompasses multiple disciplines to ensure functionality of the built environment by integrating people, place, processes and technology."

The central task of energy management is to reduce costs for the provision of energy in buildings and facilities without compromising work processes. Especially the availability and service life of the equipment and the ease of use should remain the same. The German Facility Management Association (GEFMA e.V.) has published guidelines (e.g. GEFMA 124-1 and 124–2), which contain methods and ways of dealing with the integration of energy management in the context of a successful facility management. In this topic the facility manager has to deal with economic, ecological, risk-based and quality-based targets. He tries to minimize the total cost of the energy-related processes (supply, distribution and use).

Procurement is the acquisition of goods or services. Energy prices fluctuate constantly, which can significantly affect the energy bill of organizations. Therefore, poor energy procurement decisions can be expensive. Organizations can control and reduce energy costs by taking a proactive and efficient approach to buying energy. Even a change of the energy source can be a profitable and eco-friendly alternative.

Production is the act of creating output, a good or service which has value and contributes to the utility of individuals. This central process may differ depending on the industry. Industrial companies have facilities that require a lot of energy. Service companies, in turn, do not need many materials, their energy-related focus is mainly facility management or Green IT. Therefore, the energy-related focus has to be identified first, then evaluated and optimize.

Usually, production is the area with the largest energy consumption within an organization. Therefore, also the production planning and control becomes very important. It deals with the operational, temporal, quantitative and spatial planning, control and management of all processes that are necessary in the production of goods and commodities. The "production planner" should plan the production processes so that they operate in an energy efficient way. For example, a strong power consumer can be moved into the night time. Peaks should be avoided for the benefit of a unified load profile.

The impending changes in the structure of energy production require an increasing demand for storage capacity. The Production planning and control has to deal with the problem of limited storability of energy. In principle there is the possibility to store energy electrically, mechanically or chemically. Another trend-setting technology is lithium-based electrochemical storage, which can be used in electric vehicles or as an option to control the power grid. The German Federal Ministry of Economics and Technology realized the significance of this topic and established an initiative with the aim to promote technological breakthroughs and support the rapid introduction of new energy storage.

Maintenance is the combination of all technical and administrative actions, including supervision actions, intended to retain an item in, or restore it to, a state in which it can perform a required function. Detailed maintenance is essential to support the energy management. Hereby power losses and cost increases can be avoided.

Through the energy efficiency it management is remain the key for the any industrial user across globe, to achieve the energy management goal for the federal government or industry the efficiency of water and energy resources play a vital role.

Examples of how it is possible to save energy and costs with the help of maintenance:

- Defrost the fridges.
- Check the barometer of cars and trucks.
- Insulation of hot systems.
- Improve leaks in building envelopes.

7.2.2 Benefits of Edge Computing in Smart Cities

Edge computing offers several strategic benefits for urban planners, municipal authorities, and residents.

Low Latency and Real-Time Responsiveness

Reduces data transmission delays and latency issues by processing critical data locally at the edge, enabling real-time decision-making, faster emergency response times, and improved service delivery across smart city applications.

Scalability and Resource Efficiency

Optimizes bandwidth usage, network congestion, and computing resources by distributing processing capabilities and data storage closer to IoT endpoints and edge devices, minimizing operational costs and enhancing scalability.

Enhanced Data Privacy and Security

Protects citizen privacy, personal data, and sensitive information by encrypting data, implementing access controls, and adhering to data protection regulations (e.g., GDPR, CCPA) in edge computing deployments for smart city services.

7.2.3 Challenges and Considerations

Deploying edge computing in smart cities presents challenges and considerations that require strategic planning and proactive management.

Infrastructure Interoperability

Integrates heterogeneous IoT devices, legacy systems, and cloud platforms with edge computing architectures, ensuring data interoperability, standardized protocols, and seamless integration for diverse smart city applications.

Data Governance and Regulatory Compliance

Adheres to regulatory requirements, data protection laws, and cybersecurity standards (e.g., ISO/IEC 27001) to safeguard citizen data privacy, mitigate security risks, and maintain trust in edge-driven smart city initiatives.

Community Engagement and Stakeholder Collaboration

Promotes transparency, inclusivity, and stakeholder engagement in smart city planning, ensuring citizen participation, feedback mechanisms, and ethical considerations in deploying edge computing technologies.

7.2.4 Future Trends and Innovations

Emerging trends and innovations in edge computing are shaping the future of smart city development and urban sustainability.

5G Network Integration

Leverages high-speed 5G networks and edge computing capabilities to support bandwidth-intensive smart city applications, IoT connectivity, and ultra-low latency services for autonomous vehicles, remote healthcare, and immersive experiences.

AI and Machine Learning at the Edge

Advances in edge AI algorithms, predictive analytics, and machine learning models enable predictive maintenance, urban forecasting, and personalized services delivery based on real-time data insights from edge devices and IoT sensors.

Blockchain and Distributed Ledger Technology

Integrates blockchain-based solutions for secure data sharing, decentralized identity management, and transparent governance in smart city infrastructures, enhancing trust, accountability, and data integrity across municipal services.

7.2.5 Ethical and Social Implications

Addressing ethical considerations and social impacts of edge computing in smart cities involves promoting digital inclusion, equitable access to technology, and addressing biases in AI-driven decision-making to ensure fair, transparent, and responsible urban governance.

7.3 EDGE COMPUTING IN MANUFACTURING

Edge computing is revolutionizing the manufacturing industry by enabling real-time data analytics, predictive maintenance, and process optimization at the network edge. This decentralized computing paradigm leverages edge devices, industrial IoT (IIoT) sensors, and local computing resources to enhance operational efficiency, reduce downtime, and improve production quality within manufacturing facilities.

Edge computing is transforming manufacturing operations by enabling real-time data analytics, predictive maintenance, and process optimization at the network edge. By leveraging edge computing technologies, manufacturing enterprises can enhance operational efficiency, reduce downtime, and improve production quality while addressing challenges related to cybersecurity, data governance, and regulatory compliance. As industries embrace edge-driven initiatives and deploy innovative applications, prioritizing scalable deployment strategies, workforce readiness, and ethical considerations fosters resilience, innovation, and sustainable growth in the evolving landscape of smart manufacturing ecosystems. Edge computing continues to play a pivotal role in shaping the future of manufacturing automation, digital transformation, and competitive advantage in the global marketplace.

7.3.1 Applications of Edge Computing in Manufacturing

Edge computing facilitates a wide range of applications and use cases across different stages of manufacturing processes.

Predictive Maintenance

Implements edge analytics and machine learning algorithms to monitor equipment health, detect anomalies, and predict potential failures in real-time, enabling proactive maintenance and minimizing unplanned downtime.

Quality Control and Assurance

Integrates edge AI for visual inspection, defect detection, and product quality assessment on the production line, ensuring compliance with manufacturing standards, reducing waste, and enhancing product consistency.

Real-Time Production Monitoring

Deploys edge sensors and IoT devices to capture operational data (e.g., machine performance metrics, production throughput) at the point of production, enabling real-time monitoring, process visibility, and performance optimization.

Supply Chain Optimization

Enhances logistics and inventory management with edge computing capabilities for real-time tracking of materials, parts, and finished goods, optimizing supply chain efficiency, and reducing lead times in manufacturing operations.

7.3.2 Benefits of Edge Computing in Manufacturing

Reduced Latency and Enhanced Responsiveness

Minimizes data transmission delays by processing critical data locally at the edge, ensuring real-time responsiveness for machine control, production planning, and quality assurance in dynamic manufacturing environments.

Improved Operational Efficiency

Optimizes resource utilization, energy consumption, and equipment performance through real-time analytics, predictive insights, and automated decision-making at the edge, enhancing operational efficiency and production yield.

Cost Savings and Scalability

Reduces bandwidth costs and data storage requirements by distributing computing resources and processing capabilities closer to IIoT endpoints and manufacturing devices, supporting scalable deployment and operational flexibility.

7.3.3 Challenges and Considerations

Deploying edge computing in manufacturing environments presents challenges and considerations that require strategic planning and risk management.

Integration with Legacy Systems

Integrates edge computing solutions with existing manufacturing IT infrastructure, legacy systems, and industrial control systems (ICS), ensuring compatibility, data interoperability, and seamless integration for production continuity.

Cybersecurity Risks

Mitigates cybersecurity threats, data breaches, and malicious attacks targeting IIoT devices, edge nodes, and manufacturing networks by implementing robust security controls, access management policies, and encryption standards.

Data Governance and Regulatory Compliance

Adheres to regulatory requirements (e.g., GDPR, NIST SP 800-171) for data privacy, intellectual property protection, and industry-specific compliance in manufacturing operations, ensuring secure data handling and regulatory alignment.

7.3.4 Future Trends and Innovations

Emerging trends and innovations in edge computing are shaping the future of manufacturing automation, industrial IoT, and smart factory initiatives.

Edge AI and Machine Learning

Advances in edge AI algorithms and federated learning techniques enable autonomous decision-making, adaptive manufacturing processes, and predictive analytics for continuous improvement and agile manufacturing strategies.

Digital Twins and Simulation

Integrates digital twin technologies with edge computing capabilities to create virtual replicas of manufacturing processes, equipment, and supply chain operations, enabling predictive simulations, scenario analysis, and optimization of production workflows.

5G Network Integration

Leverages high-speed 5G networks and edge computing architectures to support low-latency communication, remote monitoring, and real-time control of manufacturing systems, enhancing agility, responsiveness, and connectivity in smart factory environments.

7.3.5 Ethical and Social Implications

Addressing ethical considerations and societal impacts of edge computing in manufacturing involves promoting workforce training, skill development, and ethical AI practices to ensure safe, inclusive, and human-centric adoption of advanced technologies in industrial automation and smart manufacturing initiatives.

7.4 EDGE COMPUTING IN AUTONOMOUS VEHICLES

Edge computing is revolutionizing the automotive industry by enabling real-time data processing, decision-making, and advanced driver assistance systems (ADAS) at the network edge. This decentralized computing paradigm leverages edge devices, sensors, and local computing resources to enhance vehicle perception, navigation capabilities, and overall safety in autonomous driving environments. Edge computing is transforming autonomous vehicles by enabling real-time data processing, decision-making, and enhanced safety features at the network edge. By leveraging edge computing technologies, automotive manufacturers and developers can optimize vehicle performance, reduce latency, and improve driver experience while addressing challenges related to cybersecurity, regulatory compliance, and infrastructure reliability. As the automotive industry embraces edge-driven innovations and deploys autonomous vehicle technologies, prioritizing safety, privacy, and ethical considerations fosters trust, resilience, and sustainable development in the evolving landscape of intelligent transportation systems. Edge computing continues to play a pivotal role in shaping the future of autonomous mobility, urban transportation, and smart mobility solutions in the digital era.

7.4.1 Applications of Edge Computing in Autonomous Vehicles

Edge computing facilitates a wide range of applications and functionalities within autonomous vehicles:

Sensor Fusion and Perception

Sensor fusion is the process of combining sensor data or data derived from disparate sources such that the resulting information has less uncertainty than would be possible when these sources were used individually. For instance, one could potentially obtain a more accurate location estimate of an indoor object by combining multiple data sources such as video cameras and WiFi localization signals. The term *uncertainty reduction* in this case can mean more accurate, more complete, or more dependable, or refer to the result of an emerging view, such as stereoscopic vision (calculation of depth information by combining two-dimensional images from two cameras at slightly different viewpoints).

The data sources for a fusion process are not specified to originate from identical sensors. One can distinguish *direct fusion*, *indirect fusion* and fusion of the outputs of the former two. Direct fusion is the fusion of sensor data from a set of heterogeneous or homogeneous sensors, soft sensors, and history values of sensor data, while indirect fusion uses information sources like *a priori* knowledge about the environment and human input.

Sensor fusion is also known as *(multi-sensor) data fusion* and is a subset of *information fusion*.

Examples of Sensors

- Accelerometers.
- Electronic Support Measures (ESM).
- Flash LIDAR.
- Global Positioning System (GPS).
- Infrared / thermal imaging camera.
- Magnetic sensors.
- MEMS.
- Phased array.
- Radar.
- Radiotelescopes, such as the proposed Square Kilometre Array, the largest sensor ever to be built.
- Scanning LIDAR.
- Seismic sensors.
- Sonar and other acoustic.
- Sonobuoys.
- TV cameras.

Algorithms

Sensor fusion is a term that covers a number of methods and algorithms, including:

- Kalman filter.
- Bayesian networks.
- Dempster–Shafer.
- Convolutional neural network.
- Gaussian processes.

Centralized versus Decentralized

In sensor fusion, centralized versus decentralized refers to where the fusion of the data occurs. In centralized fusion, the clients simply forward all of the data to a central location, and some entity at the central location is responsible for correlating and fusing the data. In decentralized, the clients take full responsibility for fusing the data. "In this case, every sensor or platform can be viewed as an intelligent asset having some degree of autonomy in decision-making."

Another classification of sensor configuration refers to the coordination of information flow between sensors. These mechanisms provide a way to resolve conflicts or disagreements and to allow the development of dynamic sensing strategies. Sensors are in redundant (or competitive) configuration if each node delivers independent measures of the same properties.

This configuration can be used in error correction when comparing information from multiple nodes. Redundant strategies are often used with high level fusions in voting procedures. Complementary configuration occurs when multiple information sources supply different information about the same features. This strategy is used for fusing information at raw data level within decision-making algorithms. Complementary features are typically applied in motion recognition tasks with Neural network, Hidden Markov model, Support-vector machine, clustering methods and other techniques. Cooperative sensor fusion uses the information extracted by multiple independent sensors to provide information that would not be available from single sensors. For example, sensors connected to body segments are used for the detection of the angle between them. Cooperative sensor strategy gives information impossible to obtain from single nodes. Cooperative information fusion can be used in motion recognition, gait analysis, motion analysis,,.

Levels

There are several categories or levels of sensor fusion that are commonly used.

- **Level 0:** Data alignment
- **Level 1:** Entity assessment (e.g., signal/feature/object).
  - Tracking and object detection/recognition/identification
- **Level 2:** Situation assessment
- **Level 3:** Impact assessment
- **Level 4:** Process refinement (i.e. sensor management)
- **Level 5:** User refinement

Sensor fusion level can also be defined basing on the kind of information used to feed the fusion algorithm. More precisely, sensor fusion can be performed fusing raw data coming from different sources, extrapolated features or even decision made by single nodes.

- **Data Level:** Data level (or early) fusion aims to fuse raw data from multiple sources and represent the fusion technique at the lowest level of abstraction. It is the most common sensor fusion technique in many fields of application. Data level fusion algorithms usually aim to combine multiple homogeneous sources of sensory data to achieve more accurate and synthetic readings. When portable devices are employed data compression represent an important factor, since collecting raw information from multiple sources generates huge information spaces that could define an issue in terms of memory or communication bandwidth for portable systems. Data level information fusion tends to generate big input spaces, that slow down the decision-making procedure. Also, data level fusion often cannot handle incomplete measurements. If one sensor modality becomes useless due to malfunctions, breakdown or other reasons the whole systems could occur in ambiguous outcomes.
- **Feature Level:** Features represent information computed on board by each sensing node. These features are then sent to a fusion node to feed the fusion algorithm. This procedure generates smaller information spaces with respect to the data level fusion, and this is better in terms of computational load. Obviously, it is important to properly select features on which to define classification procedures: choosing the most efficient features set should be a main aspect in method design. Using features selection algorithms that properly detect correlated features and features subsets improves the recognition accuracy but large training sets are usually required to find the most significant feature subset.
- **Decision Level:** Decision level (or late) fusion is the procedure of selecting an hypothesis from a set of hypotheses generated by individual (usually weaker) decisions of multiple nodes. It is the highest level of abstraction and uses the information that has been already elaborated through preliminary data- or feature level processing. The main goal in decision fusion is to use meta-level classifier while data from nodes are preprocessed by extracting features from them. Typically decision level sensor fusion is used in classification an recognition activities and the two most common approaches are majority voting and Naive-Bayes. Advantages coming from decision level fusion include communication bandwidth and improved decision accuracy. It also allows the combination of heterogeneous sensors.

Applications

One application of sensor fusion is GPS/INS, where Global Positioning System and inertial navigation system data is fused using various different methods, e.g., the extended Kalman filter. This is useful, for example, in determining the attitude of an aircraft using low-cost sensors. Another example is using the data fusion approach to determine the traffic state (low traffic, traffic jam, medium flow) using road side collected acoustic, image and sensor data. In the field of autonomous driving, sensor fusion is used to combine the redundant information from complementary sensors in order to obtain a more accurate and reliable representation of the environment.

Although technically not a dedicated sensor fusion method, modern Convolutional neural network based methods can simultaneously process many channels of sensor data (such as Hyperspectral imaging with hundreds of bands) and fuse relevant information to produce classification results.

Real-Time Decision-Making

Processes sensor data locally at the edge to analyze road conditions, detect obstacles, and execute real-time driving maneuvers (e.g., braking, steering) without relying solely on centralized cloud computing, ensuring low-latency responsiveness and safety critical functions.

V2X Communication

Vehicle-to-everything (V2X) is communication between a vehicle and any entity that may affect, or may be affected by, the vehicle. It is a vehicular communication system that incorporates other more specific types of communication as V2I (vehicle-to-infrastructure), V2N (vehicle-to-network), V2V (vehicle-to-vehicle), V2P (vehicle-to-pedestrian), V2D (vehicle-to-device).

V2X can be grouped into two supergroups, V2X using common communication technologies like bluetooth or mobile networks and V2X using a dedicated special communication technology. The main motivations for the dedicated V2X technology are road safety, traffic efficiency, energy savings, and mass surveillance. The U.S. NHTSA estimates a minimum of 13% reduction in traffic accidents if a V2V system were implemented, resulting in 439,000 fewer crashes per year. Equally, V2X technology is already used in countries such as China, where different safety information is being communicated between vehicles to reduce road accidents. There are two standards for dedicated V2X communication depending on the underlying technology being used: (1) WLAN-based, and (2) cellular-based. The term V2X contains the following sub categories:

- **Vehicle-to-Everything (V2X):** "Communication between a vehicle and any entity that may affect, or may be affected by, the vehicle."

- **Vehicle-to-Device (V2D):** Bluetooth / WiFi-Direct, e.g. Apple's CarPlay and Google's Android Auto.
- **Vehicle-to-Grid (V2G):** Information exchange with the smart grid to balance loads more efficiently.
  - Vehicle-to-Building (V2B), also known as Vehicle-to-Home (V2H)
  - Vehicle-to-Load (V2L)
- **Vehicle-to-Network (V2N):** Communication based on Cellular (3GPP) / 802.11p.
  - Vehicle-to-Cloud (V2C)—e.g. OTA updates, remote vehicle diagnostics (DoIP).
  - Vehicle-to-Infrastructure (V2I)—e.g. traffic lights, lane markers and parking meters.
  - Vehicle-to-Pedestrian (V2P)—e.g. wheelchairs and bicycles, commonly also used to designate vulnerable road users (VRUs).
  - Vehicle-to-Vehicle (V2V)—real-time data exchange with nearby vehicles.

History

The history of working on vehicle-to-vehicle communication projects to increase safety, reduce accidents and driver assistance can be traced back to the 1970s with projects such as the US Electronic Road Guidance System (ERGS) and Japan's CACS. Most milestones in the history of vehicle networks originate from the United States, Europe, and Japan.

Standardization of WLAN-based V2X supersedes that of cellular-based V2X systems. IEEE first published the specification of WLAN-based V2X (IEEE 802.11p) in 2010. It supports direct communication between vehicles (V2V) and between vehicles and infrastructure (V2I). This technology is referred to as Dedicated Short Range Communication (DSRC). DSRC uses the underlying radio communication provided by 802.11p.

In 2016, Toyota became the first automaker globally to introduce automobiles equipped with V2X. These vehicles use DSRC technology and are only for sale in Japan. In 2017, GM became the second automaker to introduce V2X. GM sells a Cadillac model in the United States that also is equipped with DSRC V2X.

In 2016, 3GPP published V2X specifications based on LTE as the underlying technology. It is generally referred to as "cellular V2X" (C-V2X) to differentiate itself from the 802.11p based V2X technology. In addition to the direct communication (V2V, V2I), C-V2X also supports wide area communication over a cellular network (V2N).

As of December 2017, a European automotive manufacturer has announced to deploy V2X technology based on 802.11p from 2019. While some studies and analysis in 2017 and 2018, all performed by the 5G Automotive Association (5GAA) – the industry organisation supporting and developing the C-V2X technology – indicate that cellular-based C-V2X technology in direct communication mode is superior to 802.11p in multiple aspects, such as performance, communication range, and reliability, many of these claims are disputed, e.g. in a whitepaper published by NXP, one of the companies active in the 802.11p based V2X technology, but also published by peer-reviewed journals.

This technology can be misused to remotely control the vehicle. The Police of the Czech Republic(2024) announced, in cooperation with universities, has developed a system for remote stopping of vehicles with reference to the fact that such a procedure is legal even under the current legislation.

IEEE 802.11p (DSRC)

The original V2X communication uses WLAN technology and works directly between vehicles (V2V) as well as vehicles and traffic infrastructure (V2I), which form a vehicular ad-hoc network as two V2X senders come within each other's range. Hence it does not require any communication infrastructure for vehicles to communicate, which is key to assure safety in remote or little-developed areas. WLAN is particularly well-suited for V2X communication, due to its low latency. It transmits messages known as Cooperative Awareness Messages (CAM) or Basic Safety Message (BSM), and Decentralised Environmental Notification Messages (DENM). Other roadside infrastructure related messages are Signal Phase and Timing Message (SPAT), In Vehicle Information Message (IVI), and Service Request Message (SRM). The data volume of these messages is very low. The radio technology is part of the WLAN IEEE 802.11 family of standards and known in the US as Wireless Access in Vehicular Environments (WAVE) and in Europe as ITS-G5. To complement the direct communication mode, vehicles can be equipped with traditional cellular communication technologies, supporting V2N based services. This extension with V2N was achieved in Europe under the C-ITS platform umbrella with cellular systems and broadcast systems (TMC/DAB+).

3GPP (C-V2X)

More recent V2X communication uses cellular networks and is called cellular V2X (or C-V2X) to differentiate it from the WLAN-based V2X. There have been multiple industry organizations, such as the 5G Automotive Association (5GAA) promoting C-V2X due to its advantages over WLAN based V2X (without considering disadvantages at the same time). C-V2X is initially defined as LTE in 3GPP Release 14 and is designed to operate in several modes:

- Device-to-device (V2V or V2I), and
- Device-to-network (V2N).

In 3GPP Release 15, the V2X functionalities are expanded to support 5G. C-V2X includes support of both direct communication between vehicles (V2V) and traditional cellular-network based communication. Also, C-V2X provides a migration path to 5G based systems and services, which implies incompatibility and higher costs compared to 4G based solutions.

The direct communication between vehicle and other devices (V2V, V2I) uses so-called PC5 interface. PC5 refers to a reference point where the User Equipment (UE), i.e. mobile handset, directly communicates with another UE over the direct channel. In this case, the communication with the base station is not required. In system architectural level, proximity service (ProSe) is the feature that specifies the architecture of the direct communication between UEs. In 3GPP RAN specifications, "sidelink" is the terminology to refer to the direct communication over PC5. PC5 interface was originally defined to address the needs of mission-critical communication for public safety community (Public Safety-LTE, or PS-LTE) in release 13. The motivation of the mission-critical communication was to allow law enforcement agencies or emergency rescue to use the LTE communication even when the infrastructure is not available, such as natural disaster scenario. In release 14 onwards, the use of PC5 interface has been expanded to meet various market needs, such as communication involving wearable devices such as smartwatch. In C-V2X, PC5 interface is re-applied to the direct communication in V2V and V2I.

The Cellular V2X mode 4 communication relies on a distributed resource allocation scheme, namely sensing-based semipersistent scheduling which schedules radio resources in a stand-alone fashion in each user equipment (UE).

In addition to the direct communication over PC5, C-V2X also allows the C-V2X device to use the cellular network connection in the traditional manner over Uu interface. Uu refers to the logical interface between the UE and the base station. This is generally referred to as vehicle-to-network (V2N). V2N is a unique use case to C-V2X and does not exist in 802.11p based V2X given that the latter supports direct communication only. However, similar to WLAN based V2X also in case of C-V2X, two communication radios are required to be able to communicate simultaneously via a PC5 interface with nearby stations and via the UU interface with the network.

While 3GPP defines the data transport features that enable V2X, it does not include V2X semantic content but proposes usage of ITS-G5 standards like CAM, DENM, BSM, etc. over 3GPP V2X data transport features.

Use Cases

Through its instant communication V2X allows road safety applications such as (non-exhaustive list):

- Forward collision warning.

- Lane change warning/blind spot warning.
- Emergency electric brake light warning.
- Intersection movement assist.
- Emergency vehicle approaching.
- Roadworks warning.
- Platooning.

The US National Highway Traffic Safety Administration's (NHTSA) report "Vehicle-to-Vehicle Communications: Readiness of V2V Technology for Application" lists the initial use cases envisioned for the US. European standardisation body ETSI and SAE published standards on what they see as use cases. Early use cases focus on road safety and efficiency. New and advanced use cases are introduced by organizations such as 3GPP, 5GAA, and 5GCAR, these use cases address high levels of automation.

In the medium term V2X is perceived as a key enabler for autonomous driving, assuming it would be allowed to intervene into the actual driving. In that case vehicles would be able to join platoons, the way HGVs do. With the advent of connected and autonomous mobility, V2X discussions are seen to play an important role, especially in the context of teleoperations for autonomous vehicles and platooning

Standardisation History

IEEE 802.11p:

- WLAN-based V2X communication is based on a set of standards drafted by the American Society for Testing and Materials (ASTM). The ASTM E 2213 series of standards looks at wireless communication for high-speed information exchange between vehicles themselves as well as road infrastructure. The first standard of this series was published 2002. Here the acronym Wireless Access in Vehicular Environments (WAVE) was first used for V2X communication.
- From 2004 onwards the Institute Electrical and Electronics Engineers (IEEE) started to work on wireless access for vehicles under the umbrella of their standards family IEEE 802.11 for Wireless Local Area Networks (WLAN). Their initial standard for wireless communication for vehicles is known as IEEE 802.11p and is based on the work done by the ASTM. Later on in 2012 IEEE 802.11p was incorporated in IEEE 802.11.
- Around 2007 when IEEE 802.11p got stable, IEEE started to develop the 1609.x standards family standardising applications and a security framework (IEEE uses the term WAVE), and soon after SAE started

to specify standards for V2V communication applications. SAE uses the term DSRC for this technology (this is how the term was coined in the US). In parallel at ETSI the technical committee for Intelligent transportation system (ITS) was founded and started to produce standards for protocols and applications (ETSI coined the term ITS-G5). All these standards are based on IEEE 802.11p technology.

- Between 2012 and 2013, the Japanese Association of Radio Industries and Businesses (ARIB) specified, also based on IEEE 802.11, a V2V and V2I communication system in the 700 MHz frequency band.
- In 2015 ITU published as summary of all V2V and V2I standards that are worldwide in use, comprising the systems specified by ETSI, IEEE, ARIB, and TTA (Republic of Korea, Telecommunication Technology Association).

3GPP:

- 3GPP started standardization work of cellular V2X (C-V2X) in Release 14 in 2014. It is based on LTE as the underlying technology. Specifications were published in 2017. Because this C-V2X functionalities are based on LTE, it is often referred to as LTE-V2X. The scope of functionalities supported by C-V2X includes both direct communication (V2V, V2I) as well as wide area cellular network communication (V2N).
- In Release 15, 3GPP continued its C-V2X standardization to be based on 5G. Specifications are published in 2018 as Release 15 comes to completion. To indicate the underlying technology, the term 5G-V2X is often used in contrast to LTE-based V2X (LTE-V2X). Either case, C-V2X is the generic terminology that refers to the V2X technology using the cellular technology irrespective of the specific generation of technology.
- In Release 16, 3GPP further enhances the C-V2X functionality. The work is currently in progress. In this way, C-V2X is inherently future-proof by supporting migration path to 5G.
- Study and analysis were done to compare the effectiveness of direct communication technologies between LTE-V2X PC5 and 802.11p from the perspective of accident avoided and reduction in fatal and serious injuries. The study shows that LTE-V2X achieves higher level of accident avoidance and reduction in injury. It also indicates LTE-V2X performs higher percentage of successful packet delivery and communication range. Another link-level and system-level simulation result indicates that, to achieve the same link performance for both line-of-sight (LOS)

and non-line-of-sight (NLOS) scenarios, lower signal-to-noise-ratio (SNR) are achievable by LTE-V2X PC5 interface compared to IEEE 802.11p.

- Cellular-based V2X solution also leads to the possibility of further protecting other types of road users (e.g. pedestrian, cyclist) by having PC5 interface to be integrated into smartphones, effectively integrating those road users into the overall C-ITS solution. Vehicle-to-person (V2P) includes Vulnerable Road User (VRU) scenarios to detect pedestrians and cyclists to avoid accident and injuries involving those road users.
- As both direct communication and wide area cellular network communication are defined in the same standard (3GPP), both modes of communication will likely be integrated into a single chipset. Commercialization of those chipsets further enhances economy of scale and leads to possibilities to wider range of business models and services using both types of communications.

In United States

In 1999 the US Federal Communications Commission (FCC) allocated 75 MHz in the spectrum of 5.850-5.925 GHz for intelligent transport systems. Since then the US Department of Transportation (USDOT) has been working with a range of stakeholders on V2X. In 2012 a pre-deployment project was implemented in Ann Arbor, Michigan. 2800 vehicles covering cars, motorcycles, buses and HGV of different brands took part using equipment by different manufacturers. The US National Highway Traffic Safety Administration (NHTSA) saw this model deployment as proof that road safety could be improved and that WAVE standard technology was interoperable. In August 2014 NHTSA published a report arguing vehicle-to-vehicle technology was technically proven as ready for deployment. On 20 August 2014 the NHTSA published an Advance Notice of Proposed Rulemaking (ANPRM) in the Federal Register, arguing that the safety benefits of V2X communication could only be achieved if a significant part of the vehicles fleet was equipped. Because of the lack of an immediate benefit for early adopters, the NHTSA proposed a mandatory introduction. On 25 June 2015 the US House of Representatives held a hearing on the matter, where again the NHTSA, as well as other stakeholders argued the case for V2X.

On November 18, 2020, the FCC reallocated 45 MHz in the 5.850–5.895 GHz range to Wi-Fi, and the rest of the V2X band to C-V2X, citing the failure of DSRC to take off. The advocacy organizations ITS America and American Association of State Highway and Transportation Officials sued the FCC, arguing that the decision harms users of DSRC; on August 12, 2022, a federal court permitted the reassignment to go ahead.

In Europe

To acquire EU-wide spectrum, radio applications require a harmonised standard, in case of ITS-G5 ETSI EN 302 571, first published in 2008. A harmonised standard in turn requires an ETSI System Reference Document, here ETSI TR 101 788. Commission Decision 2008/671/EC harmonises the use of the 5875 to 5905 MHz frequency band for transport safety ITS applications. In 2010 the ITS Directive 2010/40/EU was adopted. It aims to assure that ITS applications are interoperable and can operate across national borders, it defines priority areas for secondary legislation, which cover V2X and requires technologies to be mature. In 2014 the European Commission's industry stakeholder "C-ITS Deployment Platform" started working on a regulatory framework for V2X in the EU. It identified key approaches to an EU-wide V2X security Public Key infrastructure (PKI) and data protection, as well as facilitating a mitigation standard to prevent radio interference between ITS-G5 based V2X and road charging systems. The European Commission recognised ITS-G5 as the initial communication technology in its 5G Action Plan and the accompanying explanatory document, to form a communication environment consisting of ITS-G5 and cellular communication as envisioned by EU Member States. Various pre-deployment projects exist at EU or EU Member State level, such as SCOOP@F, the Testfeld Telematik, the digital testbed Autobahn, the Rotterdam-Vienna ITS Corridor, Nordic Way, COMPASS4D or C-ROADS. There exist real scenarios of implementation V2X standard as well. The first commercial project where V2X standard is used for Intersection movement assist use-case. It has been realized in Brno City / Czech Republic where 80 pcs of cross intersections are controlled by V2X communication standard from public transport vehicles of municipality Brno.

Consideration in the Transition Period

The deployment of V2X technology (either C-V2X or 802.11p based products) will occur gradually over time. New cars will be equipped with either of the two technologies starting around 2020 and its proportion on the road is expected to increase gradually. The Volkswagen Golf 8th generation was the first passenger car to be fitted with V2X technology powered by NXP technology. In the meantime, existing (legacy) vehicles will continue to exist on the road. This implies that the V2X capable vehicles will need to co-exist with non-V2X (legacy) vehicles or with V2X vehicles of incompatible technology.

The main obstacles to its adoption are legal issues and the fact that, unless almost all vehicles adopt it, its effectiveness is limited. British weekly *The Economist* argued in 2016 that autonomous driving is more driven by regulations than by technology. However, a 2017 study indicated that there are benefits in reducing traffic accidents even during the transitional period in which the technology is being adopted in the market.

Edge AI for Autonomous Operations

Deploys machine learning models and deep learning algorithms at the edge to learn and adapt to complex driving scenarios, traffic patterns, and dynamic environments, supporting autonomous decision-making and navigation in diverse road conditions.

7.4.2 Benefits of Edge Computing in Autonomous Vehicles

Edge computing offers several strategic benefits for autonomous vehicle manufacturers, developers, and consumers.

Low Latency and Real-Time Responsiveness

Reduces data transmission delays by processing critical sensor data locally at the edge, ensuring rapid decision-making, vehicle control, and response to dynamic traffic conditions for enhanced safety and driver experience.

Enhanced Privacy and Data Security

Protects vehicle-to-cloud communications, personal data, and sensitive information by encrypting data, implementing secure protocols, and minimizing exposure to cyber threats in autonomous driving environments.

Bandwidth Efficiency and Cost Optimization

Optimizes bandwidth usage and reduces reliance on centralized cloud resources by offloading computational tasks to edge devices and onboard processing units, minimizing data latency, and operational costs for autonomous vehicle fleets.

7.4.3 Challenges and Considerations

Deploying edge computing in autonomous vehicles presents challenges and considerations that require strategic planning and regulatory compliance.

Edge Device Reliability

Ensures reliability, fault tolerance, and operational resilience of edge computing infrastructure, sensors, and onboard processing units (e.g., ECUs) to maintain continuous operation and safety critical functions in autonomous driving scenarios.

Cybersecurity Risks

Mitigates cybersecurity threats, data breaches, and vulnerabilities in connected vehicles by implementing robust security measures, intrusion detection systems (IDS), and firmware updates to protect against malicious attacks and unauthorized access.

Regulatory Compliance

Adheres to automotive safety standards (e.g., ISO 26262), data protection regulations (e.g., GDPR, CCPA), and industry guidelines for autonomous vehicle deployment, ensuring compliance with legal requirements, liability frameworks, and ethical considerations.

7.4.4 Future Trends and Innovations

Emerging trends and innovations in edge computing are shaping the future of autonomous vehicles and intelligent transportation systems.

Edge AI and Federated Learning

Advances in edge AI algorithms, federated learning techniques, and decentralized machine learning models enable collaborative data processing, model training, and knowledge sharing among autonomous vehicles while preserving data privacy and security.

5G Network Integration

Leverages high-speed 5G networks and edge computing capabilities to support vehicle-to-network (V2N) communication, ultra-low latency services, and real-time updates for autonomous driving, enhancing connectivity, and situational awareness on the road.

Edge-to-Cloud Continuum

Integrates hybrid edge-to-cloud architectures for seamless data integration, workload distribution, and scalability in autonomous vehicle fleets, optimizing computational resources, and enabling adaptive decision-making in complex driving environments.

7.4.5 Ethical and Social Implications

Addressing ethical considerations and societal impacts of edge computing in autonomous vehicles involves promoting safety, transparency, and accountability in AI-driven decision-making, ensuring public trust, regulatory compliance, and responsible deployment of autonomous driving technologies.

CHAPTER 8

EDGE COMPUTING AND INDUSTRY 4.0

8.1 EDGE COMPUTING AND THE FOURTH INDUSTRIAL REVOLUTION

Edge computing is playing a pivotal role in the Fourth Industrial Revolution (Industry 4.0) by enabling decentralized data processing, real-time analytics, and autonomous decision-making at the network edge. This transformative paradigm leverages edge devices, IoT sensors, and localized computing resources to drive innovation, enhance operational efficiency, and accelerate digital transformation across diverse industries.

Edge computing is driving the Fourth Industrial Revolution by enabling decentralized data processing, real-time analytics, and autonomous decision-making capabilities at the network edge. By leveraging edge computing technologies, industries can enhance operational efficiency, accelerate digital innovation, and foster sustainable growth while addressing challenges related to interoperability, cybersecurity, and workforce readiness in Industry 4.0 transformations. As organizations embrace edge-driven initiatives and deploy innovative applications, prioritizing scalability, security, and ethical considerations fosters trust, resilience, and inclusive development in the evolving landscape of smart manufacturing ecosystems. Edge computing continues to play a pivotal role in shaping the future of industrial automation, digital resilience, and competitive advantage in the global marketplace.

8.1.1 Understanding the Fourth Industrial Revolution

"Fourth Industrial Revolution", "4IR", or "Industry 4.0" is a buzzword and neologism describing rapid technological advancement in the 21st century. The term was popularised in 2016 by Klaus Schwab, the World Economic Forum founder and executive chairman, who says that the changes show a significant shift in industrial capitalism.

A part of this phase of industrial change is the joining of technologies like artificial intelligence, gene editing, to advanced robotics that blur the lines between the physical, digital, and biological worlds. Throughout this, fundamental shifts are taking place in how the global production and supply network operates through ongoing automation of traditional manufacturing and industrial practices, using modern smart technology, large-scale machine-to-machine communication (M2M), and the Internet of things (IoT). This integration results in increasing automation, improving communication and self-monitoring, and the use of smart machines that can analyse and diagnose issues without the need for human intervention.

It also represents a social, political, and economic shift from the digital age of the late 1990s and early 2000s to an era of embedded connectivity distinguished by the ubiquity of technology in society (i.e. a metaverse) that changes the ways humans experience and know the world around them. It posits that we have created and are entering an augmented social reality compared to just the natural senses and industrial ability of humans alone.

History

The phrase *Fourth Industrial Revolution* was first introduced by a team of scientists developing a high-tech strategy for the German government. Klaus Schwab, executive chairman of the World Economic Forum (WEF), introduced the phrase to a wider audience in a 2015 article published by *Foreign Affairs*. "Mastering the Fourth Industrial Revolution" was the 2016 theme of the World Economic Forum Annual Meeting, in Davos-Klosters, Switzerland.

On 10 October 2016, the Forum announced the opening of its Centre for the Fourth Industrial Revolution in San Francisco. This was also subject and title of Schwab's 2016 book. Schwab includes in this fourth era technologies that combine hardware, software, and biology (cyber-physical systems), and emphasises advances in communication and connectivity. Schwab expects this era to be marked by breakthroughs in emerging technologies in fields such as robotics, artificial intelligence, nanotechnology, quantum computing, biotechnology, the internet of things, the industrial internet of things, decentralised consensus, fifth-generation wireless technologies, 3D printing, and fully autonomous vehicles.

First Industrial Revolution

The First Industrial Revolution was marked by a transition from hand production methods to machines through the use of steam power and water power. The implementation of new technologies took a long time, so the period which this refers to was between 1760 and 1820, or 1840 in Europe and the United States. Its effects had consequences on textile manufacturing, which was first to adopt such changes, as well as iron industry, agriculture, and mining although it also had societal effects with an ever stronger middle class.

Second Industrial Revolution

The Second Industrial Revolution, also known as the Technological Revolution, is the period between 1871 and 1914 that resulted from installations of extensive railroad and telegraph networks, which allowed for faster transfer of people and ideas, as well as electricity. Increasing electrification allowed for factories to develop the modern production line. It was a period of great economic growth, with an increase in productivity, which also caused a surge in unemployment since many factory workers were replaced by machines.

Third Industrial Revolution

The Third Industrial Revolution, also known as the Digital Electronics Revolution, occurred in the late 20th century, after the end of the two world wars, resulting from a slowdown of industrialisation and technological advancement compared to previous periods. The production of the Z1 computer, which used binary floating-point numbers and Boolean logic, a decade later, was the beginning of more advanced digital developments.

A book titled The Third Industrial Revolution, by Jeremy Rifkin, was published in 2011, which focused on the intersection of digital communications technology and renewable energy. It was made into a 2017 documentary by Vice Media.

Characteristics

In essence, the Fourth Industrial Revolution is the trend towards automation and data exchange in manufacturing technologies and processes which include cyber-physical systems (CPS), IoT, industrial internet of things, cloud computing, cognitive computing, and artificial intelligence.

The machines cannot replace the deep expertise but they tend to be more efficient than humans in performing repetitive functions, and the combination of machine learning and computational power allows machines to carry out highly complicated tasks. The Fourth Industrial Revolution has been defined as technological developments in cyber-physical systems such as high capacity connectivity; new human-machine interaction modes such as touch interfaces and virtual reality systems; and improvements in transferring digital instructions to the physical world including robotics and 3D printing (additive manufacturing); the Internet of Things (IoT); "big data" and cloud computing; artificial intelligence-based systems; improvements to and uptake of Off-Grid / Stand-Alone Renewable Energy Systems: solar, wind, wave, hydroelectric and the electric batteries (lithium-ion renewable energy storage systems (ESS) and EV). The Fourth Industrial Revolution marks the beginning of the imagination age.

Key Themes

Industry 4.0 increases operational efficiency. Four themes are presented that summarise an Industry 4.0:

- **Decentralized Decisions:** The ability of cyber physical systems to make decisions on their own and to perform their tasks as autonomously as possible. Only in the case of exceptions, interference, or conflicting goals, are tasks delegated to a higher level

Distinctiveness

Proponents of the Fourth Industrial Revolution suggest it is a distinct revolution rather than simply a prolongation of the Third Industrial Revolution. This is due to the following characteristics:

- **Velocity:** Exponential speed at which incumbent industries are affected and displaced
- **Scope and Systems Impact:** The large amount of sectors and firms that are affected
- **Paradigm Shift in Technology Policy:** New policies designed for this new way of doing are present. An example is Singapore's formal recognition of Industry 4.0 in its innovation policies.

Critics of the concept dismiss Industry 4.0 as a marketing strategy. They suggest that although revolutionary changes are identifiable in distinct sectors, there is no systemic change so far. In addition, the pace of recognition of Industry 4.0 and policy transition varies across countries; the definition of Industry 4.0 is not harmonised. One of the most known figures is Jeremy Rifkin who "agree[s] that digitalization is the hallmark and defining technology in what has become known as the Third Industrial Revolution". However, he argues that "that the evolution of digitalization has barely begun to run its course and that its new configuration in the form of the Internet of Things represents the next stage of its development".

Components

The application of the Fourth Industrial Revolution operates through:

- Mobile devices.
- Internet of things (IoT) platforms.
- Location detection technologies (electronic identification).
- Advanced human-machine interfaces.
- Authentication and fraud detection.
- Smart sensors.
- Big analytics and advanced processes.
- Multilevel customer interaction and customer profiling.
- Augmented reality/wearables.

- On-demand availability of computer system resources.
- Data visualisation and triggered "live" training.

Mainly these technologies can be summarised into four major components, defining the term "Industry 4.0" or "smart factory":

- Cyber-physical systems.
- Internet of things (IoT).
- On-demand availability of computer system resources (e.g. cloud computing).
- Cognitive computing.

Industry 4.0 networks a wide range of new technologies to create value. Using cyber-physical systems that monitor physical processes, a virtual copy of the physical world can be designed. Characteristics of cyber-physical systems include the ability to make decentralised decisions independently, reaching a high degree of autonomy.

The value created in Industry 4.0, can be relied upon electronic identification, in which the smart manufacturing require set technologies to be incorporated in the manufacturing process to thus be classified as in the development path of Industry 4.0 and no longer digitisation.

Trends

Smart Factory

Smart Factory is the vision of a production environment in which production facilities and logistics systems are organised without human intervention. The Smart Factory is no longer a vision. While different model factories represent the feasible, many enterprises already clarify with examples practically, how the Smart Factory functions.

The technical foundations on which the Smart Factory – the intelligent factory – is based are cyber-physical systems that communicate with each other using the Internet of Things and Services. An important part of this process is the exchange of data between the product and the production line. This enables a much more efficient connection of the Supply Chain and better organisation within any production environment.

The Fourth Industrial Revolution fosters what has been called a "smart factory". Within modular structured smart factories, cyber-physical systems monitor physical processes, create a virtual copy of the physical world and make decentralised decisions. Over the internet of things, cyber-physical systems communicate and cooperate with each other and with humans in synchronic time both internally and across organizational services offered and used by participants of the value chain.

Predictive Maintenance

Industry 4.0 can also provide predictive maintenance, due to the use of technology and the IoT sensors. Predictive maintenance – which can identify maintenance issues in real time – allows machine owners to perform cost-effective maintenance and determine it ahead of time before the machinery fails or gets damaged. For example, a company in Los Angeles could understand if a piece of equipment in Singapore is running at an abnormal speed or temperature. They could then decide whether or not it needs to be repaired.

3D Printing

The Fourth Industrial Revolution is said to have extensive dependency on 3D printing technology. Some advantages of 3D printing for industry are that 3D printing can print many geometric structures, as well as simplify the product design process. It is also relatively environmentally friendly. In low-volume production, it can also decrease lead times and total production costs. Moreover, it can increase flexibility, reduce warehousing costs and help the company towards the adoption of a mass customisation business strategy. In addition, 3D printing can be very useful for printing spare parts and installing it locally, therefore reducing supplier dependence and reducing the supply lead time. The determining factor is the pace of change. The correlation of the speed of technological development and, as a result, socio-economic and infrastructural transformations with human life allows one to state a qualitative leap in the speed of development, which marks a transition to a new time era.

Smart Sensors

Sensors and instrumentation drive the central forces of innovation, not only for Industry 4.0 but also for other "smart" megatrends, such as smart production, smart mobility, smart homes, smart cities, and smart factories. Smart sensors are devices, which generate the data and allow further functionality from self-monitoring and self-configuration to condition monitoring of complex processes. With the capability of wireless communication, they reduce installation effort to a great extent and help realise a dense array of sensors.

The importance of sensors, measurement science, and smart evaluation for Industry 4.0 has been recognised and acknowledged by various experts and has already led to the statement "Industry 4.0: nothing goes without sensor systems." However, there are a few issues, such as time synchronisation error, data loss, and dealing with large amounts of harvested data, which all limit the implementation of full-fledged systems. Moreover, additional limits on these functionalities represents the battery power. One example of the integration of smart sensors in the electronic devices, is the case of smart watches, where sensors receive the data from the movement of the user, process the data and as a result, provide the user with the information about how many steps they have walked in a day and also converts the data into calories burned.

Agriculture and Food Industries

Smart sensors in these two fields are still in the testing stage. These innovative connected sensors collect, interpret and communicate the information available in the plots (leaf area, vegetation index, chlorophyll, hygrometry, temperature, water potential, radiation). Based on this scientific data, the objective is to enable real-time monitoring via a smartphone with a range of advice that optimises plot management in terms of results, time and costs. On the farm, these sensors can be used to detect crop stages and recommend inputs and treatments at the right time. As well as controlling the level of irrigation. The food industry requires more and more security and transparency and full documentation is required. This new technology is used as a tracking system as well as the collection of human data and product data.

Accelerated Transition to the Knowledge Economy

Knowledge economy is an economic system in which production and services are largely based on knowledge-intensive activities that contribute to an accelerated pace of technical and scientific advance, as well as rapid obsolescence. Industry 4.0 aids transitions into knowledge economy by increasing reliance on intellectual capabilities than on physical inputs or natural resources.

Challenges

Challenges in implementation of Industry 4.0:

Economic

- High economic cost.
- Business model adaptation.
- Unclear economic benefits/excessive investment.

Social

- Privacy concerns.
- Surveillance and distrust.
- General reluctance to change by stakeholders.
- Threat of redundancy of the corporate IT department.
- Loss of many jobs to automatic processes and IT-controlled processes, especially for blue collar workers.

- Increased risk of gender inequalities in professions with job roles most susceptible to replacement with AI.

Political

- Lack of regulation, standards and forms of certifications.
- Unclear legal issues and data security.

Organizational

- IT security issues, which are greatly aggravated by the inherent need to open up previously closed production shops.
- Reliability and stability needed for critical machine-to-machine communication (M2M), including very short and stable latency times.
- Need to maintain the integrity of production processes.
- Need to avoid any IT snags, as those would cause expensive production outages.
- Need to protect industrial know-how (contained also in the control files for the industrial automation gear).
- Lack of adequate skill-sets to expedite the transition towards a fourth industrial revolution.
- Low top management commitment.
- Insufficient qualification of employees.

Industry Applications

The aerospace industry has sometimes been characterised as "too low volume for extensive automation"; however, Industry 4.0 principles have been investigated by several aerospace companies, and technologies have been developed to improve productivity where the upfront cost of automation cannot be justified. One example of this is the aerospace parts manufacturer Meggitt PLC's M4 project.

The increasing use of the industrial internet of things is referred to as Industry 4.0 at Bosch, and generally in Germany. Applications include machines that can predict failures and trigger maintenance processes autonomously or self-organised coordination that react to unexpected changes in production. in 2017, Bosch launched the Connectory, a Chicago, Illinois based innovation incubator that specializes in IoT, including Industry 4.0. Industry 4.0 inspired Innovation 4.0, a move toward digitisation for academia and research and development. In 2017, the £81M Materials Innovation Factory (MIF) at the University of Liverpool opened as a center for computer aided materials science, where robotic formulation, data capture and modelling are being integrated into development practices.

Future

Industry 5.0

Industry 5.0 has been proposed as a strategy to create a paradigm shift for an industrial landscape in which the primary focus should no longer be on increasing efficiency but on promoting the well-being of society and sustainability of the economy and industrial production.

8.1.2 Applications of Edge Computing in Industry 4.0

Edge computing facilitates a wide range of applications and use cases within the Fourth Industrial Revolution.

Smart Manufacturing and Industrial IoT (IIoT)

Integrates edge devices with industrial sensors and production equipment to enable predictive maintenance, process optimization, and real-time monitoring of manufacturing operations, enhancing productivity, and reducing downtime.

Autonomous Systems and Robotics

Employs edge AI algorithms and machine learning models to enable autonomous robots, drones, and vehicles for automated material handling, logistics, and smart grid management in smart factories and industrial environments.

Digital Twins and Simulation

Leverages edge computing for real-time data synchronization, virtual simulations, and predictive modeling of physical assets, enabling digital twins to replicate and optimize operational processes, product design, and supply chain management.

Supply Chain Optimization

Enhances logistics, inventory management, and predictive analytics with edge computing capabilities for real-time tracking of shipments, demand forecasting, and adaptive supply chain strategies in response to market fluctuations.

8.1.3 Benefits of Edge Computing in Industry 4.0

Edge computing offers several strategic benefits for industries embarking on the Fourth Industrial Revolution.

Low Latency and Real-Time Responsiveness

Reduces data transmission delays and latency issues by processing critical data locally at the edge, ensuring rapid decision-making, operational agility, and real-time responsiveness in dynamic industrial environments.

Scalability and Resource Efficiency

Optimizes bandwidth usage, network congestion, and computational resources by distributing computing capabilities closer to IoT endpoints and edge devices, supporting scalable deployment and operational flexibility.

Enhanced Data Privacy and Security

Protects sensitive industrial data, intellectual property, and operational insights by implementing robust security protocols, encryption standards, and access controls in edge computing architectures, ensuring data integrity and regulatory compliance.

8.1.4 Challenges and Considerations

Deploying edge computing in Industry 4.0 environments presents challenges and considerations that require strategic planning and risk management.

Interoperability and Integration

Integrates heterogeneous industrial systems, legacy equipment, and cloud platforms with edge computing architectures, ensuring data interoperability, standardized protocols, and seamless integration for unified industrial automation.

Cybersecurity Risks

Mitigates cybersecurity threats, data breaches, and vulnerabilities in interconnected industrial networks by implementing advanced security measures, anomaly detection systems, and continuous monitoring to safeguard against malicious attacks and unauthorized access.

Workforce Skills and Training

Promotes workforce readiness, digital literacy, and skill development in edge computing technologies, AI-driven automation, and industrial IoT to enhance operational efficiency, employee productivity, and organizational resilience in Industry 4.0 transformations.

8.1.5 Future Trends and Innovations

Emerging trends and innovations in edge computing are shaping the future of Industry 4.0 and smart manufacturing initiatives.

Edge AI and Machine Learning

Advances in edge AI algorithms, federated learning techniques, and distributed computing enable autonomous decision-making, predictive analytics, and adaptive control systems for autonomous manufacturing processes and intelligent industrial automation.

5G Network Integration

Leverages high-speed 5G networks and edge computing capabilities to support ultra-low latency communication, high-throughput data transmission, and real-time connectivity for smart factories, autonomous vehicles, and industrial IoT applications.

Blockchain Technology

Integrates blockchain-based solutions for secure data sharing, transparent supply chain management, and decentralized trust in Industry 4.0 ecosystems, enhancing data provenance, traceability, and transactional transparency across industrial operations.

8.1.6 Ethical and Social Implications

Addressing ethical considerations and societal impacts of edge computing in Industry 4.0 involves promoting digital inclusion, ethical AI practices, and responsible automation to ensure equitable access, workforce empowerment, and socio-economic sustainability in the era of intelligent manufacturing and digital transformation.

8.2 SMART FACTORIES AND EDGE-ENABLED MANUFACTURING

Smart factories represent the future of industrial manufacturing, integrating advanced technologies such as edge computing, IoT sensors, and AI-driven automation to optimize production processes, enhance operational efficiency, and enable real-time decision-making at the network edge. Edge-enabled manufacturing is transforming smart factories by enabling real-time data processing, AI-driven automation, and operational intelligence at the network edge. By leveraging edge computing technologies, manufacturers can optimize production efficiency, reduce costs, and drive innovation while addressing challenges related to interoperability, cybersecurity, and workforce readiness in Industry 4.0 transformations. As industries embrace edge-driven initiatives and deploy innovative applications, prioritizing scalability, security, and ethical considerations fosters trust, resilience, and inclusive development in the evolving landscape of smart manufacturing ecosystems. Edge computing continues to play a pivotal role in shaping the future of industrial automation, digital resilience, and competitive advantage in the global marketplace.

8.2.1 Applications of Edge-Enabled Manufacturing

Edge computing facilitates a wide range of applications and functionalities within smart factories:

- **Predictive Maintenance:** Integrates edge devices with industrial sensors to monitor equipment performance, detect anomalies, and predict potential failures in real-time, enabling proactive maintenance, minimizing downtime, and optimizing asset lifecycle management.

- **Real-Time Quality Control:** Implements edge AI algorithms for visual inspection, defect detection, and quality assurance on the production line, ensuring product consistency, reducing waste, and enhancing manufacturing yield through automated inspection processes.
- **Supply Chain Optimization:** Enhances logistics, inventory management, and demand forecasting with edge computing capabilities for real-time data analytics, predictive insights, and adaptive supply chain strategies in response to market dynamics and customer demands.
- **Autonomous Operations:** Deploys edge AI and robotics for automated material handling, assembly line operations, and adaptive manufacturing processes, improving productivity, reducing labor costs, and optimizing resource utilization in smart factory environments.

8.2.2 Benefits of Edge-Enabled Manufacturing

Edge computing offers several strategic benefits for manufacturers adopting smart factory initiatives:

- **Low Latency and Real-Time Responsiveness:** Reduces data transmission delays by processing critical manufacturing data locally at the edge, ensuring rapid decision-making, operational agility, and real-time responsiveness to dynamic production demands and supply chain disruptions.
- **Scalability and Flexibility:** Optimizes bandwidth usage, network traffic, and computational resources by distributing processing capabilities closer to IoT endpoints and industrial devices, supporting scalable deployment, and adaptive manufacturing strategies.
- **Enhanced Data Security and Privacy:** Protects sensitive manufacturing data, intellectual property, and operational insights by implementing robust security measures, encryption standards, and access controls in edge computing architectures, ensuring data integrity and regulatory compliance.

8.2.3 Challenges and Considerations

Deploying edge-enabled manufacturing in smart factory environments presents challenges and considerations that require strategic planning and risk management:

- **Interoperability and Integration:** Integrates diverse industrial systems, legacy equipment, and cloud platforms with edge computing architectures, ensuring seamless data interoperability, standardized protocols, and unified automation for holistic smart factory operations.

- **Cybersecurity Risks:** Mitigates cybersecurity threats, data breaches, and vulnerabilities in interconnected industrial networks by implementing advanced security measures, intrusion detection systems (IDS), and continuous monitoring to safeguard against malicious attacks and unauthorized access.
- **Workforce Skills and Training:** Promotes workforce readiness, digital literacy, and skill development in edge computing technologies, AI-driven automation, and industrial IoT to enhance operational efficiency, employee productivity, and organizational resilience in smart manufacturing transformations.

8.2.4 Future Trends and Innovations

Emerging trends and innovations in edge-enabled manufacturing are shaping the future of smart factories and industrial automation:

- **Edge AI and Machine Learning:** Advances in edge AI algorithms, federated learning techniques, and distributed computing enable autonomous decision-making, predictive analytics, and adaptive control systems for agile manufacturing processes and intelligent production systems.
- **5G Network Integration:** Leverages high-speed 5G networks and edge computing capabilities to support ultra-low latency communication, high-throughput data transmission, and real-time connectivity for smart factory operations, enabling seamless integration of autonomous systems and IoT devices.
- **Digital Twins and Simulation:** Integrates digital twin technologies with edge computing for real-time data synchronization, virtual simulations, and predictive modeling of production workflows, enabling predictive maintenance, scenario analysis, and optimization of manufacturing operations.

8.2.5 Ethical and Social Implications

Addressing ethical considerations and societal impacts of edge-enabled manufacturing involves promoting safety, transparency, and accountability in AI-driven automation, ensuring ethical AI practices, and responsible deployment of advanced technologies to empower workers, protect consumer rights, and foster sustainable development in smart factory ecosystems.

8.3 PREDICTIVE MAINTENANCE WITH EDGE ANALYTICS

Predictive maintenance is a proactive approach used in various industries to predict equipment failures before they occur, thereby reducing downtime, optimizing maintenance schedules, and enhancing operational efficiency. Edge analytics plays a crucial role in enabling real-time data processing, machine learning algorithms, and predictive insights at the network edge. Predictive maintenance with edge analytics is transforming industries by enabling proactive maintenance strategies, real-time data processing, and predictive insights at the network edge. By leveraging edge computing technologies, industries can enhance equipment reliability, reduce downtime, and optimize maintenance operations while addressing challenges related to data quality, scalability, and cybersecurity. As organizations embrace predictive maintenance with edge-driven initiatives and deploy innovative applications, prioritizing reliability, efficiency, and cost savings fosters resilience, competitiveness, and sustainable growth in the evolving landscape of industrial automation and asset management. Edge analytics continues to play a pivotal role in shaping the future of predictive maintenance, operational excellence, and digital transformation across diverse industries.

8.3.1 Concepts of Predictive Maintenance

Predictive maintenance aims to predict equipment failures based on the condition of the equipment, rather than using fixed intervals or waiting for failures to happen. It leverages data analytics, machine learning models, and historical data to anticipate maintenance needs, identify anomalies, and recommend timely repairs or replacements. By analyzing real-time data from sensors and IoT devices, predictive maintenance ensures optimal asset performance, extends equipment lifespan, and reduces operational costs across industries.

8.3.2 Applications of Edge Analytics in Predictive Maintenance

Edge analytics enhances predictive maintenance capabilities by processing data locally at the network edge, near the equipment or sensors generating the data. This approach offers several advantages:

- **Real-Time Data Processing:** Analyzes streaming data from sensors and equipment in real-time, enabling immediate detection of anomalies, deviations from normal operating conditions, and early warning signs of potential failures.
- **Reduced Latency:** Minimizes data transmission delays and response times by processing critical maintenance data locally at the edge, ensuring rapid decision-making, and timely intervention to prevent equipment breakdowns and production disruptions.
- **Cost Efficiency:** Optimizes resource allocation and maintenance schedules by prioritizing critical maintenance tasks based on predictive insights and asset condition monitoring, reducing unnecessary downtime, and minimizing operational costs.

8.3.3 Benefits of Predictive Maintenance with Edge Analytics

Predictive maintenance with edge analytics offers several strategic benefits for industries:

- **Improved Equipment Reliability**: Enhances equipment reliability and uptime by proactively identifying and addressing maintenance needs, minimizing unplanned downtime, and optimizing asset utilization in manufacturing, energy, and transportation sectors.
- **Enhanced Safety and Operational Efficiency**: Ensures safe and efficient operations by detecting potential equipment failures, mitigating risks, and prioritizing maintenance activities based on real-time data analytics and predictive insights.
- **Cost Savings**: Reduces maintenance costs, repair expenses, and spare parts inventory by implementing predictive maintenance strategies that extend equipment lifespan, optimize maintenance schedules, and improve overall operational efficiency.

8.3.4 Challenges and Considerations

Deploying predictive maintenance with edge analytics presents challenges and considerations that require careful planning and implementation:

- **Data Quality and Integration**: Ensures data accuracy, reliability, and compatibility across heterogeneous systems, sensors, and edge computing platforms to maintain data integrity and facilitate seamless integration for predictive maintenance applications.
- **Scalability and Infrastructure Requirements**: Addresses scalability challenges and infrastructure requirements for deploying edge computing solutions, including edge device management, network bandwidth, and computational resources to support growing data volumes and analytics workloads.
- **Cybersecurity and Data Privacy**: Mitigates cybersecurity risks, data breaches, and unauthorized access by implementing robust security measures, encryption protocols, and access controls to protect sensitive maintenance data and ensure regulatory compliance.

8.3.5 Future Trends and Innovations

Emerging trends and innovations in predictive maintenance with edge analytics are shaping the future of asset management and industrial automation:

- **AI and Machine Learning**: Advances in AI-driven algorithms, machine learning models, and deep learning techniques enable predictive analytics, anomaly detection, and prescriptive maintenance recommendations for adaptive maintenance strategies and continuous improvement.

- **Edge-to-Cloud Integration:** Integrates hybrid edge-to-cloud architectures for seamless data integration, workload distribution, and scalability in predictive maintenance applications, optimizing computational resources and enabling real-time decision-making in dynamic industrial environments.
- **Digital Twins and Simulation:** Leverages digital twin technologies with edge analytics to create virtual replicas of physical assets, simulate operational scenarios, and predict equipment behavior for predictive maintenance, enabling scenario analysis and optimization of maintenance strategies.

8.4 SUPPLY CHAIN OPTIMIZATION WITH EDGE COMPUTING

Supply chain optimization is crucial for enhancing operational efficiency, reducing costs, and meeting customer demands in today's dynamic business environment. Edge computing plays a pivotal role in revolutionizing supply chain management by enabling real-time data processing, predictive analytics, and decision-making at the network edge.

Edge computing is revolutionizing supply chain optimization by enabling real-time data processing, predictive analytics, and autonomous operations at the network edge. By leveraging edge computing technologies, organizations can enhance operational efficiency, reduce costs, and improve supply chain resilience while addressing challenges related to data integration, cybersecurity, and scalability in dynamic business environments. As industries embrace edge-driven initiatives and deploy innovative applications, prioritizing efficiency, responsiveness, and sustainability fosters resilience, competitiveness, and growth in the evolving landscape of global supply chain management. Edge computing continues to play a pivotal role in shaping the future of supply chain optimization, digital transformation, and customer-centric logistics solutions worldwide.

8.4.1 Concepts of Supply Chain Optimization

Supply chain optimization aims to streamline logistics, inventory management, and distribution processes to maximize efficiency, minimize costs, and improve overall supply chain performance. It involves leveraging technology, data analytics, and strategic planning to optimize supply chain operations, enhance visibility, and meet customer expectations through timely delivery and responsive supply chain management practices.

8.4.2 Applications of Edge Computing in Supply Chain Optimization

Edge computing facilitates several applications and functionalities within supply chain management:

- **Real-Time Data Analytics:** Processes streaming data from IoT sensors, RFID tags, and supply chain devices locally at the edge to monitor inventory levels, track shipments, and analyze transportation routes in real-time, enabling proactive decision-making and responsive supply chain operations.
- **Predictive Analytics:** Utilizes machine learning algorithms and AI-driven models at the network edge to predict demand patterns, anticipate supply chain disruptions, and optimize inventory levels, ensuring efficient resource allocation and reducing inventory holding costs.
- **Edge AI for Autonomous Operations:** Integrates AI-powered robotics, autonomous vehicles, and smart logistics systems for automated material handling, warehouse management, and last-mile delivery, enhancing operational efficiency, and reducing dependency on manual interventions.

8.4.3 Benefits of Supply Chain Optimization with Edge Computing

Edge computing offers several strategic benefits for supply chain optimization:

- **Enhanced Operational Efficiency**: Improves resource utilization, reduces lead times, and optimizes inventory management through real-time data analytics and predictive insights, enabling agile supply chain strategies and responsive customer service.
- **Cost Reduction:** Minimizes transportation costs, inventory holding costs, and operational expenses by optimizing logistics routes, reducing waste, and enhancing supply chain visibility with edge computing capabilities, supporting cost-effective supply chain management practices.
- **Improved Customer Satisfaction:** Enhances order fulfillment, delivery reliability, and responsiveness to customer demands by leveraging real-time data analytics and autonomous operations at the network edge, ensuring timely delivery and superior customer service experiences.

8.4.4 Challenges and Considerations

Deploying edge computing for supply chain optimization presents challenges and considerations:

- **Data Integration and Interoperability:** Ensures seamless integration of diverse data sources, supply chain systems, and IoT devices with edge computing platforms, maintaining data consistency, and facilitating interoperability for effective supply chain coordination.
- **Cybersecurity Risks:** Mitigates cybersecurity threats, data breaches, and vulnerabilities in interconnected supply chain networks by implementing robust security measures, encryption protocols, and access controls to protect sensitive supply chain data and ensure regulatory compliance.
- **Scalability and Resource Management:** Addresses scalability challenges and infrastructure requirements for deploying edge computing solutions, including edge device management, network bandwidth, and computational resources to support growing data volumes and analytics workloads.

8.4.5 Future Trends and Innovations

Emerging trends and innovations in supply chain optimization with edge computing are shaping the future of logistics and supply chain management:

- **Blockchain Technology:** Integrates blockchain-based solutions for transparent supply chain traceability, secure transactions, and decentralized trust among supply chain partners, enhancing visibility, authenticity, and accountability in global supply chain operations.
- **5G Network Integration:** Leverages high-speed 5G networks and edge computing capabilities to support ultra-low latency communication, high-throughput data transmission, and real-time connectivity for autonomous logistics, smart warehouses, and intelligent transportation systems.
- **Digital Twins and Simulation:** Utilizes digital twin technologies with edge analytics to create virtual replicas of supply chain processes, simulate operational scenarios, and optimize logistics strategies, enabling predictive maintenance, risk assessment, and scenario-based decision-making.

CHAPTER 9

EDGE COMPUTING FOR CONTENT DELIVERY

9.1 CONTENT DELIVERY NETWORKS (CDNS) AND EDGE NODES

Content Delivery Networks (CDNs) play a critical role in delivering web content efficiently by distributing it across multiple geographically dispersed servers and edge nodes. These edge nodes, located closer to end-users, enhance performance, reduce latency, and improve the overall user experience by ensuring faster content delivery.

Content Delivery Networks (CDNs) and edge nodes are instrumental in optimizing content delivery, enhancing user experience, and improving network performance by leveraging distributed infrastructure, caching technologies, and edge computing capabilities. By deploying CDNs with edge nodes, content providers can achieve faster content delivery, reduce latency, and scale resources efficiently to meet growing user demands and global market expectations. As CDNs evolve with technological advancements and industry innovations, prioritizing performance, scalability, and security fosters resilience, competitiveness, and sustainable growth in the digital economy. CDNs continue to play a pivotal role in shaping the future of content delivery, digital media distribution, and interactive online experiences worldwide.

9.1.1 Concepts of Content Delivery Networks (CDNs)

A Content Delivery Network (CDN) is a distributed network of servers strategically located across various geographic locations to deliver web content, media files, and other digital assets to users based on their proximity to the nearest edge server. CDNs work by caching content at edge locations, reducing the distance between users and content servers, and improving response times for web page loading, video streaming, software downloads, and online transactions.

9.1.2 Architecture of CDNs and Edge Nodes

CDNs consist of three primary components:

- **Origin Servers:** The original source of web content and digital assets, typically hosted on centralized servers maintained by content providers or organizations.

- **Edge Servers or Nodes:** Distributed servers deployed at multiple edge locations, such as data centers, Points of Presence (PoPs), and Internet Exchange Points (IXPs), strategically positioned near end-users to cache and deliver content quickly.
- **Content Distribution Software:** Manages content caching, load balancing, and request routing across CDN edge servers to optimize content delivery performance, ensure high availability, and scale resources based on demand.

9.1.3 Benefits of CDNs and Edge Nodes

CDNs offer several strategic benefits for content delivery and performance optimization:

- **Improved User Experience:** Reduces latency, minimizes packet loss, and accelerates content delivery by serving cached content from nearby edge nodes, enhancing website performance, video streaming quality, and responsiveness for global audiences.
- **Scalability and Reliability:** Scales resources dynamically to handle traffic spikes, distribute workload efficiently, and maintain high availability of web services and digital content, ensuring seamless user access and uninterrupted content delivery during peak demand periods.
- **Cost Efficiency:** Reduces bandwidth consumption, infrastructure costs, and server load on origin servers by offloading content delivery responsibilities to distributed edge nodes, optimizing network traffic, and minimizing operational expenses for content providers.

9.1.4 Challenges and Considerations

Deploying CDNs and managing edge nodes involves challenges and considerations:

- **Complexity of Network Management:** Ensures effective CDN configuration, content synchronization, and edge node deployment across diverse geographic locations, managing network performance, and maintaining service level agreements (SLAs) for optimal content delivery.
- **Data Privacy and Security:** Protects sensitive user data, intellectual property, and digital assets stored and transmitted through CDNs by implementing robust encryption standards, access controls, and cybersecurity measures to mitigate risks of data breaches and unauthorized access.
- **Regulatory Compliance:** Adheres to data protection regulations,

content licensing agreements, and industry standards for CDN operations, ensuring legal compliance, ethical practices, and responsible content distribution across global markets.

9.1.5 Future Trends and Innovations

Emerging trends and innovations in CDNs and edge nodes are shaping the future of content delivery and digital media:

- **Edge Computing Integration:** Integrates edge computing capabilities with CDNs to support real-time data processing, edge AI algorithms, and personalized content delivery based on user preferences, enhancing interactive user experiences and adaptive content streaming.
- **5G Network Support:** Leverages high-speed 5G networks and CDNs to deliver low-latency, high-throughput content streaming, virtual reality (VR) experiences, and immersive gaming applications with enhanced network performance and seamless connectivity.
- **AI-Driven Content Optimization:** Utilizes AI-powered analytics and machine learning algorithms to optimize content caching, recommendation engines, and predictive content delivery strategies, enhancing user engagement, and personalizing digital experiences across platforms.

9.2 STREAMING SERVICES AND EDGE-BASED VIDEO DELIVERY

Streaming services have revolutionized how consumers access and enjoy digital content, such as movies, TV shows, live events, and interactive media. Edge-based video delivery plays a crucial role in enhancing streaming performance by leveraging distributed edge servers and content delivery networks (CDNs) to ensure high-quality, low-latency video streaming experiences.

Edge-based video delivery is transforming streaming services by enhancing streaming performance, optimizing content delivery, and improving user experiences through distributed edge servers and CDNs.

By leveraging edge computing technologies, streaming providers can deliver high-quality, low-latency video streaming, scale resources dynamically, and ensure seamless content delivery to global audiences.

As edge-based video delivery evolves with technological advancements and industry innovations, prioritizing performance, scalability, and security fosters resilience, competitiveness, and sustainable growth in the digital media landscape. Edge-based video delivery continues to play a pivotal role in shaping the future of streaming services, digital content distribution, and interactive media experiences worldwide.

9.2.1 Concepts of Streaming Services

Streaming services enable users to access multimedia content in real-time over the internet without downloading files to their devices. This on-demand content delivery model uses adaptive bitrate streaming protocols, such as HTTP Live Streaming (HLS) and Dynamic Adaptive Streaming over HTTP (DASH), to optimize video quality and playback performance based on available network bandwidth and device capabilities.

9.2.2 Role of Edge-Based Video Delivery

Edge-based video delivery enhances streaming services by deploying edge servers and CDNs closer to end-users, reducing latency and improving content delivery performance:

- **Edge Servers and CDNs:** Deployed at geographically distributed edge locations, edge servers and CDNs cache and deliver video content from nearby servers to users, minimizing data transmission delays, packet loss, and buffering issues during video playback.
- **Content Caching and Acceleration:** Stores popular video content, segments, and codecs at edge nodes, enabling faster content retrieval and adaptive streaming based on user location, device type, and network conditions for seamless viewing experiences.

9.2.3 Benefits of Edge-Based Video Delivery

Edge-based video delivery offers several strategic benefits for streaming services and digital media distribution:

- **Improved Streaming Performance:** Reduces buffering times, enhances video quality, and ensures smooth playback by serving content from nearby edge servers, optimizing network traffic, and minimizing latency for uninterrupted streaming experiences.
- **Scalability and Reliability:** Scales resources dynamically to accommodate fluctuating user demand, traffic spikes, and peak viewing periods, ensuring high availability, scalability, and reliability of streaming services without compromising content delivery speed or quality.
- **Cost Efficiency:** Optimizes bandwidth usage, reduces content delivery costs, and mitigates server load on origin servers by offloading video delivery responsibilities to distributed edge nodes and CDNs, supporting cost-effective streaming operations.

9.2.4 Challenges and Considerations

- **Infrastructure and Network Management:** Ensures effective CDN configuration, edge node deployment, and content synchronization across global regions to maintain consistent streaming performance, manage network congestion, and adhere to service level agreements (SLAs).

- **Content Security and Digital Rights Management (DRM):** Protects copyrighted video content, user data, and digital assets from unauthorized access, piracy, and content theft by implementing robust encryption standards, DRM solutions, and access controls in edge-based video delivery architectures.
- **Quality of Service (QoS) Optimization:** Monitors and optimizes QoS metrics, such as video resolution, bitrate adaptation, and playback stability, to deliver seamless streaming experiences across diverse devices, platforms, and network conditions for global audiences.

9.2.5 Future Trends and Innovations

Emerging trends and innovations in edge-based video delivery are shaping the future of streaming services and digital media:

- **Edge AI and Machine Learning:** Integrates AI-driven analytics, machine learning algorithms, and predictive models with edge servers to optimize video caching, content recommendation engines, and personalized streaming experiences based on user preferences and behavior.
- **5G Network Integration:** Leverages high-speed 5G networks and edge computing capabilities to support ultra-low latency, high-throughput video streaming, immersive VR/AR content, and interactive live events with enhanced network performance and real-time connectivity.
- **Interactive Video Experiences:** Enhances user engagement with interactive video content, virtual events, and social streaming features using edge-based technologies for real-time interaction, audience participation, and personalized content delivery in streaming services.

9.3 GAMING AND VIRTUAL REALITY (VR) WITH EDGE COMPUTING

Gaming and Virtual Reality (VR) experiences are increasingly reliant on real-time data processing, low-latency interactions, and immersive content delivery to enhance gameplay and user engagement. Edge computing plays a pivotal role in revolutionizing gaming and VR applications by enabling decentralized processing, edge analytics, and seamless integration of cloud resources with edge devices.

Edge computing is transforming gaming and VR industries by enhancing performance, optimizing content delivery, and enabling immersive digital experiences through decentralized data processing and real-time interactions at the network edge. By leveraging edge computing technologies, gaming developers, and VR content creators can deliver high-quality, low-latency gaming experiences, scale resources efficiently, and innovate with interactive gameplay, multiplayer engagements, and immersive VR simulations.

As gaming and VR evolve with technological advancements and user expectations, prioritizing performance, security, and innovation fosters competitiveness, growth, and digital transformation in the global gaming and entertainment markets. Edge computing continues to play a pivotal role in shaping the future of gaming, virtual reality, and interactive media experiences worldwide.

9.3.1 Concepts of Gaming and Virtual Reality (VR)

Gaming and VR technologies create interactive digital environments that simulate real-world experiences, offering users immersive gameplay, interactive storytelling, and virtual interactions through 3D graphics, spatial audio, and motion tracking sensors. These technologies rely on high-performance computing, low-latency networks, and real-time data processing to deliver responsive and lifelike experiences to players and users.

9.3.2 Role of Edge Computing in Gaming and VR

Edge computing enhances gaming and VR applications by decentralizing data processing and computation closer to users and devices:

- **Low-Latency Interactions**: Reduces network latency and improves responsiveness by processing game logic, rendering graphics, and handling user inputs locally at edge nodes, minimizing delays and enhancing real-time gaming experiences.
- **Content Delivery Optimization**: Caches game assets, textures, and updates at edge servers and CDNs, accelerating content delivery, reducing download times, and ensuring seamless gameplay with minimal interruptions or buffering.
- **Scalability and Resource Efficiency**: Scales computational resources dynamically to accommodate fluctuating player demands, multiplayer interactions, and intensive VR simulations, optimizing performance, and maintaining high availability of gaming services.

9.3.3 Benefits of Edge Computing in Gaming and VR

Edge computing offers several strategic benefits for gaming and VR applications:

- **Enhanced Performance**: Improves rendering speeds, frame rates, and graphic quality by offloading processing-intensive tasks to edge servers, enhancing visual fidelity, and optimizing gameplay performance for immersive VR experiences.

- **Real-Time Interactivity**: Facilitates real-time interactions, multiplayer gaming, and collaborative VR environments with minimal latency, enabling synchronized gameplay, multiplayer competitions, and social interactions in virtual worlds.
- **Cost Efficiency**: Reduces bandwidth costs, server expenses, and operational overheads by leveraging edge computing for localized data processing, content delivery, and resource management, supporting cost-effective gaming infrastructure and scalable service deployments.

9.3.4 Challenges and Considerations

Deploying edge computing for gaming and VR environments presents challenges and considerations:

- **Network Latency and Quality of Service (QoS)**: Ensures consistent QoS metrics, low latency, and high reliability for real-time gaming interactions, VR simulations, and multiplayer experiences across diverse network conditions and geographic locations.
- **Data Security and Privacy**: Protects sensitive player data, gaming transactions, and digital assets from cybersecurity threats, unauthorized access, and data breaches by implementing robust encryption, access controls, and security measures in edge computing architectures.
- **Device Compatibility and Integration**: Addresses compatibility issues, device fragmentation, and interoperability challenges when integrating edge computing solutions with gaming consoles, VR headsets, mobile devices, and cloud gaming platforms to ensure seamless user experiences.

9.3.5 Future Trends and Innovations

Emerging trends and innovations in gaming and VR with edge computing are shaping the future of interactive entertainment and digital experiences:

- **Edge AI and Machine Learning**: Integrates AI-driven analytics, predictive algorithms, and adaptive learning models with edge devices to personalize gaming experiences, optimize gameplay strategies, and enhance AI-driven NPCs, characters, and virtual environments.
- **5G Network Integration**: Leverages high-speed 5G networks and edge computing capabilities to support ultra-low latency, high-throughput gaming, and VR applications, enabling real-time multiplayer gaming,

cloud-based streaming, and immersive VR experiences with enhanced network performance.

- **Augmented Reality (AR) and Mixed Reality (MR):** Expands gaming and VR capabilities with AR overlays, spatial computing, and mixed reality experiences that blend physical and virtual elements, enhancing immersion, interaction, and engagement in gaming and entertainment content.

9.4 EDGE CACHING AND ACCELERATION

Edge caching and acceleration are pivotal technologies in modern content delivery networks (CDNs) and network optimization strategies. They play a crucial role in enhancing the performance, reliability, and scalability of web applications and services by reducing latency and improving overall user experience. Edge caching and acceleration represent essential strategies for optimizing content delivery, improving performance, and enhancing user experience across global networks. By leveraging these technologies, organizations can achieve faster response times, scalability, and reliability while reducing operational costs and mitigating network challenges. As technology continues to evolve, integrating edge computing, AI, and blockchain promises to further revolutionize CDN capabilities, paving the way for more efficient and resilient content delivery solutions.

9.4.1 Understanding Edge Caching

Definition and Purpose

Edge caching involves storing copies of data closer to end-users, typically at edge servers located geographically closer to the user base. This approach aims to minimize the distance data travels over the internet, thereby reducing latency and improving response times for accessing content or services.

Mechanisms and Implementation

Edge caching operates by strategically placing cache servers at various edge locations within a CDN infrastructure. These edge servers store frequently accessed content, such as web pages, images, videos, and other static resources. When a user requests content, the CDN directs the request to the nearest edge server that holds a cached copy. This proximity minimizes the time required to fetch and deliver content, significantly enhancing performance.

Benefits of Edge Caching

- **Improved Latency:** By reducing the round-trip time (RTT) between clients and servers, edge caching accelerates content delivery, making websites and applications load faster.

- **Scalability**: CDN edge servers distribute traffic load efficiently, preventing overload on origin servers during peak demand periods.
- **Reliability**: Caching at the edge enhances service reliability by mitigating the impact of network congestion, server failures, or DDoS attacks.
- **Cost Efficiency**: It reduces bandwidth consumption and operational costs associated with serving content directly from origin servers.

9.4.2 Acceleration Techniques

Content Delivery Optimization

Accelerating content delivery involves employing various techniques to optimize data transmission and improve performance across the network. Key acceleration techniques include:

- **HTTP/2 and QUIC:** Protocols that reduce latency through multiplexing, header compression, and faster connection establishment.
- **TCP Optimization:** Techniques like TCP Fast Open and TCP BBR enhance throughput and reduce latency by optimizing TCP congestion control.
- **Caching Policies:** Dynamic caching policies ensure efficient cache management, prioritizing frequently accessed or time-sensitive content for faster delivery.

Network Optimization

Network-level acceleration techniques focus on enhancing data transmission efficiency and reducing packet loss and latency:

- **Anycast Routing:** Routing requests to the nearest CDN edge server using anycast improves responsiveness and reduces network traversal time.
- **Load Balancing:** Distributing traffic across multiple edge servers optimizes resource utilization and enhances service availability and performance.
- **Route Optimization:** Minimizing the number of hops and optimizing network routes using techniques such as Border Gateway Protocol (BGP) optimizations.

9.4.3 Challenges and Considerations

Edge Caching Challenges

- **Cache Invalidation:** Ensuring cached content remains up-to-date and synchronized with origin servers poses challenges, particularly for dynamic content.

- **Storage and Scalability:** Managing large-scale caches distributed across global edge locations requires robust infrastructure and efficient storage management.

Acceleration Considerations

- **Security:** Acceleration techniques must integrate robust security measures to protect data integrity and confidentiality against threats like DDoS attacks or data breaches.
- **Compatibility:** Ensuring compatibility with diverse client devices, browsers, and network conditions to deliver consistent performance and user experience.

9.4.4 Future Trends and Innovations

Edge Computing Integration

The convergence of edge caching with edge computing enables executing compute-intensive tasks closer to end-users, further reducing latency and enhancing real-time application responsiveness.

Machine Learning and AI

Integrating machine learning algorithms into CDN operations enables predictive caching and intelligent content delivery optimizations based on user behavior and content popularity patterns.

Blockchain and Decentralization

Blockchain technology offers potential applications in CDN environments, enhancing trust, security, and transparency in content delivery and edge caching operations.

CHAPTER 10
CHALLENGES AND SOLUTIONS

10.1 LATENCY AND BANDWIDTH CONSTRAINTS

Latency and bandwidth constraints are critical factors that significantly impact the performance, responsiveness, and reliability of networks, applications, and services.

Latency and bandwidth constraints profoundly influence the performance, scalability, and reliability of modern digital infrastructures and applications. By understanding these constraints and implementing effective mitigation strategies, organizations can optimize data transmission, enhance user experience, and capitalize on emerging technologies to meet evolving connectivity demands.

As technology continues to advance, addressing latency and bandwidth challenges remains essential for unlocking new opportunities in digital transformation and network innovation.

10.1.1 Latency: Definition and Types

Latency refers to the delay or lag time between the initiation of a request and the receipt of a response in a network communication process. It is measured in milliseconds (ms) and encompasses various factors contributing to the overall delay experienced by users or applications.

Types of Latency

- **Propagation Latency:** The time it takes for data packets to travel from source to destination, influenced by the physical distance between devices and the speed of light.
- **Transmission Latency:** The delay caused by data transmission over the network medium, affected by bandwidth capacity, network congestion, and packet loss.
- **Processing Latency:** The time taken by devices or systems to process data packets, including protocol overhead, routing decisions, and computational tasks.

10.1.2 Bandwidth: Definition and Capacity

Bandwidth refers to the maximum data transfer rate of a network or internet connection, typically measured in bits per second (bps) or its multiples (Mbps, Gbps). It determines the amount of data that can be transmitted within a specified time frame.

Capacity and Utilization

- **Capacity**: The theoretical maximum data transfer rate supported by a network infrastructure or communication channel, influenced by technology standards (e.g., Ethernet, fiber optics) and hardware capabilities (e.g., routers, switches).
- **Utilization**: The actual amount of bandwidth consumed during data transmission, affected by network traffic, application demands, and quality of service (QoS) policies.

10.1.3 Factors Influencing Latency and Bandwidth Constraints

Network Infrastructure

- **Physical Distance**: Longer distances between endpoints increase propagation latency due to the finite speed of light, impacting real-time applications and interactive services.
- **Hardware and Software Components**: Network devices (routers, switches) and protocol implementations (TCP/IP stack) contribute to processing and transmission latencies, affecting overall network performance.

Network Congestion and Traffic

- **Congestion**: High network traffic levels lead to packet queuing, increased transmission delays, and potential packet loss, exacerbating latency and reducing effective bandwidth utilization.
- **Quality of Service (QoS)**: QoS mechanisms prioritize traffic based on service requirements (e.g., VoIP, video streaming), mitigating latency and ensuring reliable data delivery for critical applications.

Application Design and Optimization

- **Protocol Overheads**: Data encapsulation, error checking, and acknowledgments (e.g., TCP) introduce processing overheads and contribute to latency, necessitating efficient protocol optimization.
- **Content Delivery Strategies**: Utilizing caching, content distribution networks (CDNs), and edge computing reduces latency by storing and delivering content closer to end-users, enhancing responsiveness.

10.1.4 Mitigation Strategies and Technologies

Latency Reduction Techniques

- **Network Optimization:** Implementing efficient routing protocols (e.g., BGP), minimizing hops, and leveraging anycast routing enhance data path selection and reduce propagation delays.
- **Edge Computing:** Moving computational tasks closer to users (at the network edge) reduces round-trip times and latency for real-time applications and data-intensive processes.

Bandwidth Enhancement Strategies

- **Broadband Technologies:** Upgrading network infrastructures to higher-speed technologies (e.g., fiber optics, 5G) increases bandwidth capacity and supports growing data demands.
- **Traffic Management:** Employing traffic shaping, compression algorithms, and content caching optimizes bandwidth utilization, prioritizes critical applications, and improves overall network efficiency.

10.1.5 Challenges and Future Trends

Emerging Technologies

- **5G Networks:** Ultra-low latency and high-bandwidth capabilities of 5G networks enable transformative applications such as autonomous vehicles, augmented reality (AR), and IoT deployments.
- **AI and Machine Learning:** AI-driven network analytics and optimization algorithms enhance predictive traffic management, QoS provisioning, and dynamic bandwidth allocation.

Security and Compliance

- **Data Privacy:** Ensuring secure data transmission and compliance with regulatory requirements (e.g., GDPR, HIPAA) amid increasing cyber threats and privacy concerns.
- **Network Resilience:** Designing resilient architectures with redundancy, failover mechanisms, and disaster recovery strategies to mitigate downtime and ensure continuous service availability.

10.2 EDGE RESOURCE MANAGEMENT

Edge resource management is a critical aspect of optimizing the performance, efficiency, and reliability of edge computing environments. It involves the allocation, monitoring, and optimization of computational resources at distributed edge nodes to support diverse applications, services, and workloads effectively. Edge resource management plays a pivotal role in optimizing the performance, scalability, and reliability of edge computing environments.

By adopting efficient resource allocation strategies, leveraging automation and AI-driven analytics, and embracing emerging technologies, organizations can capitalize on the benefits of edge computing while addressing challenges related to heterogeneous environments, scalability, and dynamic workloads. As edge computing continues to evolve, embracing innovative solutions and sustainable practices will be crucial for unlocking new opportunities in digital transformation and enhancing the agility of interconnected IoT ecosystems.

Edge computing refers to the paradigm where data processing and storage are performed closer to the data source or end-user devices, rather than relying solely on centralized cloud servers. This proximity minimizes latency, enhances real-time application responsiveness, and reduces bandwidth usage by processing data locally at the network edge.

Edge nodes are decentralized computing devices deployed at various network edges, including IoT devices, routers, and small data centers. They serve as intermediate points between end-users and centralized cloud infrastructures, facilitating faster data processing and local decision-making.

10.2.1 Challenges in Edge Resource Management

Heterogeneous Environments

- **Diverse Hardware**: Managing different types of edge devices with varying computational capabilities, storage capacities, and networking capabilities poses challenges in resource allocation and workload distribution.
- **Interoperability**: Ensuring seamless integration and interoperability between edge nodes, cloud services, and legacy systems require standardized protocols and communication frameworks.

Scalability and Dynamic Workloads

- **Scalability**: Scaling edge computing deployments to accommodate fluctuating workloads and increasing data volumes while maintaining performance and reliability demands efficient resource scaling mechanisms.
- **Dynamic Workloads**: Adapting to unpredictable workload patterns and real-time demands necessitates dynamic resource provisioning, load balancing, and automated management strategies.

10.2.2 Strategies for Efficient Edge Resource Management

Resource Allocation and Optimization

- **Predictive Analytics:** Utilizing data analytics and machine learning algorithms to predict workload patterns, optimize resource allocation, and preemptively scale edge resources based on demand forecasts.
- **Containerization and Orchestration:** Implementing container-based virtualization (e.g., Docker, Kubernetes) to encapsulate applications, facilitate portability, and streamline resource management across distributed edge environments.

Edge Intelligence and Automation

- **AI-driven Management:** Leveraging artificial intelligence (AI) and automation tools for real-time monitoring, anomaly detection, and autonomous decision-making to optimize resource utilization and enhance system efficiency.
- **Policy-driven Management:** Establishing policies and governance frameworks to prioritize critical applications, allocate resources based on service-level agreements (SLAs), and enforce security and compliance standards.

10.2.3 Benefits of Effective Edge Resource Management

- **Improved Performance:** Enhancing application responsiveness, reducing latency, and achieving low-latency processing by leveraging local computation and data caching at edge nodes.
- **Cost Efficiency:** Optimizing resource utilization, minimizing data transfer costs, and reducing dependency on centralized cloud resources result in cost savings and operational efficiencies.
- **Reliability and Resilience:** Ensuring continuous service availability, mitigating network congestion, and improving fault tolerance through distributed edge architectures and redundant resource provisioning.

10.2.4 Future Trends and Innovations

Edge-to-Cloud Integration

- **Federated Learning:** Collaborative learning approaches where edge devices participate in model training while preserving data privacy and minimizing communication overheads with centralized cloud servers.
- **Edge AI:** Embedding AI capabilities directly into edge devices to support autonomous decision-making, real-time data analysis, and personalized user experiences without constant reliance on cloud connectivity.

10.3 STANDARDIZATION AND INTEROPERABILITY

Standardization and interoperability are critical aspects of edge computing ecosystems, enabling seamless integration, communication, and collaboration among diverse devices, platforms, and services. Standardization and interoperability play pivotal roles in advancing the adoption and scalability of edge computing technologies. By addressing challenges through collaborative industry efforts, open-source initiatives, and innovative frameworks, organizations can foster a cohesive edge ecosystem that promotes seamless integration, enhances operational efficiency, and accelerates innovation across diverse industry verticals. As edge computing continues to evolve, embracing standardized practices and interoperable solutions will be essential for unlocking new opportunities, overcoming barriers, and driving sustainable growth in the digital era.

10.3.1 Importance of Standardization in Edge Computing

Standardization in edge computing refers to the establishment of uniform protocols, interfaces, and frameworks that ensure consistency and compatibility across heterogeneous edge devices, applications, and infrastructure components. Its primary objectives include:

- **Facilitating Integration**: Enabling interoperability between edge devices, networks, and cloud services to streamline data exchange and application deployment.
- **Enhancing Scalability**: Promoting scalable edge deployments by defining common architectures and communication protocols that support diverse use cases and industry standards.

10.3.2 Challenges in Achieving Standardization and Interoperability

Heterogeneous Ecosystems

- **Diverse Technologies**: Integrating a wide array of edge devices (e.g., IoT sensors, gateways), networking protocols (e.g., MQTT, CoAP), and cloud platforms (e.g., AWS, Azure) poses challenges in establishing uniform standards and communication interfaces.
- **Vendor Lock-in**: Proprietary technologies and vendor-specific implementations hinder interoperability, limiting flexibility and complicating cross-platform integration.

Security and Privacy Concerns

- **Data Protection**: Ensuring secure data transmission, encryption, and access control across distributed edge environments while complying with regulatory requirements (e.g., GDPR, HIPAA).

- **Trust and Authentication:** Establishing trust relationships, identity management, and authentication mechanisms to mitigate security risks and unauthorized access to sensitive information.

10.3.3 Solutions to Enhance Standardization and Interoperability

Industry Collaboration and Consortia

- **Standards Development Organizations (SDOs):** Collaborative efforts by SDOs such as IEEE, IETF, and OMG to define open protocols, APIs, and data models that promote interoperability and compatibility across edge computing deployments.
- **Industry Consortia:** Participation in industry consortia (e.g., Edge Computing Consortium, Open Edge Computing) facilitates knowledge sharing, best practices, and guidelines for standardized edge architectures and interoperable solutions.

Open Source Initiatives and Frameworks

- **Open Standards and APIs:** Embracing open-source frameworks (e.g., EdgeX Foundry, Akraino Edge Stack) that provide reference architectures, APIs, and interoperability layers to accelerate edge application development and deployment.
- **Middleware and Integration Platforms:** Adopting middleware solutions (e.g., MQTT, AMQP) and integration platforms (e.g., Apache Kafka) that support data aggregation, protocol translation, and seamless communication between edge devices and cloud services.

10.3.4 Benefits of Standardization and Interoperability in Edge Computing

- **Ecosystem Growth:** Fostering a vibrant ecosystem of edge computing technologies, solutions, and services through standardized interfaces and interoperable architectures.
- **Flexibility and Scalability:** Enabling organizations to scale edge deployments, integrate new technologies, and adapt to evolving business requirements without being constrained by proprietary solutions.
- **Cost Efficiency:** Reducing development costs, time-to-market, and operational complexities associated with managing heterogeneous edge environments through standardized practices and interoperable solutions.

10.3.5 Future Directions and Emerging Trends

Edge-to-Cloud Integration

- **Edge AI and Machine Learning**: Integrating AI and machine learning capabilities at the edge to perform real-time data analytics, predictive maintenance, and autonomous decision-making without constant reliance on cloud connectivity.
- **5G and Mobile Edge Computing (MEC)**: Leveraging ultra-low latency and high-bandwidth capabilities of 5G networks to support latency-sensitive applications (e.g., AR/VR, autonomous vehicles) and distributed edge computing deployments.

Security and Compliance

- **Blockchain Technology**: Implementing blockchain-based solutions for secure data sharing, immutable transaction records, and decentralized trust management in edge computing environments.
- **Edge Security Frameworks:** Developing robust edge security frameworks with advanced encryption, zero-trust architectures, and anomaly detection mechanisms to mitigate cyber threats and protect sensitive data.

10.4 ADDRESSING EDGE COMPLEXITY

Addressing edge complexity is crucial for optimizing the performance, manageability, and scalability of edge computing environments. As organizations increasingly deploy edge computing solutions to support real-time applications and data-intensive workloads, managing the diverse array of devices, networks, and services at the edge presents significant challenges. Addressing edge complexity requires a holistic approach encompassing unified management, automation, scalable architectures, robust security measures, and compliance frameworks. By adopting strategies to simplify deployment, enhance operational efficiency, and embrace emerging technologies like AI and cloud-native approaches, organizations can overcome challenges associated with edge computing complexity and unlock new opportunities for innovation, agility, and competitive advantage in the digital era. As edge computing continues to evolve, collaboration among industry stakeholders and adherence to standardized practices will be crucial for driving sustainable growth and accelerating digital transformation across diverse industry verticals.

10.4.1 Understanding Edge Computing Complexity

Diverse Ecosystem

- **Heterogeneous Devices:** Managing a wide range of edge devices, including IoT sensors, gateways, and edge servers, each with varying computational capabilities, storage capacities, and connectivity protocols.

- **Network Diversity**: Integrating diverse network infrastructures, from wired and wireless networks to 5G and satellite communications, to ensure seamless connectivity and data transmission across distributed edge nodes.

Data Management and Processing Challenges

- **Data Volume and Variety**: Handling massive volumes of real-time data generated by edge devices and applications, including structured and unstructured data formats, necessitating efficient data aggregation, filtering, and analytics.
- **Edge-to-Cloud Integration**: Balancing local data processing and storage at the edge with cloud-based services for centralized data management, analytics, and long-term storage while minimizing latency and bandwidth constraints.

10.4.2 Strategies for Simplifying Edge Computing

Unified Management and Orchestration

- **Centralized Control**: Implementing centralized management platforms and orchestration tools (e.g., Kubernetes, OpenStack) to streamline provisioning, configuration, and monitoring of edge resources and applications.
- **Automation and AI**: Leveraging automation workflows and AI-driven analytics for proactive resource allocation, workload optimization, and anomaly detection to enhance operational efficiency and reduce manual intervention.

Edge-as-a-Service (EaaS)

- **Managed Service Providers**: Partnering with EaaS providers to outsource edge infrastructure management, application hosting, and maintenance, allowing organizations to focus on core business objectives and innovation.
- **Service Level Agreements (SLAs)**: Establishing SLAs with EaaS providers to ensure performance guarantees, uptime reliability, and compliance with industry regulations, mitigating risks associated with edge complexity.

10.4.3 Simplified Deployment Architectures

Modular and Scalable Designs

- **Microservices Architecture:** Adopting microservices-based architectures that decouple applications into smaller, independently deployable services, facilitating easier updates, scaling, and fault isolation at the edge.
- **Containerization:** Utilizing containerization technologies (e.g., Docker) to package and deploy applications with their dependencies, promoting portability, consistency, and efficient resource utilization across diverse edge environments.

Edge Cloud Integration

- **Cloud-Native Approaches:** Embracing cloud-native development principles (e.g., serverless computing, DevOps practices) to extend cloud capabilities to the edge, enabling rapid application deployment and continuous integration/continuous deployment (CI/CD) pipelines.
- **Federated Edge Architectures:** Implementing federated edge architectures that distribute computing resources and data processing across multiple edge locations while maintaining data locality, compliance, and regulatory requirements.

10.4.4 Overcoming Security and Compliance Challenges

Enhanced Security Measures

- **Zero-Trust Security:** Implementing zero-trust architectures that authenticate and authorize every device and user accessing the edge network, mitigating insider threats, and unauthorized access.
- **End-to-End Encryption:** Ensuring data confidentiality and integrity through robust encryption mechanisms (e.g., TLS/SSL, AES) for secure data transmission and storage across distributed edge nodes.

Regulatory Compliance

- **Data Governance:** Establishing comprehensive data governance frameworks to adhere to regulatory requirements (e.g., GDPR, HIPAA) concerning data privacy, retention policies, and cross-border data transfers in edge computing environments.
- **Auditing and Monitoring:** Conducting regular audits, vulnerability assessments, and real-time monitoring of edge infrastructure to detect and respond to security incidents, compliance breaches, and operational anomalies promptly.

10.4.5 Future Directions and Innovations

Edge AI and Automation

- **AI-driven Operations:** Integrating AI and machine learning algorithms to automate decision-making processes, predictive maintenance, and proactive resource management at the edge, enhancing operational agility and efficiency.
- **Edge-to-Cloud Synergies:** Expanding edge-to-cloud synergies through hybrid cloud architectures, enabling seamless workload migration, disaster recovery, and elastic scalability based on dynamic business demands.

Sustainable Edge Computing

- **Energy Efficiency:** Implementing energy-efficient edge computing solutions, renewable energy sources, and green computing practices to minimize environmental impact and operational costs while maximizing resource utilization.
- **Edge Robotics and IoT Integration:** Leveraging edge computing capabilities for autonomous robotics and IoT deployments in industries such as manufacturing, healthcare, and smart cities, enhancing productivity and service delivery.

CHAPTER 11

FUTURE TRENDS AND DEVELOPMENTS

11.1 EDGE COMPUTING IN 6G NETWORKS

Edge computing is poised to play a transformative role in 6G networks by enabling ultra-low latency, high-bandwidth applications, and distributed computing capabilities closer to end-users. As the next generation of wireless technology, 6G promises to revolutionize connectivity, digital experiences, and industry applications through advanced edge computing architectures and capabilities. Edge computing in 6G networks represents a paradigm shift in connectivity, enabling unprecedented levels of performance, reliability, and innovation across industries. By leveraging ultra-low latency, high-bandwidth capabilities, and advanced edge computing architectures, organizations can unlock new opportunities for real-time applications, enhanced user experiences, and transformative digital services. As 6G networks continue to evolve, addressing technical challenges, fostering industry collaboration, and embracing emerging technologies like AI and green computing will be crucial for realizing the full potential of edge computing in shaping the future of connected societies and digital ecosystems.

11.1.1 Evolution from 5G to 6G Networks

Ultra-Low Latency

Reducing latency to microseconds, enabling real-time applications such as autonomous vehicles, augmented reality (AR), and industrial automation with minimal delay.

High-Bandwidth Connectivity

Offering multi-terabit-per-second speeds, supporting massive data transfers, high-definition video streaming, and immersive media experiences.

11.1.2 Role of Edge Computing in 6G Networks

Proximity to End-Users

Deploying edge computing nodes closer to users and IoT devices, reducing data transmission distances, and minimizing latency for critical applications.

Real-Time Data Processing

Enabling edge AI and machine learning for instant data analysis, decision-making, and personalized services without constant reliance on centralized cloud infrastructures.

11.1.3 Benefits of Edge Computing in 6G Networks

Autonomous Vehicles

Facilitating low-latency communication between vehicles, infrastructure, and traffic management systems to ensure safe, efficient autonomous driving experiences.

Telemedicine and Healthcare

Supporting remote patient monitoring, teleconsultations, and real-time diagnostics through edge-enabled medical devices and health monitoring systems.

11.1.4 Challenges in Implementing Edge Computing in 6G Networks

Infrastructure Requirements

Building robust edge computing infrastructure capable of supporting high-density deployments, scalable architectures, and interoperable solutions across diverse environments.

Security and Privacy

Ensuring data confidentiality, integrity, and regulatory compliance in distributed edge environments with stringent security measures and encryption protocols.

11.1.5 Solutions and Innovations

Edge AI

Embedding AI capabilities at the edge for autonomous decision-making, predictive analytics, and anomaly detection to optimize resource utilization and enhance operational efficiency.

Federated Learning

Collaborative AI model training across distributed edge nodes while preserving data privacy and reducing communication overheads with centralized cloud servers.

11.1.6 Future Trends and Research Directions

Energy Efficiency

Implementing energy-efficient edge computing solutions, renewable energy sources, and green computing practices to minimize environmental impact and operational costs.

Dynamic Resource Management

Developing adaptive resource allocation algorithms, workload scheduling policies, and predictive analytics for efficient resource utilization and workload distribution in dynamic 6G edge environments.

11.2 QUANTUM EDGE COMPUTING

Quantum edge computing represents a fusion of quantum computing principles with edge computing architectures, aiming to leverage quantum phenomena to enhance computational power, security, and efficiency at the network edge. This emerging field holds promise for revolutionizing data processing, cryptography, and optimization tasks that traditional computing methods struggle to handle efficiently.

Quantum edge computing represents a frontier in computing technologies, promising to redefine the capabilities of edge computing by leveraging quantum principles for enhanced performance, security, and efficiency. As research and development continue to advance in quantum computing hardware, algorithms, and applications, the integration of quantum capabilities into edge architectures holds immense potential for driving innovation across industries, unlocking new opportunities for real-time data processing, secure communications, and transformative digital services. Embracing quantum edge computing requires addressing technical challenges, fostering interdisciplinary collaborations, and exploring novel applications to harness its full potential in shaping the future of connected societies and intelligent edge ecosystems.

11.2.1 Understanding Quantum Computing Basics

Quantum Principles and Quantum Bits (Qubits):

- **Superposition**: Qubits can exist in multiple states simultaneously, allowing quantum computers to perform parallel computations and explore multiple solutions simultaneously.
- **Entanglement**: Interconnected qubits exhibit correlations where the state of one qubit instantaneously affects the state of another, enabling faster data processing and communication.

11.2.2 Integration of Quantum Computing with Edge Architectures

Benefits and Advantages:

- **Enhanced Computational Power**: Quantum computing's ability to handle complex algorithms and perform calculations exponentially faster than classical computers enhances edge applications' performance and scalability.

- **Improved Security:** Quantum cryptography protocols offer unbreakable encryption methods, safeguarding sensitive data transmitted and processed at the network edge against potential cyber threats.

11.2.3 Applications of Quantum Edge Computing

Real-World Use Cases:

- **Optimization Algorithms:** Solving optimization problems in logistics, finance, and resource allocation with quantum algorithms that outperform classical optimization techniques.
- **Machine Learning and AI:** Enhancing machine learning models with quantum computing's capability to process and analyze vast datasets, leading to more accurate predictions and decision-making at the edge.

11.2.4 Challenges in Quantum Edge Computing

Technical and Practical Considerations:

- **Hardware Constraints:** Developing reliable quantum processors, qubit coherence, error correction mechanisms, and scalability to support practical quantum edge computing applications.
- **Integration Complexity:** Bridging quantum computing technologies with existing edge infrastructures, software frameworks, and deployment models while ensuring compatibility and interoperability.

11.2.5 Quantum Edge Computing Solutions and Innovations

Research and Development Initiatives:

- **Quantum Cloud Services:** Offering quantum computing capabilities as a service (QCaaS) to democratize access and facilitate experimentation with quantum algorithms and applications at the network edge.
- **Hybrid Quantum-Classical Approaches:** Integrating classical computing resources with quantum processors to address quantum-specific tasks while leveraging traditional computing for supporting operations and data handling.

11.2.6 Future Directions and Potential Impact

Advancing Technologies and Applications:

- **Quantum Internet:** Developing quantum communication networks to enable secure data transmission and distributed quantum computing across global edge nodes, enhancing connectivity and collaboration.
- **Quantum AI and IoT Integration:** Combining quantum computing with AI-driven IoT devices to enable autonomous decision-making,

predictive maintenance, and personalized user experiences at the network edge.

11.3 EDGE-AS-A SERVICE (EAAS) MODELS

Edge-as-a-Service" (EaaS) models represent a significant evolution in computing architecture, catering to the increasing demand for real-time data processing and low-latency applications. This concept leverages edge computing infrastructure to bring computational capabilities closer to the data source, reducing latency and enhancing performance.

Edge-as-a-Service (EaaS) models represent a transformative approach to deploying computing resources closer to the point of data generation and consumption. By reducing latency, enhancing reliability, and enabling scalable, real-time applications, EaaS accelerates digital transformation across various industries. However, addressing security challenges, managing complexity, and fostering interoperability are crucial for realizing the full potential of EaaS in shaping the future of decentralized computing landscapes. As organizations continue to adopt edge computing strategies, innovations in technology and collaboration will drive the evolution of EaaS towards more efficient, resilient, and responsive digital ecosystems.

11.3.1 Definition of Edge-as-a-Service (EaaS)

Edge-as-a-Service (EaaS) refers to a cloud service model where computing resources, such as storage and processing power, are deployed at the edge of the network. Unlike traditional cloud computing models that centralize resources in data centers, EaaS brings these resources closer to the users or devices generating the data. This proximity reduces the latency associated with data transmission to centralized cloud servers, enabling faster response times and improved performance for applications requiring real-time data processing.

11.3.2 Key Components of EaaS

Edge Computing Infrastructure

At the core of EaaS is edge computing infrastructure, which includes edge servers, gateways, and devices equipped with computational capabilities. These edge nodes serve as localized points of presence (PoPs) for processing data near its source, such as IoT devices, sensors, or mobile endpoints.

Virtualization and Orchestration

EaaS relies on virtualization technologies to abstract physical hardware resources into virtual instances that can be dynamically allocated and managed. Orchestration tools automate the provisioning, scaling, and management of these virtual resources across distributed edge environments.

Connectivity and Networking

Robust connectivity and networking technologies, including 5G networks and SD-WAN (Software-Defined Wide Area Network), play a crucial role in EaaS models. They ensure reliable data transmission between edge devices, centralized data centers, and cloud services while maintaining low latency and high bandwidth.

11.3.3 Benefits of Edge-as-a-Service Models

Reduced Latency

By processing data closer to its source, EaaS models minimize latency, ensuring faster response times for critical applications like autonomous vehicles, industrial automation, and real-time analytics.

Enhanced Reliability

Distributed edge infrastructure improves application reliability by reducing dependency on centralized data centers. This resilience is crucial for mission-critical applications where downtime or network disruptions can have significant consequences.

Cost Efficiency

EaaS optimizes operational costs by minimizing data transmission expenses associated with sending large volumes of data to centralized cloud servers. It also reduces bandwidth consumption and infrastructure overhead, especially in bandwidth-constrained environments.

Scalability and Flexibility

Scalability is inherent in EaaS models, allowing organizations to dynamically scale computing resources based on fluctuating demand or geographical distribution. This flexibility supports agile deployment of new services and accommodates varying workloads effectively.

11.3.4 Challenges of Implementing EaaS

Security and Privacy Concerns

Distributed edge environments pose challenges related to data security and privacy. Ensuring robust security measures across diverse edge nodes, including data encryption, access control, and threat detection, is critical to safeguard sensitive information.

Management Complexity

Managing a decentralized edge infrastructure requires sophisticated orchestration and monitoring capabilities. Organizations must implement comprehensive management frameworks to ensure seamless operation, resource optimization, and compliance with service-level agreements (SLAs).

Interoperability and Standards

The diversity of edge devices and platforms complicates interoperability between different EaaS solutions. Establishing common standards and protocols for communication, data exchange, and application deployment is essential to foster compatibility and seamless integration across heterogeneous environments.

11.3.5 Applications of Edge-as-a-Service Models

Industrial IoT (IIoT)

EaaS facilitates real-time monitoring, predictive maintenance, and operational efficiency in industrial IoT deployments. Edge computing capabilities enable local data processing within manufacturing plants, warehouses, and remote facilities, enhancing production uptime and reducing maintenance costs.

Smart Cities and Urban Infrastructure

In smart city initiatives, EaaS supports connected infrastructure, including smart grids, traffic management systems, and public safety solutions. Edge computing enables local decision-making and responsiveness to dynamic urban conditions, improving citizen services and resource utilization.

Retail and Customer Engagement

Retailers leverage EaaS to deliver personalized customer experiences through real-time analytics and location-based services. Edge computing enables in-store inventory management, customer behavior analysis, and targeted promotions, enhancing operational efficiency and customer satisfaction.

Healthcare and Telemedicine

Edge computing in healthcare facilitates remote patient monitoring, medical diagnostics, and telemedicine applications. EaaS enables healthcare providers to deliver timely interventions, transmit sensitive medical data securely, and improve patient outcomes through continuous monitoring and analysis.

11.3.6 Future Trends and Innovations

Edge AI and Machine Learning

Integrating artificial intelligence (AI) and machine learning (ML) at the edge enhances decision-making capabilities and autonomous operation in EaaS models. Edge AI enables real-time inference, anomaly detection, and predictive analytics without relying on centralized cloud resources.

Edge-to-Cloud Integration

Hybrid EaaS solutions that integrate edge computing with centralized cloud services will become more prevalent. This integration optimizes resource allocation, workload distribution, and data synchronization across distributed environments, ensuring seamless operation and scalability.

Edge Security and Privacy Enhancements

Advancements in edge security technologies, including decentralized identity management, blockchain-based authentication, and secure data processing frameworks, will bolster trust and compliance in EaaS deployments. These innovations mitigate risks associated with data breaches, unauthorized access, and regulatory compliance.

11.4 CONTINUOUS INNOVATIONS AND EMERGING TECHNOLOGIES

"Continuous Innovations and Emerging Technologies" encompass a broad spectrum of advancements that shape various industries, redefine business models, and enhance everyday life. Continuous innovations and emerging technologies are catalysts for transformation, driving progress, economic growth, and societal well-being globally. From AI and IoT to blockchain, quantum computing, and renewable energy, these innovations shape industries, redefine business models, and address global challenges. Embracing ethical considerations, addressing regulatory challenges, and fostering collaborative partnerships are essential to harnessing the full potential of technology for a sustainable and inclusive future. As organizations and stakeholders navigate the evolving landscape of continuous innovations, opportunities abound to leverage technology for positive impact and drive meaningful change in the years to come.

11.4.1 Introduction to Continuous Innovations and Emerging Technologies

Continuous innovations refer to ongoing improvements, breakthroughs, and advancements across various domains driven by technological progress, research, and development. These innovations often introduce disruptive changes, enabling new capabilities, efficiencies, and opportunities for businesses, governments, and individuals alike. Emerging technologies, on the other hand, are novel technological developments that have the potential to significantly impact society, economy, and culture as they mature and gain widespread adoption.

11.4.2 Artificial Intelligence (AI) and Machine Learning (ML)

Artificial Intelligence (AI) and Machine Learning (ML) represent transformative technologies that enable machines to learn from data, make decisions, and perform tasks traditionally requiring human intelligence. AI algorithms power applications ranging from virtual assistants and recommendation systems to autonomous vehicles and predictive analytics. Continuous innovations in AI/ML algorithms, deep learning frameworks, and neural network architectures drive advancements in natural language processing, computer vision, and personalized user experiences.

11.4.3 Internet of Things (IoT) and Smart Devices

The Internet of Things (IoT) ecosystem continues to expand with the proliferation of interconnected smart devices, sensors, and actuators. IoT enables real-time data collection, monitoring, and control of physical environments across industries such as healthcare, agriculture, and manufacturing. Emerging technologies in IoT include edge computing, 5G networks, and blockchain integration, enhancing scalability, security, and efficiency in connected ecosystems.

11.4.4 Blockchain and Distributed Ledger Technology (DLT)

Blockchain and Distributed Ledger Technology (DLT) innovations are reshaping financial services, supply chain management, and digital identity verification. Blockchain's decentralized architecture enables transparent, secure, and tamper-resistant transactions, reducing fraud and improving trust in peer-to-peer transactions. Continuous innovations in blockchain scalability, interoperability, and smart contract capabilities drive adoption in diverse sectors, including healthcare, logistics, and energy management.

11.4.5 Augmented Reality (AR) and Virtual Reality (VR)

Augmented Reality (AR) and Virtual Reality (VR) technologies merge digital content with the physical world and immersive virtual environments, respectively. AR enhances real-world experiences with interactive overlays, while VR creates simulated environments for training, gaming, and virtual meetings. Continuous innovations in AR/VR hardware, software development kits, and spatial computing enable new applications in education, retail, entertainment, and remote collaboration.

11.4.6 Quantum Computing

Quantum Computing represents a revolutionary approach to processing information using quantum bits (qubits) instead of traditional binary bits. Quantum computers promise exponentially faster computation for complex problem-solving in cryptography, material science, and optimization. Continuous innovations in quantum hardware, error correction algorithms, and quantum software development aim to overcome technical challenges and accelerate commercialization for practical applications.

11.4.7 Renewable Energy and Sustainable Technologies

Renewable Energy and Sustainable Technologies drive continuous innovations in clean energy generation, storage, and distribution. Advancements in solar photovoltaics, wind turbines, battery technologies, and smart grid solutions promote energy efficiency, reduce carbon emissions, and enhance resilience to climate change.

Emerging technologies such as green hydrogen production, carbon capture and storage (CCS), and circular economy principles contribute to global sustainability efforts and transition towards a low-carbon future.

11.4.8 Biotechnology and Healthcare Innovations

Biotechnology and Healthcare Innovations encompass breakthroughs in genomics, personalized medicine, and therapeutic advancements. Continuous innovations in CRISPR gene editing, mRNA vaccines, regenerative medicine, and wearable health technologies revolutionize disease diagnosis, treatment, and patient care. Emerging technologies like AI-driven drug discovery, telemedicine platforms, and digital health solutions enhance healthcare accessibility, efficiency, and personalized outcomes globally.

11.4.9 Challenges and Ethical Considerations

Despite the transformative potential of continuous innovations and emerging technologies, several challenges and ethical considerations must be addressed:

Data Privacy and Security

The proliferation of interconnected devices and digital platforms raises concerns about data privacy, cybersecurity threats, and unauthorized access. Ensuring robust data encryption, user consent mechanisms, and regulatory compliance frameworks are essential to safeguarding personal and sensitive information.

Ethical AI and Bias Mitigation

AI algorithms and automated decision-making systems may exhibit biases based on training data and algorithmic design.

Addressing ethical concerns, promoting algorithmic transparency, and implementing bias mitigation strategies are crucial to fostering equitable AI applications and societal trust.

Technological Inequality and Digital Divide

Disparities in access to technology, digital literacy, and infrastructure contribute to technological inequality and digital divide challenges. Bridging these gaps through inclusive policies, affordable broadband connectivity, and digital skills training initiatives is essential for equitable participation in the digital economy.

Regulatory Frameworks and Governance

The rapid pace of technological innovation outpaces regulatory frameworks and governance structures, posing challenges in areas such as data protection, intellectual property rights, and ethical standards. Collaborative efforts among governments, industry stakeholders, and academia are necessary to establish adaptive regulatory frameworks that balance innovation with ethical, legal, and social implications.

11.4.10 Future Trends and Opportunities

Looking ahead, continuous innovations and emerging technologies will continue to drive transformative changes across industries, society, and global economies.

Convergence of Technologies

Increasing convergence of AI, IoT, blockchain, and quantum computing will unlock synergistic opportunities for innovation in smart cities, autonomous systems, and personalized digital experiences.

Sustainable Development Goals (SDGs)

Technological advancements in renewable energy, healthcare, and sustainable agriculture contribute to achieving the United Nations Sustainable Development Goals (SDGs), promoting environmental stewardship, social equity, and economic resilience.

Ethical AI and Responsible Innovation

Promoting ethical AI practices, responsible innovation, and inclusive design principles will foster trust, mitigate risks, and ensure positive societal impacts of technological advancements.

CHAPTER 12

CASE STUDIES AND SUCCESS STORIES

12.1 REAL-WORLD IMPLEMENTATIONS OF EDGE COMPUTING

Edge computing has gained significant traction across various industries due to its ability to process data closer to the source, reduce latency, and support real-time applications. Real-world implementations of edge computing demonstrate its transformative impact across industries, enabling real-time data processing, reducing latency, and supporting mission-critical applications. From manufacturing and smart cities to healthcare and autonomous vehicles, edge computing enhances operational efficiency, improves decision-making, and drives innovation in diverse sectors. Addressing security challenges, ensuring data privacy, and embracing emerging technologies like AI and hybrid cloud architectures are key to unlocking the full potential of edge computing in shaping the future of digital transformation and advancing towards a connected, intelligent, and decentralized computing landscape.

12.1.1 Introduction to Edge Computing

Edge computing extends cloud computing capabilities to the edge of the network, where data is generated and consumed, such as IoT devices, sensors, and mobile endpoints. This decentralized approach enhances data processing efficiency, minimizes latency, and supports applications requiring immediate insights and responses.

12.1.2 Industrial IoT and Manufacturing

In Industrial IoT (IIoT) and manufacturing sectors, edge computing enables real-time monitoring, predictive maintenance, and operational efficiency. Edge nodes installed on factory floors collect and analyze data from machinery and sensors, optimizing production workflows and reducing downtime. Manufacturers leverage edge analytics to detect anomalies, improve quality control, and ensure safety compliance without relying on centralized cloud resources.

12.1.3 Smart Cities and Urban Infrastructure

Edge computing enhances smart city initiatives by supporting connected infrastructure, including smart grids, traffic management systems, and public safety applications. Edge nodes deployed in urban environments process data from sensors, cameras, and IoT devices, enabling local decision-making and responsiveness to real-time events. Smart cities leverage edge analytics to optimize traffic flow, enhance energy efficiency, and improve emergency response times, thereby enhancing citizen services and urban sustainability.

12.1.4 Telecommunications and 5G Networks

Telecommunications providers integrate edge computing with 5G networks to deliver low-latency, high-bandwidth services and applications. Edge servers deployed at network edges support content delivery, video streaming, and augmented reality (AR)/virtual reality (VR) experiences with minimal latency. Edge computing enables mobile edge computing (MEC) capabilities, allowing telecom operators to offer localized services, reduce network congestion, and enhance user experience in densely populated areas.

12.1.5 Retail and Customer Engagement

In retail, edge computing supports personalized customer experiences, inventory management, and real-time analytics. Edge devices installed in stores analyze customer behavior, optimize shelf stocking, and deliver targeted promotions based on real-time data insights. Retailers leverage edge AI to implement cashierless checkout systems, enhance in-store navigation, and improve operational efficiency. Edge computing transforms retail operations by bridging online and offline customer interactions while ensuring data privacy and security.

12.1.6 Healthcare and Telemedicine

Edge computing facilitates remote patient monitoring, medical diagnostics, and telemedicine applications in healthcare settings. Edge devices equipped with healthcare IoT sensors collect and process patient data locally, ensuring timely interventions and reducing healthcare costs. Healthcare providers leverage edge analytics to analyze medical images, monitor vital signs, and deliver personalized treatments without transmitting sensitive data to centralized cloud servers. Edge computing enhances healthcare accessibility, patient outcomes, and operational efficiency while complying with regulatory requirements.

12.1.7 Autonomous Vehicles and Transportation

Edge computing plays a crucial role in enabling autonomous vehicles (AVs) and intelligent transportation systems (ITS). Edge nodes installed along roadways process real-time traffic data, communicate with AVs, and support vehicle-to-everything (V2X) connectivity. Edge AI algorithms enable AVs to make split-second decisions, navigate complex environments, and ensure passenger safety without relying solely on cloud-based data processing. Edge computing in transportation enhances traffic management, reduces congestion, and supports sustainable mobility solutions, accelerating the adoption of AVs and enhancing transportation efficiency.

12.1.8 Edge Security and Privacy Considerations

Implementing edge computing introduces security and privacy challenges due to distributed data processing and decentralized architecture. Organizations must implement robust security measures, including data encryption, access control, and threat detection at edge nodes and network edges. Addressing privacy concerns involves data anonymization, user consent mechanisms, and compliance with data protection regulations to safeguard sensitive information and mitigate cybersecurity risks in edge computing deployments.

12.1.9 Future Trends and Innovations

Looking ahead, several trends and innovations are shaping the future of edge computing:

Edge AI and Machine Learning

Integration of AI and machine learning at the edge enhances decision-making capabilities, supports real-time analytics, and enables autonomous operation across diverse industries. Edge AI algorithms optimize resource allocation, improve data processing efficiency, and unlock new opportunities for innovation in smart devices, predictive maintenance, and personalized user experiences.

Hybrid Cloud and Edge Computing

Emerging hybrid cloud and edge computing architectures enable seamless integration of edge devices with centralized cloud services. Hybrid deployments optimize workload distribution, ensure data synchronization, and support scalable, distributed applications in dynamic and heterogeneous environments. Organizations leverage hybrid cloud and edge computing to achieve operational agility, enhance scalability, and capitalize on the benefits of both centralized and distributed computing paradigms.

Edge-to-Cloud Orchestration and Management

Advancements in edge-to-cloud orchestration tools and management platforms simplify deployment, monitoring, and maintenance of edge computing infrastructure. Edge-native management solutions enable automated provisioning, scaling, and optimization of edge resources, ensuring reliability, resilience, and performance consistency across distributed edge environments. Integrated edge-to-cloud management frameworks enhance operational efficiency, reduce complexity, and support diverse use cases in industrial IoT, telecommunications, and smart city deployments.

12.2 LESSONS LEARNED FROM DEPLOYMENTS

Deployments of edge computing have provided valuable insights and lessons across various industries, shaping best practices, addressing challenges, and optimizing operational efficiencies. Lessons learned from deployments of edge computing underscore its transformative impact on optimizing data processing, enhancing reliability, scaling infrastructure, and addressing security challenges across diverse industries. By leveraging these lessons, organizations can effectively deploy, manage, and optimize edge computing solutions to drive innovation, improve operational efficiency, and deliver seamless user experiences in an increasingly interconnected and data-driven world. Embracing emerging trends, advancing edge AI capabilities, and prioritizing security and interoperability will shape the future of edge computing, enabling organizations to unlock new opportunities and achieve sustainable growth in the digital era.

12.2.1 Introduction to Edge Computing Deployments

Edge computing deployments involve placing computing resources closer to the data source, enabling real-time data processing, minimizing latency, and supporting applications requiring immediate insights and responses. Lessons learned from these deployments provide valuable insights into optimizing infrastructure, enhancing performance, and addressing operational challenges in diverse use cases.

12.2.2 Optimizing Data Processing and Latency Reduction

One of the primary lessons learned from edge computing deployments is the optimization of data processing and reduction of latency. By placing computational resources closer to where data is generated, organizations can achieve significant reductions in latency, enabling faster response times and enhancing user experiences. Edge nodes facilitate local data processing, reducing reliance on centralized cloud resources and improving application performance for latency-sensitive applications such as autonomous vehicles, industrial automation, and real-time analytics.

12.2.3 Enhancing Reliability and Resilience

Edge computing deployments enhance reliability and resilience by decentralizing computing resources and distributing workload processing across edge nodes. This distributed architecture reduces single points of failure, improves fault tolerance, and ensures continuous operation in dynamic and challenging environments. Lessons learned emphasize the importance of implementing redundant edge nodes, failover mechanisms, and disaster recovery strategies to maintain service continuity and mitigate downtime in critical applications such as smart grid management, healthcare monitoring, and emergency response systems.

12.2.4 Scaling Edge Infrastructure and Workload Management

Scalability is a crucial lesson learned from edge computing deployments, enabling organizations to dynamically scale infrastructure and manage fluctuating workloads efficiently. Edge nodes support elastic scaling, allowing resources to be provisioned based on demand and geographical distribution. Lessons emphasize the adoption of edge orchestration tools, containerization technologies, and microservices architectures to automate workload management, optimize resource allocation, and ensure scalability in industrial IoT, retail analytics, and telecommunications applications.

12.2.5 Securing Edge Environments and Data Privacy

Edge computing deployments highlight the importance of securing edge environments and protecting sensitive data from cybersecurity threats and privacy breaches. Lessons learned emphasize implementing robust security measures such as data encryption, access control, and threat detection at edge nodes and network edges. Organizations must address security vulnerabilities, adhere to regulatory compliance requirements, and adopt best practices for securing distributed edge infrastructure to safeguard data integrity, confidentiality, and trust in edge computing deployments across industries.

12.2.6 Integrating Edge with Cloud and Hybrid Architectures

Integrating edge computing with cloud and hybrid architectures is a key lesson learned to optimize data synchronization, workload distribution, and application performance. Hybrid deployments enable seamless integration of edge devices with centralized cloud services, supporting scalable, distributed applications and enhancing operational flexibility. Lessons emphasize leveraging edge-to-cloud orchestration platforms, edge-native management frameworks, and hybrid cloud strategies to streamline deployment, monitoring, and management of edge computing infrastructure in smart cities, retail analytics, and autonomous vehicle deployments.

12.2.7 Addressing Interoperability and Standards

Interoperability and standards play a critical role in edge computing deployments, facilitating seamless integration and compatibility across diverse edge devices, platforms, and ecosystems. Lessons learned emphasize establishing common protocols, data formats, and communication standards to promote interoperability, facilitate data exchange, and enable collaboration among edge computing stakeholders. Organizations must address interoperability challenges, foster industry collaboration, and adhere to emerging standards to accelerate innovation, enhance scalability, and unlock new opportunities in edge computing applications such as industrial automation, healthcare IoT, and smart grid management.

12.2.8 Embracing Edge AI and Machine Learning

Edge computing deployments underscore the adoption of edge AI and machine learning technologies to enhance decision-making, predictive analytics, and autonomous operation at the edge. Lessons learned emphasize deploying AI models locally on edge devices to analyze real-time data, derive actionable insights, and support intelligent decision-making in healthcare diagnostics, predictive maintenance, and retail analytics. Edge AI capabilities enable organizations to optimize resource utilization, improve operational efficiency, and deliver personalized user experiences while reducing dependency on centralized cloud resources and mitigating bandwidth constraints.

12.2.9 Future Considerations and Emerging Trends

Looking ahead, edge computing deployments continue to evolve with emerging trends and future considerations, including:

Edge-to-Cloud Integration and Management

Advancements in edge-to-cloud integration and management platforms enable seamless orchestration, synchronization, and management of distributed edge computing infrastructure. Organizations leverage integrated management solutions to optimize resource allocation, automate workload provisioning, and ensure consistency in performance across heterogeneous edge environments.

Edge Security and Privacy Enhancements

Enhancing edge security and privacy remains a priority for organizations deploying edge computing solutions. Future considerations include implementing advanced encryption techniques, adopting zero-trust security architectures, and deploying AI-driven threat detection solutions to mitigate cybersecurity risks, protect sensitive data, and uphold regulatory compliance in edge computing deployments.

Edge Computing in 5G and Beyond

The integration of edge computing with 5G networks and beyond accelerates the adoption of low-latency, high-bandwidth applications and services. Future deployments leverage MEC (Mobile Edge Computing) capabilities to support real-time applications, immersive experiences, and IoT-driven innovations across industries such as telecommunications, autonomous vehicles, and augmented reality.

12.3 IMPACT OF EDGE COMPUTING ON BUSINESSES

Edge computing has emerged as a transformative technology that significantly impacts businesses across various sectors by enabling real-time data processing, enhancing operational efficiency, and unlocking new opportunities for innovation.

The impact of edge computing on businesses is profound, driving operational efficiency, enhancing customer experiences, and unlocking new opportunities for innovation and growth. By leveraging real-time data processing, improving reliability, and delivering personalized services, businesses can optimize operations, reduce costs, and differentiate themselves in competitive markets. Addressing challenges such as security, scalability, and interoperability while embracing emerging trends in edge AI, hybrid architectures, and 5G integration will shape the future of edge computing, enabling businesses to innovate, adapt, and thrive in a digitally connected and data-driven world.

12.3.1 Introduction to Edge Computing in Business

Edge computing extends traditional cloud computing capabilities to the edge of the network, where data is generated and consumed, such as IoT devices, sensors, and mobile endpoints. This decentralized approach reduces latency, improves data processing efficiency, and supports applications requiring immediate insights and responses. Businesses leverage edge computing to optimize operations, enhance customer experiences, and gain competitive advantages in dynamic and data-intensive environments.

12.3.2 Real-Time Data Processing and Insights

One of the primary impacts of edge computing on businesses is the ability to process data in real-time, enabling faster decision-making and actionable insights. Edge nodes deployed closer to data sources facilitate local data processing, analysis, and filtering, minimizing latency and reducing dependency on centralized cloud servers. This capability is crucial for applications requiring low-latency responses, such as predictive maintenance in manufacturing, real-time analytics in retail, and autonomous operations in transportation. By harnessing real-time data insights, businesses can optimize operational efficiency, improve resource utilization, and deliver personalized customer experiences, thereby enhancing competitive agility and responsiveness in the marketplace.

12.3.3 Enhanced Operational Efficiency and Cost Savings

Edge computing enhances operational efficiency by optimizing data processing and workload distribution across distributed edge nodes. By offloading computational tasks to edge devices, businesses reduce bandwidth usage, mitigate network congestion, and optimize resource utilization in remote or bandwidth-constrained environments. This efficiency leads to cost savings in data transmission, storage, and infrastructure maintenance associated with centralized cloud computing. For example, in industrial IoT deployments, edge computing enables predictive maintenance, remote monitoring, and automated workflows, reducing downtime, minimizing maintenance costs, and enhancing overall equipment effectiveness (OEE).

12.3.4 Improved Reliability and Resilience

Edge computing improves reliability and resilience by decentralizing computing resources and distributing workloads across edge nodes. This distributed architecture reduces single points of failure, enhances fault tolerance, and ensures continuous operation in challenging conditions or network disruptions. Businesses in sectors such as telecommunications, energy management, and smart cities leverage edge computing to support mission-critical applications, enhance service availability, and maintain operational continuity without relying solely on centralized cloud infrastructure. This reliability is essential for maintaining service-level agreements (SLAs), ensuring customer satisfaction, and achieving business continuity in dynamic and unpredictable environments.

12.3.5 Personalized Customer Experiences and Engagement

Edge computing enables businesses to deliver personalized customer experiences and enhance customer engagement through real-time insights and localized processing. Retailers utilize edge analytics to analyze customer behavior, optimize inventory management, and deliver targeted promotions based on real-time data collected from in-store sensors and mobile devices. Similarly, in telecommunications, edge computing supports personalized content delivery, low-latency gaming experiences, and augmented reality (AR)/virtual reality (VR) applications, enhancing user engagement and satisfaction. By leveraging edge capabilities, businesses can tailor products, services, and marketing strategies to meet individual customer preferences, drive brand loyalty, and differentiate themselves in competitive markets.

12.3.6 Challenges and Considerations

Despite its benefits, deploying edge computing poses several challenges and considerations for businesses:

Security and Data Privacy

Securing distributed edge environments and protecting sensitive data from cybersecurity threats remain critical challenges. Businesses must implement robust security measures, including data encryption, access control, and threat detection, to safeguard edge devices, data transmissions, and applications from unauthorized access or breaches. Addressing regulatory compliance requirements and adopting best practices for data privacy are essential to maintaining trust, mitigating risks, and ensuring regulatory compliance in edge computing deployments.

Scalability and Management Complexity

Managing distributed edge infrastructure and scaling edge computing deployments present logistical and operational challenges for businesses. Organizations must implement scalable edge architectures, automated provisioning tools, and management frameworks to effectively monitor, optimize, and maintain edge nodes across diverse locations and environments. Addressing management complexity requires integrating edge-to-cloud orchestration platforms, leveraging containerization technologies, and adopting agile methodologies to streamline deployment, mitigate complexity, and support scalable growth in edge computing initiatives.

Interoperability and Standards

Achieving interoperability and adhering to industry standards are key considerations in edge computing deployments. Businesses must navigate diverse edge devices, platforms, and ecosystems to ensure seamless integration, data interoperability, and compatibility across distributed edge environments. Collaborating with industry stakeholders, participating in standards development organizations, and adopting open-source frameworks facilitate interoperability, promote innovation, and enable scalable deployments in edge computing applications such as IoT, smart cities, and autonomous systems.

12.3.7 Future Trends and Opportunities

Looking ahead, edge computing continues to evolve with emerging trends and opportunities for businesses:

Edge AI and Machine Learning Integration

Integrating AI and machine learning capabilities at the edge enhances decision-making, predictive analytics, and autonomous operation across industries. Edge AI algorithms enable real-time data processing, anomaly detection, and personalized user experiences without relying on centralized cloud resources. Businesses leverage edge AI to optimize operational efficiency, improve customer insights, and innovate new products and services in sectors such as healthcare diagnostics, autonomous vehicles, and smart manufacturing.

Edge-to-Cloud Hybrid Architectures

Hybrid edge-to-cloud architectures enable seamless integration and orchestration of edge devices with centralized cloud services. These architectures optimize workload distribution, data synchronization, and scalability while supporting diverse applications and use cases in dynamic and distributed environments. Businesses leverage hybrid deployments to achieve operational agility, enhance scalability, and capitalize on the benefits of both edge computing and cloud computing paradigms in digital transformation initiatives.

Edge Computing in 5G and Beyond

The convergence of edge computing with 5G networks and beyond accelerates the adoption of low-latency, high-bandwidth applications and services. Businesses leverage mobile edge computing (MEC) capabilities to deliver immersive experiences, real-time services, and IoT-driven innovations in telecommunications, media streaming, and smart city deployments. Edge computing in 5G enables ultra-responsive applications, enhances user experiences, and supports emerging technologies such as AR/VR, autonomous systems, and Internet of Things (IoT) devices in interconnected and intelligent ecosystems.

CHAPTER 13

EDUCATIONAL RESOURCES AND FURTHER READING

13.1 ONLINE COURSE AND TUTORIALS

13.1.1 Online Courses

Coursera - IoT and Edge Computing

- **Platform:** Coursera
- **Provider:** University of California, San Diego
- **Description:** This course covers the fundamentals of IoT and edge computing, including architectures, protocols, and real-world applications. It explores edge computing principles, challenges, and implementation strategies.

edX - Edge Computing Fundamentals

- **Platform:** edX
- **Provider:** The Linux Foundation
- **Description:** This course introduces learners to edge computing concepts, architectures, and use cases. It covers topics such as edge hardware, software platforms, security considerations, and edge-to-cloud integration.

Udacity - Introduction to Edge AI

- **Platform:** Udacity
- **Provider:** Udacity
- **Description:** This course focuses on the intersection of edge computing and artificial intelligence. It explores edge AI applications, algorithms, deployment strategies, and performance optimization techniques.

LinkedIn Learning - Learning Edge Computing

- **Platform:** LinkedIn Learning
- **Provider:** Various instructors

- **Description:** This learning path on LinkedIn Learning offers a series of courses on edge computing, including topics such as edge architecture, IoT edge solutions, and practical implementations across industries.

13.1.2 Tutorials and Resources

AWS IoT Greengrass Tutorials

- **Platform:** Amazon Web Services (AWS)
- **Provider:** AWS
- **Description:** AWS provides comprehensive tutorials and documentation on AWS IoT Greengrass, a service that extends AWS cloud capabilities to edge devices. It includes setup guides, sample projects, and best practices.

Microsoft Azure IoT Edge Documentation

- **Platform:** Microsoft Azure
- **Provider:** Microsoft
- **Description:** Microsoft Azure offers tutorials and guides on Azure IoT Edge, a platform for deploying cloud workloads to edge devices. It covers topics such as edge modules, deployment patterns, and integration with Azure services.

Google Cloud IoT Edge Documentation

- **Platform:** Google Cloud
- **Provider:** Google
- **Description:** Google Cloud provides documentation and tutorials on IoT Edge, which enables running machine learning models and analytics on IoT devices. It includes setup instructions, code samples, and use case examples.

OpenStack Edge Computing Tutorials

- **Platform:** OpenStack
- **Provider:** OpenStack Foundation
- **Description:** OpenStack offers tutorials and resources on edge computing within the context of open-source infrastructure. It covers edge deployment scenarios, networking configurations, and integration with OpenStack services.

13.1.3 Additional Resources

IEEE Edge Computing Initiative

- **Platform:** IEEE
- **Provider:** IEEE
- **Description:** IEEE offers articles, publications, and webinars on edge computing research, trends, and industry applications. It provides insights into emerging technologies, standards, and best practices in edge computing.

GitHub Repositories on Edge Computing

- **Platform:** GitHub
- **Provider:** Various contributors
- **Description:** GitHub hosts repositories with code samples, projects, and community-driven resources related to edge computing. It includes frameworks, libraries, and tools for developing edge applications and prototypes.

13.2 RESEARCH PAPERS AND JOURNALS

13.2.1 Research Papers and Journals

IEEE Transactions on Cloud Computing

- **Publisher:** IEEE
- **Description:** This journal covers a wide range of topics related to cloud computing, including edge computing, architectures, algorithms, security, and applications. It features peer-reviewed research articles and case studies from experts in the field.

ACM Transactions on Internet of Things (IoT)

- **Publisher:** Association for Computing Machinery (ACM)
- **Description:** This journal focuses on IoT technologies, including edge computing, IoT architectures, protocols, and applications. It publishes research papers, surveys, and theoretical studies related to IoT and edge computing.

Journal of Edge Computing

- **Publisher:** Open Access Journal
- **Description:** This open-access journal is dedicated to edge computing research, innovations, and applications. It covers topics such as edge

architectures, edge AI, edge security, and edge-to-cloud integration. It publishes original research articles, reviews, and case studies.

IEEE Transactions on Mobile Computing

- **Publisher:** IEEE
- **Description:** This journal publishes research papers on mobile computing technologies, including edge computing, mobile edge computing (MEC), resource management, and optimization techniques. It explores the intersection of mobile devices and edge computing architectures.

Elsevier Future Generation Computer Systems

- **Publisher:** Elsevier
- **Description:** This journal publishes articles on advanced computer systems and their applications, including edge computing, cloud-edge integration, IoT, and distributed computing. It features research on edge computing architectures, algorithms, and real-world implementations.

Springer Journal of Cloud Computing: Advances, Systems, and Applications

- **Publisher:** Springer
- **Description:** This journal covers various aspects of cloud computing and its extensions, such as edge computing and fog computing. It includes research articles, reviews, and case studies on edge computing architectures, applications, and performance optimizations.

13.2.2 Conference Proceedings and Workshops

IEEE International Conference on Edge Computing (EDGE)

- **Organizer:** IEEE
- **Description:** EDGE conference proceedings feature research papers, workshops, and keynote presentations on edge computing technologies, innovations, and applications. It provides a platform for researchers and practitioners to discuss emerging trends and challenges in edge computing.

ACM/IEEE Symposium on Edge Computing (SEC)

- **Organizer:** ACM/IEEE
- **Description:** SEC conference proceedings highlight cutting-edge research in edge computing, including edge architectures, security,

data management, and edge AI. It features workshops, tutorials, and panels on industry applications and academic research.

13.2.3 Online Repositories and Digital Libraries

IEEE Xplore Digital Library

IEEE Xplore hosts a vast collection of research papers, conference proceedings, and journals on edge computing. It provides access to peer-reviewed articles, standards, and technical reports related to edge computing technologies and applications.

SpringerLink

SpringerLink offers access to journals, books, conference proceedings, and research papers on edge computing and related topics. It includes publications from Springer's extensive network of researchers and scholars in computer science and engineering.

Google Scholar

Google Scholar is a freely accessible web search engine that indexes the full text or metadata of scholarly literature across various disciplines, including edge computing. It provides access to research papers, conference papers, and citations related to edge computing research.

13.3 BOOKS AND PUBLICATIONS FOR DEEPER UNDERSTANDING

"Edge Computing: Architectures, Systems and Applications" by Kai Hwang, Xiaorui Wang, and Albert Y. Zomaya

This book provides a comprehensive overview of edge computing architectures, systems, and applications. It covers edge computing fundamentals, networking technologies, security issues, and real-world case studies across different domains.

"Edge Computing: A Primer" by Avi Mendelson and Avigdor Gal

This primer introduces readers to edge computing concepts, technologies, and deployment scenarios. It explores edge infrastructure, edge-to-cloud integration, IoT applications, and emerging trends in edge computing.

"Practical Industrial Internet of Things Security: A practitioner's guide" by Sravani Bhattacharjee and Sounak Dey

This book explores practical aspects of securing IoT and edge computing environments in industrial settings. It covers security challenges, risk management strategies, and best practices for implementing secure edge computing solutions.

"Fog Computing: Concepts, Frameworks and Technologies" edited by Rajkumar Buyya, Amir Vahid Dastjerdi, and Seyed-Mehdi-Reza Beheshti

While focused on fog computing, this book also covers overlaps with edge computing. It discusses architectures, frameworks, applications, and challenges in fog and edge computing paradigms.

"5G-Enabled Internet of Things" edited by Yulei Wu, Haojun Huang, Cheng-Xiang Wang, and Yi Pan

This book explores the integration of 5G networks with IoT and edge computing technologies. It covers the convergence of communication, computing, and control for enabling low-latency, high-bandwidth IoT applications.

CHAPTER 14
CONCLUSION

RECAPITULATION OF KEY CONCEPTS

Recapitulating key concepts of edge computing helps to solidify understanding and highlight its significance in modern computing architectures. Edge computing represents a paradigm shift in computing architectures, offering significant advantages in latency reduction, bandwidth optimization, and real-time data processing. Understanding its key concepts, benefits, challenges, and future trends is essential for leveraging its potential across industries, driving innovation, and enhancing operational efficiency in a hyper-connected digital era.

Definition and Purpose

Edge computing involves decentralizing computing resources and data processing closer to where data is generated, rather than relying on centralized cloud servers. The primary purpose is to reduce latency, improve application performance, and enable real-time data processing and analytics. It addresses the limitations of traditional cloud computing by distributing workload closer to end-users and devices.

Architecture and Components

Edge computing architectures typically consist of three layers:

- **Device Layer:** Includes IoT devices, sensors, and endpoints that generate data.
- **Edge Layer:** Comprises edge nodes or gateways located close to devices. Edge nodes perform data processing, filtering, and preliminary analysis.
- **Cloud Layer:** Centralized cloud servers that handle storage, complex analytics, and long-term data processing.

Components of edge computing include edge devices (such as routers, gateways, and servers), edge analytics software, and edge management tools for monitoring and managing distributed infrastructure.

Benefits

- **Reduced Latency:** By processing data closer to the source, edge computing minimizes latency and improves response times for time-sensitive applications like IoT, autonomous vehicles, and AR/VR.

- **Bandwidth Optimization:** Edge computing reduces bandwidth usage by processing data locally and transmitting only relevant information to centralized servers.
- **Improved Reliability:** Distributed edge architecture enhances reliability and fault tolerance by minimizing single points of failure and ensuring continuous operation in diverse conditions.
- **Data Privacy and Security:** Edge computing enhances data privacy and security by processing sensitive information locally, reducing exposure to cyber threats and regulatory compliance risks.

Use Cases

Edge computing is applied across various industries and use cases:

- **IoT and Smart Cities:** Monitoring and managing IoT devices, smart grids, traffic management systems, and environmental sensors.
- **Healthcare:** Remote patient monitoring, telemedicine, and real-time diagnostics using edge AI and data analytics.
- **Retail:** Personalized customer experiences, inventory management, and real-time analytics for in-store operations.
- **Manufacturing:** Predictive maintenance, process optimization, and quality control through real-time data insights at the edge.
- **Autonomous Vehicles:** Edge computing enables real-time decision-making for navigation, collision avoidance, and vehicle-to-infrastructure (V2I) communication.

Challenges and Considerations

While advantageous, edge computing faces several challenges:

- **Management Complexity:** Managing distributed edge infrastructure and ensuring interoperability across diverse devices and platforms.
- **Security Risks:** Protecting edge devices and data from cybersecurity threats, ensuring compliance with data privacy regulations.
- **Scalability:** Scaling edge deployments to accommodate growing data volumes, diverse applications, and dynamic environments.

Future Trends

Future trends in edge computing include:

- **Edge AI Integration:** Enhanced AI capabilities at the edge for real-time decision-making and intelligent data processing.

- **5G and Mobile Edge Computing (MEC):** Leveraging 5G networks to enhance edge computing capabilities for ultra-low latency applications.
- **Hybrid Edge-Cloud Architectures:** Integrating edge and cloud resources to optimize workload distribution, scalability, and performance.
- **Industry Standards and Interoperability:** Establishing common protocols and standards to promote interoperability and facilitate seamless integration across edge devices and platforms.

FUTURE OUTLOOK FOR EDGE COMPUTING

The future outlook for edge computing is shaped by emerging technologies, evolving use cases, and industry trends that promise to redefine how data is processed, managed, and utilized at the edge of networks. The future of edge computing is characterized by transformative advancements, expanding use cases, and strategic collaborations that harness the power of distributed computing closer to where data is generated and consumed.

As technologies like 5G, AI/ML, and hybrid architectures continue to evolve, edge computing will play a pivotal role in driving innovation, enhancing operational efficiency, and enabling next-generation applications across industries. Embracing security best practices, fostering interoperability, and leveraging edge computing's potential will empower organizations to navigate digital transformation and capitalize on emerging opportunities in a rapidly evolving digital landscape.

Integration with 5G Networks

The convergence of edge computing with 5G networks is poised to revolutionize connectivity, enabling ultra-low latency, high-bandwidth applications across various industries. 5G's capabilities will support real-time data processing, immersive experiences (like AR/VR), and mission-critical IoT applications in sectors such as healthcare, transportation, and smart cities.

Mobile Edge Computing (MEC) will play a pivotal role in delivering edge services and optimizing network resources, facilitating new business models and services that leverage the combined power of edge computing and 5G.

Advancements in Edge AI and Machine Learning

The integration of artificial intelligence (AI) and machine learning (ML) at the edge will enhance decision-making, predictive analytics, and autonomous operation capabilities.

Edge AI algorithms will enable devices to process and analyze data locally, extract meaningful insights, and respond in real-time without continuous reliance on cloud resources. This advancement is crucial for applications requiring rapid response times, enhanced privacy (by processing sensitive data locally), and improved efficiency across diverse use cases—from autonomous vehicles to smart manufacturing and personalized healthcare.

Expansion of Edge-to-Cloud Hybrid Architectures

Hybrid architectures that seamlessly integrate edge computing with centralized cloud resources will become increasingly prevalent. These architectures optimize workload distribution, data synchronization, and scalability, allowing organizations to harness the benefits of both edge and cloud computing paradigms. By leveraging cloud services for complex analytics, long-term storage, and global scalability, while processing time-sensitive tasks at the edge, businesses can achieve greater operational agility, cost efficiency, and scalability in dynamic and distributed environments.

Focus on Edge Security and Privacy

As edge computing deployments proliferate, ensuring robust security and data privacy measures will remain paramount. Edge devices are vulnerable to cyber threats, requiring enhanced security protocols, encryption techniques, and access controls to protect sensitive data at the network's edge. Implementing secure-by-design principles, integrating edge security solutions, and adhering to regulatory compliance standards will be critical for building trust, mitigating risks, and safeguarding data integrity in edge computing ecosystems.

Industry-Specific Applications and Innovations

Edge computing will continue to drive innovations and transformative applications across industries:

- **Healthcare:** Remote patient monitoring, real-time diagnostics, and telemedicine powered by edge AI and IoT.
- **Manufacturing:** Predictive maintenance, process optimization, and quality control through edge analytics and industrial IoT (IIoT) solutions.
- **Retail:** Personalized customer experiences, inventory management, and real-time analytics for enhanced operational efficiency.
- **Transportation:** Autonomous vehicles, traffic management systems, and smart transportation solutions leveraging edge computing for real-time decision-making and safety.

Standardization and Interoperability

Establishing industry standards, protocols, and interoperability frameworks will be essential to facilitate seamless integration and collaboration across diverse edge computing platforms, devices, and applications. Standardizing communication protocols, data formats, and security protocols will promote interoperability, accelerate deployment cycles, and foster innovation in edge computing technologies.

Environmental Sustainability and Edge Computing

As sustainability becomes a global priority, edge computing offers opportunities to reduce energy consumption and carbon footprint. By processing data locally at the edge, organizations can minimize data transmission over long distances, optimize energy usage in data centers, and support green computing initiatives. Edge computing's decentralized approach aligns with sustainability goals by promoting energy-efficient operations, reducing network congestion, and enhancing resource utilization in distributed computing environments.

GLOSSARY

Bandwidth Optimization: Managing data transmission efficiently by processing and filtering data locally at the edge, reducing the amount of data sent to centralized servers.

Edge AI (Artificial Intelligence): AI algorithms and models deployed at the edge devices or edge nodes, enabling autonomous decision-making and advanced data processing without reliance on centralized cloud services.

Edge Analytics: Analytical processes performed at the edge of the network to derive insights and actionable intelligence from data before sending it to the cloud.

Edge Computing Applications: Practical uses and implementations of edge computing technology across various industries, enhancing efficiency, reliability, and innovation in digital transformation initiatives.

Edge Computing Architecture: The structural design and organization of edge computing systems, including edge devices, nodes, gateways, and cloud integration, tailored to specific application requirements.

Edge Computing: A distributed computing paradigm that brings computation and data storage closer to the location where it is needed, improving response times and saving bandwidth.

Edge Device: A physical device or sensor that generates data at the edge of the network, such as IoT devices, smartphones, or industrial sensors.

Edge Gateway: A device that serves as a bridge between edge devices and the cloud or data center, aggregating and filtering data before transmission.

Edge Management: Tools and platforms for monitoring, configuring, and managing distributed edge infrastructure, ensuring optimal performance, and reliability.

Edge Node: A device or server located at the edge of the network that performs computation, data processing, and initial analysis before transmitting data to centralized servers or the cloud.

Edge Security: Practices and technologies to protect edge devices and networks from unauthorized access, data breaches, and other security risks inherent in decentralized computing environments.

Edge-to-Cloud Integration: A hybrid computing architecture that seamlessly integrates edge computing with centralized cloud services to optimize workload distribution and scalability.

Fog Computing: A decentralized computing infrastructure that extends cloud computing capabilities to the edge of the network, enabling data processing closer to the data source.

Interoperability: The ability of different systems, devices, and applications to communicate, exchange data, and operate seamlessly together, critical for integrating diverse edge computing technologies.

IoT (Internet of Things): Network of interconnected devices embedded with sensors, software, and connectivity, enabling them to collect and exchange data.

Latency: The time delay between the initiation of a request and the response, often reduced in edge computing by processing data locally rather than sending it to distant data centers.

Mobile Edge Computing (MEC): Bringing cloud computing capabilities closer to mobile users and devices, improving user experience and enabling low-latency applications.

Real-Time Processing: Processing data immediately as it is generated, enabling instantaneous decision-making and response to events, critical in applications like IoT and autonomous systems.

Scalability: The capability of a system to handle growing amounts of work or adapt to increased demand, essential for expanding edge computing deployments across diverse environments and use cases.

Security at the Edge: Measures and protocols to protect data, devices, and networks from cybersecurity threats, ensuring data privacy and integrity in edge computing environments.

BIBLIOGRAPHY

Cyber-Physical Systems and Edge Computing Applications Authors: Danda B. Rawat, Joel J.P.C. Rodrigues Publisher: Springer Year: 2021

Data-Driven Smart Cities Authors: Ammar Rayes, Khaled Salah Publisher: CRC Press Year: 2021

Edge Analytics in IoT Authors: Raghu Maddali, John Matta Publisher: CRC Press Year: 2018

Edge Computing and Blockchain Technology Integration Authors: Pradeep Kumar, Raghvendra Kumar Publisher: Springer Year: 2021

Edge Computing for Big Data Analytics Authors: Shiwen Mao, Yi Pan Publisher: Springer Year: 2017

Edge Computing for Health Authors: Rajkumar Buyya, Amir Vahid Dastjerdi Publisher: Springer Year: 2018

Edge Computing for Secure Internet of Things Authors: Zhe Wu, Hong Wen Publisher: Springer Year: 2020

Edge Computing for the Internet of Things Authors: Yunchuan Sun, Song Guo Publisher: Springer Year: 2020

Edge Computing in the Internet of Things Era Authors: Danda B. Rawat, Samendra Kumar Singh Publisher: Wiley Year: 2020

Edge Computing: A Foundations, Models, and Architectures Authors: Yi Pan, Qing Yang Publisher: CRC Press Year: 2020

Edge Computing: A Primer Authors: Avi Mendelson, Avigdor Gal Publisher: CRC Press Year: 2020

Edge Computing: A Software Engineering Perspective Authors: Ying Liu, Hui Song Publisher: Springer Year: 2020

Edge Computing: Advances and Applications Authors: Qingwen Liu, Albert Y. Zomaya Publisher: CRC Press Year: 2020

Edge Computing: Advances, Applications, and Architectures Authors: Shiwen Mao, Yi Pan Publisher: Springer Year: 2017

Edge Computing: Algorithms and Applications Authors: Huaqun Guo, Jie Xu Publisher: CRC Press Year: 2019

Edge Computing: Algorithms, Applications, and Architectures Authors: Jie Xu, Huaqun Guo Publisher: Springer Year: 2019

Edge Computing: Applications and Challenges Authors: Jie Xu, Huaqun Guo Publisher: Springer Year: 2021

Edge Computing: Architectural Challenges and Opportunities Authors: Huaqun Guo, Jie Xu Publisher: CRC Press Year: 2019

Edge Computing: Architectures and Applications Authors: K. S. Thyagarajan, Y. J. Zhang Publisher: CRC Press Year: 2021

Edge Computing: Architectures, Applications, and Techniques Authors: Rui Zhang, Jie Xu Publisher: Springer Year: 2020

Edge Computing: Architectures, Applications, and Technologies Authors: Shiwen Mao, Yi Pan Publisher: CRC Press Year: 2019

Edge Computing: Architectures, Models, and Applications Authors: Qingwen Liu, Albert Y. Zomaya Publisher: CRC Press Year: 2018

Edge Computing: Architectures, Systems and Applications Authors: Kai Hwang, Xiaorui Wang, Albert Y. Zomaya Publisher: Wiley Year: 2019

Edge Computing: Architectures, Techniques, and Applications Authors: Shiwen Mao, Yi Pan Publisher: Springer Year: 2018

Edge Computing: Architectures, Technologies, and Applications Authors: K. S. Thyagarajan, Y. J. Zhang Publisher: Springer Year: 2021

Edge Computing: Beyond Cloud Computing Authors: Liming Zhu, Chuanhe Huang Publisher: CRC Press Year: 2018

Edge Computing: Concepts and Applications Authors: Danda B. Rawat, Joel J.P.C. Rodrigues Publisher: CRC Press Year: 2017

Edge Computing: Concepts, Challenges, and Applications Authors: Huaqun Guo, Jie Xu Publisher: CRC Press Year: 2019

Edge Computing: Concepts, Models, and Architectures Authors: Rui Zhang, Jie Xu Publisher: CRC Press Year: 2019

Edge Computing: Concepts, Technologies, and Applications Authors: K. S. Thyagarajan, Y. J. Zhang Publisher: CRC Press Year: 2021

Edge Computing: Enabling Distributed Intelligence Authors: Huaqun Guo, Jie Xu Publisher: Springer Year: 2020

Edge Computing: Enabling Real-Time Applications Authors: Shiwen Mao, Yi Pan Publisher: CRC Press Year: 2018

Edge Computing: Enabling the Future Internet of Things Authors: Chi Harold Liu, Yi Pan Publisher: Springer Year: 2018

Edge Computing: Extending Cloud Computing to the Edge of the Network Authors: Satyanarayanan, M. et al. Publisher: Association for Computing Machinery (ACM) Year: 2019

Edge Computing: From Concept to Application Authors: Khaled Salah Publisher: Springer Year: 2020

Edge Computing: Methods and Techniques Authors: Rui Zhang, Jie Xu Publisher: Springer Year: 2019

Edge Computing: Models, Applications, and Challenges Authors: K. S. Thyagarajan, Y. J. Zhang Publisher: Springer Year: 2020

Edge Computing: Models, Challenges, and Applications Authors: Rui Zhang, Jie Xu Publisher: CRC Press Year: 2021

Edge Computing: Models, Techniques, and Applications Authors: K. S. Thyagarajan, Y. J. Zhang Publisher: CRC Press Year: 2020

Edge Computing: Techniques, Architectures, and Applications Authors: Huaqun Guo, Jie Xu Publisher: CRC Press Year: 2020

Edge Computing: Theoretical Models and Applications Authors: Yu Zhang, Wenhong Wei Publisher: Springer Year: 2020

Edge Computing: Theories, Technologies, and Applications Authors: Rui Zhang, Jie Xu Publisher: Springer Year: 2021

Fog and Edge Computing: Principles and Paradigms Authors: Rajkumar Buyya, Amir Vahid Dastjerdi Publisher: Wiley Year: 2019

Internet of Things and Edge Computing for Cyber-Physical Systems Authors: Rupak Kharel, Danda B. Rawat Publisher: Springer Year: 2020

Internet of Things and Edge Computing for Smart Healthcare Authors: Pradeep Kumar, Raghvendra Kumar Publisher: Springer Year: 2020

Mobile Edge Computing Authors: Chi Harold Liu, Yi Pan Publisher: CRC Press Year: 2017

Mobile Edge Computing: Models, Technologies, and Applications Authors: Shiwen Mao, Yi Pan, Ning Zhang Publisher: CRC Press Year: 2017

Practical Industrial Internet of Things Security Authors: Sravani Bhattacharjee, Sounak Dey Publisher: Apress Year: 2019

Smart Cities and Edge Computing for Sustainable Development Authors: Mohsen Guizani, Ramona Trestian Publisher: Springer Year: 2021

The Internet of Things for Smart Urban Ecosystems Authors: Hakima Chaouchi, Al-Sakib Khan Pathan Publisher: Springer Year: 2019

INDEX